Achievement and Motivation is a review of recent research on the topic from a social-developmental perspective. The basic theme concerns the relation between motivation (why one does something) and achievement in educational settings (how one performs on a variety of tasks and activities). Given current concerns about the educational system and student interest in learning, this is a timely and crucial subject.

Cambridge Studies in Social and Emotional Development

General Editor: Martin L. Hoffman

Achievement and motivation: A social-developmental perspective

Achievement and motivation

A social-developmental perspective

Edited by

ANN K. BOGGIANO
University of Colorado

THANE S. PITTMAN
Gettysburg College

Published by the Press Syndicate of the University of Cambridge
The Pitt Building, Trumpington Street, Cambridge CB2 1RP
40 West 20th Street, New York, NY 10011-4211, USA
10 Stamford Road, Oakleigh, Victoria 3166, Australia

First published 1992

Printed in Canada

Library of Congress Cataloging-in-Publication Data

Achievement and motivation / edited by Ann K. Boggiano, Thane S. Pittman.
p. cm. – (Cambridge studies in social and emotional development)
Includes index.
ISBN 0-521-32220-0
1. Achievement motivation. 2. Intrinsic motivation.
3. Achievement motivation in children. I. Pittman, Thane S.
II. Series.
BF503.A22 1992
370.15′4 – dc20 91-43220

A catalog record for this book is available from the British Library.

ISBN 0–521–32220–0 hardback

We dedicate this book to our respective children:

To my daughters, Kristin and Keri, and in memory of my son, Bobby, whose intrinsic motivation for learning inspired all who knew him.

To Kathleen and Walter.

Contents

Part III Motivation and achievement

Contributors

Teresa Amabile
Department of Psychology
Brandeis University

Marty Barrett
Department of Psychology
University of Colorado

Ann K. Boggiano
Department of Psychology
University of Colorado

Renae Cohen
Department of Psychology
New York University

James P. Connell
Department of Psychology
River Campus
University of Rochester

Philip Costanzo
Psychology Department
Duke University

Edward Deci
Department of Psychology
University of Rochester

Cheryl Flink
5942 Puma Drive
Loveland, Colorado 80538

Karin S. Frey
Department of Psychology
University of Washington

Wendy S. Grolnick
Department of Psychology
Clark University

Ellen H. Grosovsky
Department of Psychology
New York University

Judith M. Harackiewicz
Department of Psychology
University of Wisconsin

Susan Harter
Department of Psychology
University of Denver

Beth A. Hennessey
Department of Psychology
Wellesley College

Phyllis A. Katz
Institute for Research on Social
Problems
Boulder, Colorado

Deborah S. Main
University of Colorado
Health Sciences Center

George Manderlink
Department of Psychology
Columbia University

Thane S. Pittman
Department of Psychology
Gettysburg College

Janet Morgan Riggs
Department of Psychology
Gettysburg College

Diane N. Ruble
Department of Psychology
New York University

Richard M. Ryan
Department of Psychology
River Campus
University of Rochester

Carol Sansone
Department of Psychology
University of Utah

Pamela M. Slater
Department of Psychology
Charles River Hospital

Erik Woody
Department of Psychology
University of Waterloo

1 Psychological perspectives on motivation and achievement

Thane S. Pittman and Ann K. Boggiano

The study of human motivation explores an intriguing phenomenon: Given an abundance of alternatives, why do individuals choose to act and react in particular ways? This book offers some bold answers to that question. The distinction between intrinsic and extrinsic motivation, for example, is elegantly simple but rich in its implications. Although not constrained to a particular setting, much of the research has targeted the nature of human motivation in one vital context: the classroom. Ignoring the implications of the findings in this field may hinder our efforts to educate today's students, which ultimately could place our future in jeopardy. However, we offer no quick fixes; instead, we examine a variety of perspectives on the fundamental motivating forces affecting human behavior offered by the leading researchers in the field of motivation.

As we write this chapter, the U.S. faces a crisis in education. We are alarmed by a skyrocketing high-school dropout rate and a declining interest in science among college students. To reverse these trends, we must endeavor to understand what educational techniques may suffocate students' interest in learning, then work to rekindle that interest. The research discussed in these chapters offers a clearer understanding of our successes and failures in motivating young and often gifted students.

In this initial chapter, we offer a brief review of the history of research on human motivation and achievement. (For more extensive historical reviews, see Buck, 1988; Mook, 1987; Pittman & Heller, 1987.) In an effort to guide the reader in his or her exploration of this challenging field, we also will briefly discuss the major constructs relevant to motivation and achievement examined in the research presented here: intrinsic and extrinsic motivation, self-determination, and perceptions of competence.

Motivation and achievement research

The most basic source of human motivation is physical need – for food, oxygen, warmth, and sleep. Hunger motivates us to seek food; cold and fatigue compel us to fulfill other basic life requirements. Recognition of this physical component of motivation was an integral part of Pavlov's (1927) investigations in classical conditioning and of Skinner's (1953) research on instrumental conditioning. In each approach, tissue deficits were regarded as the impetus for action, and satisfaction of physical needs was thought to be the primary reward. These theorists assumed that other stimuli might acquire secondary reinforcing properties through association with these primary rewards. Behaviorists consequently attempted to explain all of human behavior in terms of fundamental bodily needs, but this is clearly only one dimension of complex human behavior. Motivation researchers, then, endeavored to explore other aspects of human motivation, and two early theories set the stage for the research presented in this volume.

In the 1950s, research teams began to investigate why individuals whose bodily needs were satisfied nevertheless engaged in goal-oriented behavior. One line of inquiry assumed that curiosity was an innate motive, as natural as the drives for food, warmth, and sleep (Harlow, Harlow, & Meyer, 1950; Berlyne, 1960; Hunt, 1965). Curiosity, then, would move an otherwise satisfied person to read a novel or seek some form of "stimulating" entertainment. In one seminal paper, Robert White suggested a second fundamental motive: the desire for effective commerce with and control over the environment (White, 1959). Effectance motivation might lead our physically satisfied individual to struggle to master the Sunday crossword puzzle, for example. These perspectives differ from a strict behaviorist view in that both curiosity and effectance motives prompt actions that are controlled by internal interests and individual characteristics, rather than by external forces. These two early theories comprise the foundation of today's extensive research on intrinsic and extrinsic motivation.

Achievement motivation theory took this notion of internal processes one step further by suggesting that people also were moved to action by a need to achieve or to be successful (McClelland, Atkinson, Clark & Lowell, 1958; Atkinson & Feather, 1966; Atkinson & Raynor, 1978). This theory, which is reviewed in Chapters 10 and 11, suggests a balance between an individual's desire to succeed and his or her need to avoid failure, a balance which determines responses to achievement situations. According to this perspective, a second major determinant of achievement behavior is the availability of extrinsic incentives. Atkinson and Raynor propose that the tendency to undertake an achievement-oriented activity increases when extrinsic incentives, such as social approval or monetary compensation, are present. Such incentives may enhance a student's willingness to undertake an achievement-related task at a given time. Of critical concern, however, is the question of the effect of such extrinsic incentives on a student's subsequent willingness to undertake such activities, in the absence of the incentive. The focus of the research presented in this volume addresses the effect of extrinsic incentives on subsequent intrinsic interest in activities, as well as on the quality of performance.

Intrinsic and extrinsic motivation

In 1971, Ed Deci reported the results of a set of ingenious and revolutionary experiments that spawned an extensive and influential body of literature on intrinsic and extrinsic motivation. Deci's initial findings pointed to a paradoxical effect of reward, later dubbed the "overjustification effect" (Lepper, Greene & Nisbett, 1973). Deci and Lepper have demonstrated that rewarding college students (Deci, 1971) and children (Lepper, Greene, & Nisbett, 1973) for engaging in activities the subjects inherently enjoyed caused a loss of interest in that activity, as indexed by the amount of time subjects spent with that activity during a subsequent free period in which there were no rewards or other external incentives for task performance. Because psychologists had assumed that rewards reinforced behavior, and thus enhanced interest and perseverance, the results of these studies seemed counterintuitive. However, Deci's and Lepper's revolutionary results were compatible with other early theoretical stances. Both effectance and curiosity theories suggested that people engaged in activities for two very different reasons. An individual may be moved to satisfy curiosity or to achieve effectance and control; activities of this kind are regarded as ends in themselves (Kruglanski, 1975) and constitute an individual's intrinsically motivated behavior. Other activities may be pursued for reward or recognition and are regarded as means to an end; these are extrinsically motivated behaviors. The overjustification effect, then, reflects a shift in a person's motivational orientation, from intrinsic to extrinsic, after he or she is rewarded for a particular activity. Because the person no longer experiences a sense of self-determination for initiation or regulation of the activity (Deci & Ryan, 1987), continued interest in the task becomes contingent on the promise of further rewards.

The two decades of research following Deci's initial publication outlined a number of vital processes and consequences of adopting an intrinsic versus extrinsic motivational orientation: a feeling of self-determination, the experience of competence, and enhanced quality of learning as indexed by conceptual reasoning, creativity, and achievement.

Self-determination

White's (1959) seminal theoretical work proposed that the desire to have effective control over the environment was a fundamental impetus to human behavior. This desire for efficacy has become a central assumption spanning a wide variety of theories, including Bandura's (1982) self-efficacy theory and Seligman's (1975) theory of learned helplessness. DeCharms (1968) also relied on the notion of self-determination in his analysis of perceptions of control and motivation in the classroom. The assumption was that students who perceived themselves to be in control of the process of learning would experience feelings of efficacy that would motivate them to explore and learn. DeCharms called these students "origins." Alternatively, students who perceived their achievement-related behaviors to be controlled by external forces (e.g., teachers' use of highly controlling behaviors) would be less likely to initiate and explore. DeCharms called these students "pawns." This view set the stage for Deci's cognitive evaluation theory (Deci, 1975), in which the concept of self-determination was central.

The research discussed in the following chapters clearly shows that when external rewards or other controlling strategies are used, behavior is no longer seen as self-determined, and an individual's interest in pursuing the activity in his or her free time declines (see Chapter 2). Even when the reason for performing an activity is affected by internally controlling processes (e.g., "I *should* do well") self-determination decreases and motivation is impaired (see Chapters 2 and 8). This detrimental effect also has been documented in interpersonal interactions (Chapter 3), in creativity (Chapter 4), and in overall achievement (Chapter 5).

Perceptions of competence

The question of self-determination could be expressed as, "Why am I doing this? Who or what controls whether I engage in this activity?" By contrast, the question of competence might be, "How well am I doing?" Like feelings of self-determination, an individual's perception of his or her competence is an important element in maintaining intrinsic motivation. The functional significance of competence feedback, (i.e., whether it is interpreted by an individual as informational or controlling) is the major determinant of the impact of evaluative feedback on a child's motivation. The conditions under which feedback relevant to competence will be beneficial versus detrimental to motivation and achievement are explained in a number of studies described in Chapters 5–10 and 11. The relationship between perceived competence and affect has also been documented and will be discussed (Chapter 5).

References

Atkinson, J.W., & Feather, N. T. (1966). *A theory of achievement motivation.* New York: Wiley.

Atkinson, J. W., & Raynor, J. O. (1978). *Personality, motivation, and achievement.* New York: Wiley.

Bandura, A. (1982). Self-efficacy mechanism in human agency. *American Psychologist, 37,* 122–147.

Berlyne, D.D. (1960). *Conflict, arousal, and curiosity.* New York: McGraw-Hill.

Buck, R. (1988). *Human motivation and emotion.* New York: Wiley.

DeCharms, R. (1968). *Personal causation.* New York: Academic Press.

Deci, E. L. (1971). Effects of externally mediated rewards on intrinsic motivation. *Journal of Personality and Social Psychology, 18,* 105–115.

Deci, E. L. (1975). *Intrinsic motivation.* New York: Plenum.

Deci, E. L., & Ryan, R. M. (1987). The support of autonomy and the control of behavior. *Journal of Personality and Social Psychology, 53,* 1024–1037.

Harlow, H. F., Harlow, M. K., & Meyer, D. R. (1950). Learning motivated by a manipulation drive. *Journal of Experimental Psychology, 40,* 228–234.

Hunt, J. M. (1965). Intrinsic motivation and its role in psychological development. *Nebraska Symposium on Motivation, 13,* 189–282.

Kruglanski, A. W. (1975). The endogenous-exogenous partition in attribution theory. *Psychological Review, 83,* 387–406.

Lepper, M. R., Greene, D., & Nisbett, R. E. (1973). Undermining children's intrinsic interest with extrinsic reward: A test of the overjustification hypothesis. *Journal of Personality and Social Psychology, 28,* 129–137.

McClelland, D. C., Atkinson, J. W., Clark, R. A., & Lowell, E. L. (1958). *The achievement motive.* New York: Appleton-Centry-Crofts.

Mook, D. G. (1987). *Motivation: The organization of action.* New York: W. W. Norton.

Pavlov, I. P. (1927). *Conditioned reflexes* (G. V. Anrep, trans.). London: Oxford University Press.

Pittman, T. S., & Heller, J. F. (1987). Social motivation. In M. Rosenzweig and L. Porter (Eds.), *Annual Review of Psychology,* Volume 38. Palo Alto, CA: Annual Reviews, Inc.

Seligman, M. E. P. (1975). *Helplessness: On depression, development, and death.* San Francisco: Freeman.

Skinner, B. F. (1953). *Science and human behavior.* New York: Macmillan.

White, R. W. (1959). Motivation reconsidered: The concept of competence. *Psychological Review, 66,* 297–333.

Part I

Intrinsic motivation

The *development* of intrinsic motivation as it relates to the experiences of competence and autonomy is the subject of Chapter 2, by Edward Deci and Richard Ryan. They argue that although intrinsic motivation is innate, it becomes differentiated with development such that an individual's interest is directed at certain activities and not at others. Consistent with their previous explications of cognitive evaluation theory (Deci, 1975, 1980; Deci & Ryan, 1980, 1985, 1987), Deci and Ryan assume that environmental factors influence which activities an individual selects through the processes of experiencing competence and self-determination. A variety of effects of competence versus incompetence and autonomy versus control are reviewed, including effects on self-esteem, motivation, and achievement. One of the many interesting distinctions made in this chapter concerns the development of individual differences in habitual orientations toward experiences, such that one event may be experienced by different people as having different informational, controlling, or motivating connotations, depending on the individual's motivational orientation and the functional significance of the event for the person.

Thane Pittman, Ann Boggiano, and Deborah Main (Chapter 3) discuss factors that promote intrinsic and extrinsic orientations in interpersonal relationships. Like achievement situations, interpersonal interactions may be approached with intrinsic or extrinsic motivational orientations, which can affect both an individual's interest in sustaining peer interactions as well as the quality of the interaction. Thus, feelings about a peer may be positive or negative, depending on the child's developmental level in conjunction with his or her motivational orientation. After extending the existence of overjustification effects to the realm of interpersonal interactions, the authors discuss the results of several studies in terms of their developmental implications.

In the final chapter in this section on intrinsic motivation, Teresa Amabile and Beth Hennessey (Chapter 4) investigate the proposition that children are more creative when they are intrinsically motivated. The authors first report on research showing how extrinsic constraints, such as rewards, evaluation, competition, and lack of choice, may interfere with both verbal and artistic creativity. They then describe research investigating some highly innovative and promising methods of maintaining creativity by fostering intrinsic motivation, and discuss the practical implications of their findings.

References

Deci, E.L. (1975). *Intrinsic motivation.* NY: Plenum.

Deci, E.L. (1980). *The psychology of self-determination.* Lexington, MA: Heath.

Deci, E.L. & Ryan. R.M. (1980). The empirical investigation of intrinsic motivational processes. In L. Berkowitz (Ed.), *Advances in experimental social psychology* (Vol. 13, pp. 40–80). New York: Academic Press.

Deci, E.L. & Ryan. R.M. (1985). *Intrinsic motivation and self determination in human behavior.* New York: Plenum.

Deci, E.L., & Ryan. R.M. (1987). The support of autonomy and the control of behavior. *Journal of Personality and Social Psychology, 53,* 1024–1037.

2 The initiation and regulation of intrinsically motivated learning and achievement

Edward L. Deci and Richard M. Ryan

Children are by nature active, and through their natural activity they learn. By spontaneously exercising their capacities, children expand and refine those capacities and acquire new knowledge. This learning proceeds at its own pace and, as Montessori (1965) stated it, "in accordance with the tendency of nature" (p., 164).

In motivational terms, we say that this learning is intrinsically motivated. The innate psychological needs to be competent and self-determining are manifested as curiosity and interest, and they lead children to explore and manipulate. Through continually taking on new challenges and working to master them, children not only experience spontaneous, intrinsic satisfactions, they also develop skills that allow them to function more effectively and autonomously.

The concept of intrinsic motivation arose during the 1950s (e.g., Berlyne, 1950; Harlow, 1953; Koch, 1956; White, 1959) in opposition to the focus on external rewards or reinforcers as the sole motivators of learning. Whether defined in terms of their role in drive reduction (Hull, 1943) or as operationally separable events that change the rate of responding (Skinner, 1938), external reinforcers were said to be necessary for learning. It became increasingly clear that much learning occurs in the absence of reinforcers and, indeed, that the opportunity for spontaneous learning can even serve as a reinforcer for other behaviors.

Along with the recognition of the importance of intrinsic motivation came an acceptance of the fact that people's inner experience is the appropriate focal point for a psychological analysis of human functioning. In the area of human motivation, for example, it has become clear that people's *experiences* of effectance and autonomy are critical determinants of motivational processes and of the concomitants and consequences of those processes.

In considering the issues of learning and achievement, we assume that *some* of children's learning and achievement is intrinsically motivated – in other words, is prompted by their interest and their desire to be effective and self-initiating. Consequently, we will explore the developmental progression of intrinsic motivation and the relationship of the experiences of competence and autonomy to that development. In addition, we will discuss the contextual factors that influence those experiences and, accordingly, affect the development of intrinsic motivation.

While intrinsically motivated learning is the earliest and most natural form of learning, it is not the only form. Especially as children grow older and enter institutional settings, extrinsic motivation plays an increasingly critical role in learning and achievement. The issues involved in the development of extrinsic motivation will be discussed in Chapter 8. Here we will concentrate only on the development of intrinsic motivation.

The active organism

In studying the development of intrinsic motivation our analysis begins with the person – with the assumption that humans are active and strive to be effective and autonomous. Since this activity is assumed to be inherent to the organism, we view the development of intrinsic motivation with an unfolding or "opening out" metaphor. Thus we suggest that the forms of one's intrinsic motivation or the areas where one's intrinsic motivation is displayed are best conceptualized in terms of the differentiation or channeling of a global motivation, rather than in terms of acquiring or "taking in" individual motivations.

Intrinsic motivation is innate, yet the differentiation of this motivation depends on three sets of factors that affect the child's experience of competence and autonomy: the relation of the child's abilities to the task demands, the affordances available in the environment and the degree to which the social context is supportive of autonomy versus controlling of behavior. In this chapter, we will focus primarily on the environmental factors that affect the development of intrinsic motivation; thus, we review research studies that have explored how various contextual factors have tended to facilitate or diminish intrinsic motivation for target activities. Because the differentiation of intrinsic motivation is a process whereby one's intrinsic interests become directed toward specific activities or classes of activities, the studies of increases and decreases in intrinsic motivation allow us to make direct inferences about the environmental factors that are likely to affect differentiation. To summarize, we are arguing that intrinsic motivation is innate; that children's general intrinsic motivation becomes differentiated such that their interest is directed toward certain activities; and that environmental factors influence the activities toward which their intrinsic interest is directed by affecting their experience of competence and self-determination.

Because this volume pertains to achievement, the development of intrinsic motivation is germane only insofar as intrinsic motivation has a clear relationship to learning and achievement. Consequently, we will review research that has compared the quality of intrinsically motivated versus externally controlled learning and achievement, and that also has related intrinsic motivation to a variety of personal and adjustment variables. In short, then, we address the development of intrinsically motivated learning and achievement in two parts: First we discuss the development of intrinsic motivation, then we discuss the relation of intrinsic motivation to qualities of learning, achievement, and adjustment.

The experience of competence versus incompetence

When intrinsically motivated, people seek interesting stimuli that function as nutriments for their growth and development. Because intrinsic motivation relates to the psychological needs to feel competent and self-determining, the experiences of competence and autonomy are important for maintaining intrinsic motivation and for influencing the developmental process of differentiating interests.

The experience of competence as a mediator has been studied in two broad ways: first, in the relationship between the target activity and the person's capabilities; and, second, as a function of feedback that is provided either by the activity itself or by another person. We will consider these in turn.

Optimal challenge

According to theories of intrinsic motivation (e.g., Csikszentmihalyi, 1975; Deci, 1975), activities must be optimally challenging to be interesting and to promote intrinsic motivation. Activities that are too easy lead to boredom, and those that are too difficult lead to frustration and the experience of anxiety and incompetence. Developmentally, this means that the differentiation of intrinsic motivation is, in part, influenced by what stimulating and optimally challenging activities are available in children's surroundings. In the words of Montessori (1965), stimulation must be "organized in direct relation to the child's internal organization" for it to be interesting and thus for the child to develop a preference for it.

The issue of optimal challenge is extremely important for children's learning and achievement; children will learn new material or perform effectively on a project only insofar as it is optimal for, and thus challenges, their abilities. This of course highlights the necessity to treat each child individually, which, unfortunately, represents a problem for teachers who have insufficient resources.

Several studies have explored the relationship between optimal challenge and intrinsic motivation. For example, Shapira (1976) found that subjects who were offered puzzles that ranged from very easy to very difficult tended to choose fairly difficult ones – ones that were challenging without being overly difficult. Stated differently, he found that when subjects were free to select their own activities, they indicated clear preferences for challenging ones. Similarly, Harter (1974) reported that when children worked on moderately difficult anagram problems they expressed greater pleasure than when they worked on very easy or very difficult ones.

Finally, Danner and Lonky (1981) directly tested the hypothesis that children would be more intrinsically motivated for optimally challenging tasks. First, they graded tasks in terms of cognitive complexity, and they pretested the children's ability levels. Then they introduced the children to activities with a range of difficulty levels and left the children free to participate in whichever ones they chose. Subsequently they asked the children to rate their interest in the various activities. Results confirmed that children spent the greatest amount of time with, and rated as most interesting, those tasks that were one step more difficult than their pretested skill level. Children seem to be intrinsically motivated for optimally challenging activities.

In terms of the differentiation of intrinsic interest, these studies imply that children will tend to channel their interests and intrinsic motivation toward those available activities that represent optimal challenges and therefore permit them to experience a sense of competence. Accordingly, the practical import of affording opportunities for choice of challenge level in achievement settings, and of offering moderately difficult tasks when directing learning activities, follows directly.

It is also true, however, that choice of activities is influenced by the social surroundings. Children seem especially curious about the activities that their parents, teachers, and friends seem to enjoy freely. If those activities, or modified versions of them, are optimally challenging for the children, the activities are likely to become the objects of an enduring preference. Children from homes in which adults spend a lot of time reading, for example, are more likely to be interested in reading than children from homes in which books are not part of the social milieu. Here we see that although the issue of optimal challenge is crucial for the differentiation of intrinsic motivation, so is the psychological need for *relatedness*. Other factors aside, people tend toward activities that are meaningful to others in their social context.

Feedback

When children try activities, they are likely to receive feedback about their effectance either directly from the activity (e.g., when they push a toy, it moves) or from other people (e.g., when they make the toy move, Mommy says, "That's very good!"). Anything that contributes to their experience of being competent will tend to enhance their intrinsic motivation for the target activity, and anything that contributes to their experience of being incompetent will tend to diminish their intrinsic motivation for the activity. Thus the differentiation of intrinsic motivation is hypothesized to be influenced by people's experiences of competence; their interests will tend to differentiate toward those optimally challenging activities at which they experience a sense of competence.

Harter (1982) provided some support for this hypothesis by finding that perceived competence and intrinsic motivation were positively correlated for children in late elementary and junior high school classes. Most of the support, however, has come from experimental, rather than correlational, paradigms. These studies have explored the effects on intrinsic motivation of positive and negative feedback and of success and failure.

Positive feedback. In one study, Deci (1971) reported that college student subjects who were told that they had performed well at an interesting activity were more intrinsically motivated for the activity than subjects who received no feedback. Blanck, Reis, and Jackson (1984) found similar results with college student subjects, as did Russell, Studstill, and Grant (1979). Anderson, Manoogian and Reznick (1976) reported comparable findings with kindergarten children. It appears that positive feedback tends to increase intrinsic motivation, presumably because it enhances people's experience of competence.

A study by Fisher (1978), however, illustrated that the positive competence feedback needs to occur within the context of self-determination if it is to enhance intrinsic motivation. When performance outcomes were constrained, there was no relationship between competence and intrinsic motivation, whereas when performance outcomes were self-determined, there was a positive relationship between the two variables. More recently, Sansone (1987) also provided evidence indicating that the effects of competence feedback on intrinsic motivation were stronger in a context of self-determination. When people feel responsible for the outcomes about which they receive positive competence feedback, intrinsic motivation is likely to be enhanced.

Negative feedback. When tasks are too difficult for a person, or when situations are structured so that desired outcomes do not follow reliably from a person's behavior, the person is likely to fail in his or her attempts to achieve the outcome. These failure experiences, as well as experiences of receiving negative feedback from another person, are predicted to undermine intrinsic motivation; indeed, they are predicted to result in amotivation and the sense of incompetence.

Deci, Cascio, and Krusell (1973) reported that subjects who failed to solve puzzles evidenced less subsequent intrinsic motivation for the puzzles than subjects who succeeded. The researchers also found that negative feedback to subjects about their performance, administered verbally by the experimenter, decreased intrinsic motivation for the target activity. Evidence of incompetence, whether from failure or from verbal feedback, led subjects to lose interest in the activity and thus to engage in it less during the free-choice period than subjects who did not have the experiences of incompetence.

Seligman and his colleagues (e.g., Garber & Seligman, 1980) have conducted numerous studies of failure and ineffectance. Their theory suggests that when people fail in their attempts to achieve desired outcomes, they tend to lose motivation and to act helpless. In one study (Hiroto & Seligman, 1975), subjects who performed an activity under conditions of unattainable outcomes lost the motivation to perform effectively such that in subsequent situations in which outcomes were attainable they were less effective in achieving those outcomes. The experience with failure left them amotivated.

Finally, Vallerand and Reid (1984) conducted a study in which subjects who worked on an interesting motor activity received either positive or negative verbal feedback about their performance. In addition to assessing the subjects' subsequent intrinsic motivation, these researchers also assessed subjects' perceived competence. Path analyses of the data confirmed not only that the subjects who received positive feedback were more intrinsically motivated than those who received negative feedback, but also that these effects were mediated by perceived competence.

In sum, a central theme thus far has been that people need to feel effective or competent and that the differentiation of intrinsic motivation will be toward endeavors that permit feelings of competence. These feelings seem to occur when people engage in challenging activities; when they receive evidence of being effective at the activities; and when they think they are personally responsible for these successes. Having focused primarily on competence thus far, we turn now to a discussion of self-determination.

The experience of autonomy versus control

Because the need for self-determination underlies intrinsic motivation, we have hypothesized that contextual factors supporting self-determination will maintain or enhance intrinsic motivation for that activity, whereas those that control one's behavior vis-à-vis the activity will undermine intrinsic motivation. Thus, we suggest, children's intrinsic interest will tend to differentiate toward those activities (especially the optimally challenging ones that they perform competently) from which they experience a sense of self-determination and away from those in which they feel pressured or controlled.

Much of the research on intrinsic motivation has explored the effects on intrinsic motivation of specific external, initiating or regulatory events that affect people's experience of self-determination (Deci & Ryan, 1987). In dozens of experiments, external events such as the offer of a reward or the imposition of a deadline have been manipulated for subjects working on some activity, and subsequent intrinsic motivation for the activitiy has been assessed. We will now review those experiments to draw conclusions about the types of events that tend to be experienced as autonomy-supportive versus controlling. We will then relate this research to the development of intrinsic motivation.

Choice

When intrinsically motivated, people not only choose the activities they engage in, they also choose how to carry out those activities. They display initiative, and that initiative leaves them feeling self-determined and further enhances their intrinsic motivation. This suggests that the opportunity to make choices – assuming the choices are meaningful and relevant – will enhance intrinsic motivation.

To test this hypothesis, Zuckerman, Porac, Lathin, Smith, and Deci (1978) asked subjects to work on puzzle problems. Half of the subjects were given a choice about which three of six puzzles to work on, and they were allowed to apportion the thirty minutes of puzzle-solving time among the three puzzles. The remaining subjects were yoked to these subjects in such a way that each subject in the second group was assigned the puzzles and time allotments that had been chosen by the yoked subject in the first group.

Subsequent to the puzzle-solving period, subjects were left alone and told that they could do whatever they liked. There were additional puzzles available as well as a selection of magazines. Unbeknownst to the subjects, they were being surreptitiously observed during this free-choice period, and the amount of time they spent working with the puzzles was used as a reflection of their intrinsic motivation.

Results of the experiment revealed that those subjects who had been given a choice about how to do an activity were significantly more likely to return to the activity during a free-choice period than were subjects who had not been given a choice. We interpret this as indicating that the opportunity for choice regarding an activity enhances intrinsic motivation for the activity. In other words, self-determination appears to facilitate a high level of intrinsic motivation.

In a study with children, Swann and Pittman (1977) found complementary results. Children in one group were shown three activities and were told that they could select the one they preferred to work on, although the experimenter then suggested that they might begin by working on "Activity B," because they were sitting closest to it. This was done so that all subjects would work on the same activity while feeling as if they had been given a choice. Children in a control group were merely assigned Activity B with no mention of choice. Results revealed that those children who had been told they could choose were more intrinsically motivated for the activity than those who had not.

In contrast to these two studies of choice, each of which showed that the experience of choice tended to facilitate intrinsic motivation, most studies have been of events that tend to be experienced as controlling, rather than as supportive of self-determination. One cannot easily "manipulate" self-determination, for by definition it must emanate from the subject as agent. By contrast, obstacles to self-determination are easier to operationalize and are thus more amenable to social psychological inquiry.

Rewards

The earliest studies of intrinsic motivation with humans explored the effects of rewards on intrinsic motivation. For example, Deci (1971) reported that when college students were paid for working on interesting puzzles, they displayed less subsequent intrinsic motivation for the puzzles than did others who were not paid. Yoshimura (1979) replicated the finding with

Japanese students, and Anderson et al. (1976) reported a similar finding with kindergarten children.

Ryan, Mims, and Koestner (1983) reviewed the literature on the effects of rewards on intrinsic motivation and noted that a variety of different reward structures have been used. Consequently, they developed a typology of reward structures, organized in accord with what the rewards are contingent upon. After reviewing the research they concluded that most reward structures tend to be evaluative and controlling and thus to undermine intrinsic motivation relative to comparable control conditions. However, if the reward is structured to convey positive competence feedback in the absence of evaluative pressure, it is least likely to be undermining; indeed, it may even enhance intrinsic motivation (Harackiewicz, Manderlink, & Sansone, 1984).

Numerous rewards, other than money, have been found to produce decrements in intrinsic motivation. Food (Ross, 1975), prizes (Harackiewicz, 1979), awards (Lepper, Greene, & Nisbett, 1973), avoidance of punishment (Deci & Cascio, 1972), and tokens (Greene, Sternberg, & Lepper, 1976) have been shown to be controlling, as evidenced by their undermining of intrinsic motivation. Rewards have been found to be most disruptive when they are anticipated before performance of the activity (Lepper et al., 1973) and when they are made salient (Ross, 1975). It appears that although rewards motivate behavior, the motivation they induce is extrinsic. Behavior becomes dependent upon the rewards, and in certain situations people come to function more like pawns controlled by the rewards than like origins of their own behavior (deCharms, 1968).

Other controlling events

Rewards are not the only events that control behavior. Surveillance, whether by video camera (Lepper & Greene, 1975; Plant & Ryan, 1985) or in person (Pittman, Davey, Alafat, Wetherill, & Kramer, 1980), has been shown to undermine intrinsic motivation, as have deadlines (Amabile, DeJong, & Lepper, 1976) and goal imposition (Mossholder, 1980). Any external event that is experienced as pressure to perform in a particular way or to attain a particular outcome seems to limit people's self-determination and correspondingly to undermine their intrinsic motivation.

Evaluations

One thing common to events that are experienced as controlling is that they involve evaluation. They pressure people to perform, and the performance is evaluated. On the surface these evaluations are of people's performance and may often contain useful competence-relevant feedback. All too often, however, such evaluations are experienced by the recipients as evaluations of them as persons. In a society such as ours, so strongly oriented toward achievement, individuals' personal value may be judged, even if inadvertently, in terms of their performance. To the degree that this is so, evaluations, even when they are positive and are not accompanied by rewards, surveillance, or deadlines, are likely to be experienced as highly controlling.

Smith (1974) conducted a study that supported this hypothesis. In his study, subjects learned about art and were told that they would be evaluated. At the end of the task, all subjects received positive evaluations; yet these subjects evidenced lower levels of subsequent intrinsic motivation than did subjects who had not been evaluated. A study by Amabile (1979) showed that the expectation of evaluations also decreased the creativity of art projects that subjects produced.

The Smith study is particularly interesting because subjects received positive feedback, yet their intrinsic motivation decreased. This serves to emphasize that although positive feedback may foster intrinsic motivation, it will do so only when it is experienced as noncontrolling. An emphasis on evaluation, on performing up to someone else's standards, tends to make the positive feedback controlling and thus to diminish intrinsic motivation. If the feedback were negative, the negative effects would likely be even worse.

Competition

Competition, like evaluation, is quite prevalent within the institutions of our society. From an early age, children are encouraged to compete in games as well as in a variety of achievement-related activities. Motivationally, competition is quite complex. On the one hand, competition offers people optimal challenges and feedback that may facilitate competence. Winning, of course, can affirm one's competence, as can performing well even when one loses. For all these reasons, competition can foster intrinsic motivation; and, indeed, it often does. On the other hand, competition can be quite controlling. The focus on defeating another, for example, is extrinsic to performing effectively; and when defeating another takes on central importance, competitive behavior is likely to be more extrinsically motivated and thus undermining of intrinsic interest and motivation.

To explore the effects of competition on intrinsic motivation, Deci, Betley, Kahle, Abrams, and Porac (1981) had subjects work on interesting puzzle problems in the presence of a confederate. Subjects in half the dyads were instructed to try to beat the other person, and subjects in the other half were instructed merely to do as well as they could. In all cases, the confederates let the subjects finish first, so that those who competed won, and those who did not compete received what can be thought of as self-administered positive feedback. Results of the experiment indicated that the competition subjects displayed less subsequent intrinsic motivation than did the noncompetition subjects. In other words, it appears that people's experience of competing in this situation tended to be controlling, even though subjects won the competition. If they had lost, the feedback would have been negative and would, no doubt, have been even more detrimental. In fact, a study by Reeve, Olson, and Cole (1985) demonstrated that losers of a competition were significantly less intrinsically motivated than winners.

To summarize this research on the effects of external initiating or regulatory events, we can conclude that controlling events are those that pressure people to think, feel, or behave in particular ways. When events are experienced in this way, they impinge upon people's self-determination and decrease their intrinsic motivation. Controlling events may serve to motivate behavior, but they motivate extrinsically, at the expense of intrinsic motivation.

The implications for development are as follows: When a child encounters an optimally challenging activity, the child will more likely develop a preference for, and the child's intrinsic motivation will more likely be directed toward, the activity if the child experienced choice with regard to the activity and if the child did not experience his or her behavior as being pressured or controlled.

In terms of learning and achieving in schools, the implications would seem to be extremely important. Schools place heavy emphasis on evaluation, and the competition for good grades – for doing better than other children – often is quite strong. Under these conditions, there seems to be a great risk that the children will lose a sense of intrinsic value and self-determination for learning. Children who receive positive feedback may show heightened extrinsic motivation but less intrinsic motivation; those who receive negative feedback may lose motivation altogether.

Interpersonal contexts

Two types of studies have moved beyond the effects of specific events to investigate the influence of interpersonal contexts on motivational processes. The first was a set of field studies in which the classroom climate was assessed, either by questionnaires completed by the teachers or by children's descriptions of classroom characteristics, and then related to motivational processes. The second was a set of laboratory experiments in which external events were presented within different interpersonal contexts and motivational processes measured.

In one study (Deci, Nezlek, & Sheinman, 1981), teachers' orientations toward supporting children's autonomy versus controlling children's behavior were assessed using an instrument developed by Deci, Schwartz, Sheinman, and Ryan (1981). The reasoning was that if teachers were more oriented toward supporting autonomy they would tend to create an interpersonal climate that promoted the children's self-determination, whereas if they were more oriented toward controlling behavior, they would tend to provide a controlling context. The hypothesis, of course, was that when children experienced the interpersonal context as supporting self-determination, they would be more intrinsically motivated than when they experienced it as being controlling.

Children in the classrooms of these teachers completed Harter's intrinsic versus extrinsic motivation scale (Harter, 1981) and her perceived competence scale (Harter, 1982). Analyses of the data revealed strong positive correlations between teachers' orientations and children's motivational variables. Children whose teachers were more autonomy-supporting tended to display more intrinsic motivation – in the form of more curiosity, preference for challenge, and independent mastery attempts – as well as higher levels of perceived competence and self-esteem, than did children in the classrooms with more controlling teachers. The teachers' orientations impacted children's motivation within the first six to eight weeks of the school year, and the influence remained strong throughout the year.

Ryan and Grolnick (1986) explored the relation between elementary-school children's perceptions of their classroom climate and a variety of variables relevant to their motivation. Because our theory emphasizes that it is the *functional significance* of one's environment, rather than its objective properties, that affects motivational processes, these researchers assessed perceptions directly, rather than inferring what these perceptions must be from an assessment of environmental factors, such as teachers' orientations. Results of the study confirmed that children who perceived their classrooms to be more supportive of autonomy, as measured by deCharms' (1976) classroom climate measure, were more intrinsically motivated and had higher self-esteem than children who perceived their classrooms to be more controlling. Furthermore, when children wrote stories about hypothetical classrooms, those who perceived their classrooms to be supportive of autonomy projected more autonomy into the hypothetical classrooms than those who perceived their classrooms to be controlling.

DeCharms (1976) reported that when teachers were trained to be more supportive of children's autonomy, the children did indeed perceive the classroom to be more supportive of their autonomy, and these children became more intrinsically motivated. It appears, then, that teacher training is one route toward developing classrooms that will facilitate children's self-determination and intrinsic motivation.

Contexts and events

Several laboratory studies have explored the effects of specific events within different experimentally created interpersonal contexts. Ryan, Mims, and Koestner (1983), for example, administered performance-contingent rewards in both noncontrolling and controlling interpersonal contexts. Performance-contingent rewards are those that are administered contingent upon the attainment of a specified level of performance. For example, if a person received a dollar for each problem he or she solved faster than, say, 90 percent of the subjects, the reward would be performance-contingent. This type of reward is quite widely used and highly motivating, and it represents an interesting case for study because it is double-edged. By containing inherent positive feedback, the reward affirms one's competence. However, by requiring a specified level of performance, the structure may also be experienced as quite controlling.

Ryan et al. (1983) hypothesized that the interpersonal context would determine which of these two aspects of the reward would be more salient for the subjects. The contexts were created through the style and locution used by the experimenter. Specifically, the controlling context was formulated by conveying to subjects what they "should" do. For example, people were told that they would be rewarded for performing well, "as they should," whereas the noncontrolling context was created by not utilizing this controlling language.

Results revealed a significant difference between the two reward groups, with the controlling context leading to a lower level of intrinsic motivation. Further, a no-reward, no-feedback control group was midway between the two reward groups, thus showing that, depending upon the interpersonal context, performance-contingent rewards can either enhance or diminish intrinsic motivation, relative to a situation with no reward and no feedback.

Since performance-contingent rewards are structured in such a way that there is positive feedback inherent in them, Ryan and colleagues (1983) included two positive feedback control groups, one receiving positive feedback in a controlling context and one in a noncontrolling context. Relative to the corresponding positive feedback, the performance-contingent rewards decreased intrinsic motivation in each context. It appears, then, that although administered in a noncontrolling way, performance-contingent rewards increased intrinsic motivation relative to a situation of no rewards and no feedback, and that they decreased intrinsic motivation relative to a situation of positive feedback without rewards. Thus, although rewards do tend to be controlling, as we previously concluded, the context within which they are administered has an important influence upon how they are experienced and thus upon how they affect intrinsic motivation.

In another experiment, Ryan (1982) explored the effects of positive feedback in a noncontrolling versus a controlling context. As we mentioned earlier, positive feedback tends to enhance intrinsic motivation unless it is experienced as controlling. Ryan tested the hypothesis that a controlling interpersonal context may lead positive feedback to be experienced as controlling. Results of the study confirmed the hypothesis: when feedback was administered in a controlling context, it resulted in a significantly lower level of intrinsic motivation than when it was administered in a noncontrolling context.[1] Pittman and colleagues (1980) reported comparable results.

Finally, a study by Koestner, Ryan, Bernieri and Holt (1984) investigated the effects of setting limits when done in a noncontrolling versus a controlling context. The study was done with first and second grade children who painted pictures, and the limits related to their being neat with the painting materials. The researchers reasoned that, in order to relieve the possible controlling pressure created by the existence of the limits, it was important to avoid controlling locution – words like "should" and "must" – and to acknowledge the fact that the children might not want to conform to the limits. Indeed, emotional acknowledgment is one way of conveying respect for a child's autonomy and experience (Ginott, 1961). With limits being presented in this way, the children were able to experience them as less controlling, and as a result their subsequent intrinsic motivation for painting was higher than that of the children whose limits were presented in a controlling way. The results further revealed, in line with previous work by Amabile (1983), that controlling limits led the children to produce paintings that were judged to be less creative. The study by Koestner and

[1] There is some evidence from studies by Deci, Cascio, and Krusell (1975) and Kast (1983) that females are more inclined to experience positive feedack as controlling than are males. Nonetheless, males and females alike tend to lose intrinsic motivation when the positive feedback is administered in a controlling context.

colleagues was particularly important because it was the first one to demonstrate that it is possible to constrain children's behavior in a way that does not necessarily undermine their sense of self-determination, their intrinsic motivation, and their creativity.

In summary, research suggests that interpersonal contexts can be experienced as either autonomy-supportive or controlling and will thus have correspondingly different effects on intrinsic motivation. Furthermore, events (such as the offer of a reward or the provision of feedback) that tend to have a particular impact on intrinsic motivation may have a somewhat different impact if they are administered within a different interpersonal context. For example, competence-enhancing events such as positive feedback may not facilitate intrinsic motivation – indeed, may undermine it – if the context is controlling. On the other hand, events such as monetary rewards or limits that tend to be controlling may not undermine intrinsic motivation if the context is autonomy-supportive.

All of these results on the effects of external initiating and regulatory events have been integrated by Deci and Ryan (1980, 1985b, 1987) using *cognitive evaluation theory.* This theory suggests that the experience of autonomy (versus being controlled) and the experience of competence (versus incompetence) are critical factors in determining motivational processes and that inputs relevant to the initiation or regulation of behavior are experienced in one of three characteristic ways, thus prompting one of three sets of motivational processes. Inputs that are experienced as supporting autonomy and facilitating competence are labeled *informational;* they tend to maintain or enhance intrinsic motivation. Inputs that are experienced as pressures to think, feel, or behave in specific ways are labeled *controlling;* they tend to undermine intrinsic motivation, though they may strengthen extrinsic motivation. Finally, inputs that are experienced as promoting or signifying incompetence are labeled *amotivating;* they tend to undermine both intrinsic and extrinsic motivation.

Any input, such as a praise statement, for example, may be experienced in any one of these three ways. It may be experienced as affirmation of one's competence without evaluative or pressuring overtones, in which case it would be informational. Alternatively, it may be experienced as an evaluation, as something that pressures one to do as others think one should do, in which case it would be controlling. Finally, it may be experienced as patronizing, or as the type of praise for effort which implies that the person is really not competent. In such cases, it could be amotivating. The research reviewed here suggests that each external event can be classified as tending, on average, to be experienced in one of the three ways; however, many factors can affect how it will actually be experienced. Most notably, the interpersonal context within which the event occurs can lead it to have varying kinds of functional significance. Further, as we will see later, there are individual differences in people's tendency to experience inputs in the three different ways.

From a developmental perspective, the research we have reviewed suggests that the differentiation of intrinsic motivation will be influenced by how an initiating or regulatory event is experienced. Other things being equal, intrinsic motivation will tend to be directed toward activities encountered in contexts that are experienced as autonomy supportive (i.e., informational) and away from those encountered in contexts that are experienced as either controlling or amotivating.

Internal events

The most criticial factor involved with intrinsic motivation seems to be self-determination. When intrinsically motivated, people are active and self-determined, and an abundance of research indicates that the most significant experience for maintaining intrinsic motivation is that of self-determination. Any factor that undermines this experience will decrease intrinsic motivation.

An emphasis on external evaluations seems quite likely to undermine people's sense of self-determination. When they believe their esteem is dependent upon evaluations of their performance, they are likely to feel controlled and to lose interest in the target activity. Covington and Beery (1976) suggested that an additional cost of controlling evaluations is that they lead children to hinge their own self-esteem on performance. This, according to our perspective, is likely to have quite undesirable consequences. For the child who performs badly, the results will be deleterious, since he or she will experience a lowered sense of self-worth and confidence. And even for the child who performs well, the results can be quite negative, because that child may end up feeling like a pawn to performance outcomes. By *having* to perform well to feel worthy, the child may lose his or her sense of self-determination and intrinsic value for the activity.

According to cognitive evaluation theory (Ryan, 1982), hinging one's self-esteem on performance outcomes is an instance of *internally controlling regulation.* We have suggested that internal events such as thoughts or feelings that are involved in the initiation or regulation of behavior can be experienced in qualitatively different ways and can be classified as being informational, controlling, or amotivating, just as external events can be experienced in these ways. Contingent self-esteem, we assert, is a type of control not unlike the control implicit in esteem from others being made contingent. Both are predicted to undermine intrinsic motivation.

This is an important point theoretically, for it highlights the fact that just because an initiating or regulatory event is internal does not mean that the regulation is self-determined. Indeed, internal events can be experienced as controlling or amotivating, in which case they will be antagonistic to self-determination.

Consider as an example a girl who loves science and enjoys working on science projects. There is an upcoming science fair in the girl's city, and she has decided to enter a project and has begun working on it. Given the girl's love for science, it is possible that she would be very much task-involved in this project, working out of interest in the activity and the inherent rewards it contains. Alternatively, however, suppose that for some reason she is very invested in the science fair and has come to believe that she *has* to do well to maintain her self-image. This would be a case of ego involvement; her self-esteem would be on the line. We assert that in these two cases the quality of her involvement with the activity would be quite different and would have different motivational consequences. In the latter case she would feel pressured and would not experience a true sense of self-determination. Thus, we predict that in the former case she would maintain her love for science and her intrinsic interest in science projects, whereas in the latter case these would be to some extent undermined.

Ryan (1982) provided the first test of the hypothesis that internally controlling regulation can undermine intrinsic motivation. He reasoned that ego involvement, which is an instance of contingent self-esteem, is likely to be experienced as controlling and thus will undermine intrinisc motivation relative to task involvement. Ryan stimulated ego involvement by telling college student subjects that performance on hidden-figures puzzles, such as the ones they were about to begin working on, reflects creative intelligence. He induced task involvement simply by telling subjects about the puzzles and their creator. As predicted, ego-involved subjects displayed less intrinsic motivation in a subsequent free-choice period than did task-involved subjects. The experience of pressuring themselves to do well in order to maintain self-esteem decreased subjects' intrinsic motivation, presumably by diminishing their experience of self-determination.

Plant and Ryan (1985) suggested that another internal process that tends to be controlling in nature is what Carver and Scheier (1981) called public self-awareness. This phenomenon, which is ubiquitous in daily life, involves regulating oneself on the basis of what one imagines others must think. It involves being aware of oneself as if seen through the eyes of another, and it is perhaps the primary means by which conformity and the loss of self-determination are anchored in the psyche and experience of individuals.

Plant and Ryan (1985) reported a study in which they used a factorial design to cross task involvement versus ego involvement with type of self-focused attention. The self-focused attention subjects were seated either in front of a mirror or in front of a video camera, each of which can induce public self-awareness. Control group subjects had no self-focusing stimuli. The reasoning was that focusing attention on oneself with the mirror or camera would lead people to become controlling with themselves. Results of the study replicated the Ryan (1982) main effect for the task versus ego variable, and also showed a main effect for self-focus. The video camera led to the lowest level of intrinsic motivation and the mirror to the next lowest, and both were lower than the non-self-focused attention group.

Most recently, Koestner, Zuckerman, and Koestner (1987) provided further support for the task- versus ego-involved distinction. Their study reported that task involvement enhanced intrinsic motivation relative to ego-involvement. In addition, task-involved subjects were more likely to seek higher levels of challenge at the activity. However, these authors also showed that the orientation of subjects' involvement (task versus ego) interacted with the type of feedback that was administered (ability versus effort). Under task-involving conditions, subjects were more motivated by effort-relevant feedback, while ego-involved subjects were more motivated by ability-oriented praise. This interactive result bespeaks the self-esteem contingency that underlies the extrinsic, but internal, motivational orientation of those who are ego-involved.

Taken together, the results of these studies support the assertion that not all internal regulatory processes represent self-determination. Ego involvement and public self-awareness, for example, are modes of self-regulation that tend to be extrinsic and controlling in character. Accordingly, they have been found to undermine intrinsic motivation. On the other hand, as Ryan, Koestner, and Deci (in press) have recently argued, ego-involvement can lead to persistence at activities because of its internally controlling nature. Distinguishing between intrinsic motivation and internally controlled persistence will represent an increasing area of interest as the field of motivation grows toward greater differentiation with regard to the various forms of self-regulation (Deci & Ryan, 1985b; Anderson & Rodin, 1989; Olson, 1985).

Personality orientations

The implications of the work reported thus far are two: first, that people's intrinsic motivation for activities is to some extent a function of their experiences of self-determination and competence with respect to those activities; and second, that people may, through the cumulative effects of these experiences, develop enduring orientations toward causality that relate to a wide variety of characteristics and behaviors.

For example, if children continually have experiences of being competent and autonomous, they may develop a general orientation that entails being intrinsically motivated and self-determined. If, however, their continued experiences are of being controlled and having their self-esteem hinged to performance, they may develop an orientation toward being controlled. And finally, if their continued experiences are of incompetence, they may become generally amotivated.

In our work (e.g., Deci, 1980; Deci & Ryan, 1985a), we use the concept of causality orientations, by which we mean enduring motivational orientations. These involve characteristic ways of understanding and orienting to inputs, and they are hypothesized to have implications for a variety of motivationally relevant processes. There are three such orientations: the *autonomy orientation* involves the tendency to experience inputs as informational; the *control orientation* involves the tendency to experience inputs as controlling; and the *impersonal orientation* involves the tendency to experience inputs as amotivating. The three orientations were illustrated, respectively, by the three descriptions in the preceding paragraph. An instrument developed to assess causality orientations (Deci & Ryan, 1985a) has allowed us to confirm that, indeed, young adults have developed different orientations toward the initiation and regulation of their behavior.

Research using the instrument has indicated that the autonomy orientation was positively associated with self-actualization (Shostrom, 1966), with people's tendency to support the autonomy of children (Deci et al., 1981), with self-esteem (Janis & Field, 1959), and with ego development (Loevinger, 1976). The control orientation was positively associated with the Type A coronary-prone behavior pattern (Jenkins, Rosenman, & Friedman, 1967) and with public self-consciousness (Fenigstein, Scheier, & Buss, 1975). It was negatively correlated with performance on a psychology examination. Finally, the impersonal orientation, which describes the ongoing experience of incompetence, was positively associated with self-derogation (Kaplan & Pokorny, 1969), with depression (Beck & Beamesderfer, 1974), with social anxiety (Fenigstein, Scheier, & Buss, 1975), and with an external locus of control (Rotter, 1966).

The mapping of these results onto the earlier experimental ones is somewhat complex, yet one can see that the tendencies and behaviors that correlated positively with the autonomy orientation are ones that tend to be displayed in informational contexts and that tend to be associated with intrinsic motivation. Further, the tendencies and behaviors that correlated positively with the control orientation are ones that tend to be observed in controlling contexts. Finally, the tendencies and behaviors that correlated positively with the impersonal orientation are ones that characterize amotivation and helplessness. Thus one can see a clear parallel between the motivational processes that tend to be operative in the presence of events or contexts that are experienced as informational, controlling, or amotivating, and those processes that tend to be associated with the autonomy, control, and impersonal causality orientations, respectively.

The concomitants and consequences of intrinsic motivation

Thus far, our discussion has focused on the conditions that influence the differentiation of intrinsic motivation. We turn our attention now to research on other variables that have been found to be concomitants or consequences of intrinsic motivation. Some of the studies have entailed correlating intrinsic motivation with other variables, whereas others have been more indirect, investigating the effects on relevant dependent variables (e.g., creativity and cognitive flexibility) of the independent variables that have reliably impacted intrinsic motivation. This latter strategy has allowed us to infer that intrinsic motivation is a mediating variable in the observed relationship, although of course this is appropriate only if the inference is theoretically meaningful within the emerging network of findings concerning intrinsic motivation and self-determination.

Learning

Intrinsic motivation is directly applicable to the area of education. It is clear that young children are intrinsically motivated to learn and that classroom variables and teachers' orientations affect children's intrinsic motivation. Following up on this issue, we have designed studies to explore the relationship between intrinsic motivation and learning.

In one study (Benware & Deci, 1984) college student subjects were asked to learn the contents of a passage on neuroanatomy. Some subjects were told that they would have the opportunity to teach the material to other students, and others were told that they would be tested on the material.

The reasoning underlying the study was that those subjects who expected to use the material in some meaningful way (i.e., to teach it) would be more active and more intrinsically motivated in their learning than those who expected to be tested. Because tests and evaluations tend to be experienced as controlling, we expected the test subjects to lose intrinsic motivation for learning and thus to learn less well.

After the two groups of subjects spent about three hours learning the material with the different expectations, all subjects took an exam on the material. Some questions required conceptual responses; others required mere rote memorization. Results of the experiment indicated that subjects who learned in order to teach had significantly higher conceptual learning scores than those who learned in order to be tested; however, the two groups did not differ in their rote memorization scores. Furthermore, a measure of intrinsic motivation revealed that there was greater intrinsic motivation in the learning-in-order-to-teach group than in the learning-in-order-to-be-tested group.

Grolnick and Ryan (1987) studied the conceptual and rote learning of fifth grade children using an experimental paradigm. Children read a passage under one of three learning sets. The first was a controlling set in which they were told that they would be tested and graded on the material. The second was a noncontrolling set in which children were told that this was an opportunity to read and learn the material. And the final group received a nondirected learning set in which the children were not given an instruction to learn the material. Thus, any learning that took place in this condition was incidental, in the sense that it was presumed to be a function of the subjects' interest rather than of external directions. Both the controlling and noncontrolling groups represented directed learning; however, both the noncontrolling and spontaneous learning groups were expected to represent autonomous learning. Following the learning, all children took a test on the material in the passage.

Results of the experiment showed that both groups that had been given the directed learning set (the controlling and noncontrolling) did better on rote recall than the nondirected group; however, both the noncontrolling-directed and the spontaneous groups did better than the controlling group on conceptual learning. It appears, then, that while direction and control may facilitate rote learning, conceptual understanding requires that children feel relatively self-determined. Furthermore, it is interesting to note that in a one-week follow-up, the researchers found that the children in the controlling condition had forgotten the most material: there was no longer any difference among the three groups on rote recall. "Force feeding" of material, it seems, may promote short-term recall at the expense of conceptual understanding; but even that "advantage" may be quickly lost.

Creativity and cognitive flexibility

Several studies have focused on creativity or cognitive flexibility as dependent variables. They have typically used experimental paradigms similar to the intrinsic motivation paradigm in which initiating or regulatory events are manipulated and then the dependent variable is assessed during an ensuing performance period.

Amabile (1983) has reported several studies in which children produced paintings or collages under different experimental conditions. Subsequently, these artistic productions were rated for creativity by a set of judges who used a consensual assessment technique. The studies showed consistently that the same initiating and regulatory events that decrease intrinsic motivation also decrease creativity. When subjects were told that their collages would be evaluated, the collages were less creative than when there was no mention of evaluation. Similarly, when children competed to make the best collage, the collages were less creative than when there was no competition. Finally, when limits were set in a controlling manner on the children's neatness in painting, they led to less creativity than when limits were set informationally (Koestner et al., 1984).

In a complementary study, McGraw and McCullers (1979) explored the effects of rewards on cognitive flexibility. Subjects were asked to solve a series of problems, each of which had the same solution. After several such problems, they were given a problem with a different though easier solution. The dependent variable of interest was the amount of time it took to solve the easier problem. Subjects who are more flexible in their thinking would be expected to break the set they have developed and solve the problem quickly, whereas those who are more rigid would be expected to have a more difficult time doing so. In this experiment, half the subjects were given monetary rewards for solving the puzzles and half were not, and the question was whether rewards (which are typically experienced as controlling) would affect subjects' cognitive flexibility as reflected in the time it took them to break set. The results indicated that rewarded subjects spent longer solving the final, easy problem than did the nonrewarded subjects. The controlling nature of the extrinsic rewards seemed to create a more rigid relationship to the problem solution; in other words, it decreased subjects' flexible, conceptual thinking about the problem.

In general, then, these various studies seem to point to the same conclusion, namely, that the addition of extrinsic controls to a learning or problem-solving situation tends to limit people's creative, conceptual, flexible engagement with the activity.

Emotional tone and self-esteem

In our view of the achievement process, the quality of people's experience, as well as the achievement itself, is extremely important. Consequently, we give primary consideration to people's feelings while they are engaged with the achievement activity.

In one study, Garbarino (1975) found that sixth grade girls who were rewarded for tutoring younger girls tended to be more critical and to evidence a more negative emotional tone than comparable tutors who were not rewarded. Correspondingly, Ryan (1982) and Ryan, Mims, and Koestner (1983) found that subjects in controlling conditions reported experiencing more pressure and tension than subjects in noncontrolling conditions. It seems that the experiences associated with being controlled are relatively negative.

Further, controlling experiences can also have a more enduring negative effect. For example, Deci, Nezlek, and Sheinman (1981) reported that children in classrooms of more controlling teachers had lower self-esteem than children in classrooms with less controlling teachers, and Ryan and Grolnick (1986) reported that children who perceived their classrooms to be more controlling had lower self-esteem than children who perceived their classrooms to be more supportive of autonomy.

All things considered, then, it is clear that controlling conditions have a negative relationship not only with conceptual learning and creative thinking, but with experiential and adjustment variables as well.

Summary

Traditionally, the study of motivation and achievement has utilized the construct of achievement motivation, which describes the strength of one's tendency to achieve. This fails to recognize, however, that the motivational bases of achievement can be quite varied. Some achievement is instrinsically motivated, while other achievement is based in some form of extrinsic motivation. In the present chapter we have discussed only the former; the latter will be addressed in Chapter 8.

Intrinsic motivation represents a generalized tendency to be active in one's encounters with the environment. It is based, we have suggested, in the human needs to be competent and self-determining. Further, activity that is so motivated develops in such a way that people's interests tend to differentiate toward specific activities or classes of activities. Here we have focused first on the factors that affect the differentiation process, concluding that children's intrinsic motivation tends to be directed toward, and that children develop preferences for, activities that are optimally challenging, that are available in their environment and engaged in by significant adults, that leave them feeling competent, and that they are able to undertake in a relatively self-determined manner. Finally, we have reviewed research on the quality of intrinsically motivated learning and achievement. Evidence indicates that intrinsically motivated activity tends to be associated with greater conceptual learning, more creativity, increased cognitive flexibility, a more positive emotional tone, and higher self-esteem than does externally controlled activity.

The topic of intrinsic motivation brings an important aspect of human nature into clear focus. Humans are by innate inclination active, curious, and desirous of challenges. Such tendencies are the natural wellsprings of growth, activity, and accomplishment. All too often, in a culture that strongly emphasizes achievement, parents and teachers become impatient while waiting for intrinsically motivated learning and achievement to occur. To the detriment of all, they supply prods and pressures to motivate the children. Evidence presented here and elsewhere (Deci & Ryan, 1985b) attests to the importance of intrinsic motivation as a human resource, and highlights the significance of intrinsic motivation for effective functioning and psychological well-being. However, this research also attests to the frailty of intrinsic motivation and to people's susceptibility to social controls. It seems to us that the centrality of intrinsic motivation in psychological theories of achievement cannot be overemphasized, and that each of us concerned with children's learning and achievement needs to work toward the types of social contexts that facilitate intrinsic motivation.

References

Amabile, T.M. (1979). Effects of external evaluations on artistic creativity. *Journal of Personality and Social Psychology, 37,* 221–233.

Amabile, T.M. (1983). *The social psychology of creativity.* New York: Springer-Verlag.

Amabile, T.M., DeJong, W., & Lepper, M.R. (1976). Effects of externally imposed deadlines on subsequent intrinsic motivation. *Journal of Personality and Social Psychology, 34,* 92–98.

Anderson, R., Manoogian, S.T., & Reznick, J.S. (1976). The undermining and enhancing of intrinsic motivation in preschool children. *Journal of Personality and Social Psychology, 34,* 915–922.

Anderson, S. & Rodin, J. (1989). Is bad news always bad?: Cue and feedback effects on intrinsic motivation. *Journal of Applied Social Psychology, 19,* 449–467.

Beck, A.T. & Beamesderfer, A. (1974). Assessment of depression: The depression inventory. *Modern Problems of Pharmacopsychiatry, 7,* 151–169.

Benware, C. & Deci, E.L. (1984). The quality of learning with an active versus passive motivational set. *American Educational Research Journal, 21,* 755–765.

Berlyne, D.E. (1950). Novelty and curiosity as determinants of exploratory behavior. *British Journal of Psychology, 41,* 68–80.

Blanck, P.D., Reis, H.T., & Jackson, L. (1984). The effects of verbal reinforcements on intrinsic motivation for sex-linked tasks. *Sex Roles, 10,* 369–387.

Carver, C.S., & Scheier, M.F. (1981). *Attention and self-regulation: A control theory approach to human behavior.* New York: Springer-Verlag.

Covington, M.V., & Beery, R.G. (1976). *Self-worth and school learning.* New York: Holt, Rinehart, & Winston.

Csikszentmihalyi, M. (1975). *Beyond boredom and anxiety.* San Francisco: Jossey-Bass.

Danner, F.W. & Lonky, E. (1981). A cognitive-developmental approach to the effects of rewards on intrinsic motivation. *Child Development, 52,* 1043–1052.

deCharms, R. (1968). *Personal causation: The internal affective determinants of behavior.* New York: Academic Press.

deCharms, R. (1976). *Enhancing motivation: Change in the classroom.* New York: Irvington.

Deci, E.L. (1971). Effects of externally mediated rewards on intrinsic motivation. *Journal of Personality and Social Psychology, 18,* 105–115.

Deci, E.L. (1975). *Intrinsic motivation.* New York: Plenum.

Deci, E.L. (1980). *The psychology of self-determination.* Lexington, MA: D.C. Heath (Lexington Books).

Deci, E.L. (in press). Interest and the intrinsic motivation of behavior. In K.A. Renninger, S. Hidi, & A. Krapp (Eds.), *The role of interest in learning and development.* Hillsdale, NJ: Eribaum.

Deci, E.L., Betley, G., Kahle, J., Abrams, L., & Porac, J. (1981). When trying to win: Competition and intrinsic motivation. *Personality and Social Psychology Bulletin, 7,* 79–83.

Deci, E.L., & Cascio, W.F. (1972, April). Changes in intrinsic motivation as a function of negative feedback and threats. Paper presented at the meeting of the Eastern Psychological Association, Boston, MA.

Deci, E.L., Cascio, W.F., & Krusell, J. (1973, May). Sex differences, verbal reinforcement, and intrinsic motivation. Paper presented at the meeting of the Eastern Psychological Association, Washington, DC.

Deci, E.L., Cascio, W.F., & Krusell, J. (1975). Cognitive evaluation theory and some comments on the Calder and Staw critique. *Journal of Personality and Social Psychology, 31,* 81–85.

Deci, E.L., Nezlek, J., & Sheinman, L. (1981). Characteristics of the rewarder and intrinsic motivation of the rewardee. *Journal of Personality and Social Psychology, 40,* 1–10.

Deci, E.L. & Ryan, R.M. (1980). The empirical exploration of intrinsic motivational processes. In L. Berkowitz (Ed.), *Advances in experimental social psychology* (Vol. 13, pp. 39–80). New York: Academic Press.

Deci, E.L., & Ryan, R.M. (1985a). The general causality orientations scale: Self-determination in personality. *Journal of Research in Personality, 19,* 109–134.

Deci, E.L. & Ryan, R.M. (1985b). *Intrinsic motivation and self-determination in human behavior.* New York: Plenum.

Deci, E.L. & Ryan, R.M. (1987). The support of autonomy and the control of behavior. *Journal of Personality and Social Psychology, 53,* 1024–1037.

Deci, E.L., Schwartz, A.J., Sheinman, L., & Ryan, R.M. (1981). An instrument to assess adults' orientations toward control versus autonomy with children: Reflections on intrinsic motivation and perceived competence. *Journal of Educational Psychology, 73,* 642–650.

Fenigstein, A., Scheier, M.F., & Buss, A.H. (1975). Public and private self-consciousness: Assessment and theory. *Journal of Consulting and Clinical Psychology, 43,* 522–527.

Fisher, C.D. (1978). The effects of personal control, competence, and extrinsic reward systems on intrinsic motivation. *Organizational Behavior and Human Performance, 21,* 273–288.

Garbarino, J. (1975). The impact of anticipated reward upon cross-aged tutoring. *Journal of Personality and Social Psychology, 32,* 421–428.

Garber, J. & Seligman, M.E.P. (Eds.). (1980). *Human helplessness.* New York: Academic Press.

Ginott, H.G. (1961). *Group psychotherapy with children.* New York: McGraw Hill.

Greene, D., Sternberg, B., & Lepper, M.R. (1976). Overjustification in a token economy. *Journal of Personality and Social Psychology, 34,* 1219–1234.

Grolnick, W.S. & Ryan, R.M. (1987). Autonomy in children's learning: An experimental and individual difference investigation. *Journal of Personality and Social Psychology, 52,* 890–898.

Harackiewicz, J. (1979). The effects of reward contingency and performance feedback on intrinsic motivation. *Journal of Personality and Social Psychology, 37,* 1352–1363.

Harackiewicz, J., Manderlink, G., & Sansone, C. (1984). Rewarding pinball wizardry: The effects of evaluation on intrinsic interest. *Journal of Personality and Social Psychology, 47,* 287–300.

Harlow, H.F. (1953). Motivation as a factor in the acquisition of new responses. In *Current theory and research on motivation.* Lincoln, NB: University of Nebraska Press.

Harter, S. (1974). Pleasure derived by children from cognitive challenge and mastery. *Child Development, 45,* 661–669.

Harter, S. (1981). A new self-report scale of intrinsic versus extrinsic orientation in the classroom: Motivational and informational components. *Developmental Psychology, 17,* 300–312.

Harter, S. (1982). The perceived competence scale for children. *Child Development, 53,* 87–97.

Hiroto, D.S. & Seligman, M.E.P. (1975). Generality of learned helplessness in man. *Journal of Personality and Social Psychology, 31,* 311–327.

Hull, C.L. (1943). *Principles of behavior: An introduction to behavior theory.* New York: Appleton-Century-Crofts.

Janis, I.L. & Field, P.B. (1959). The Janis and Field personality questionnaire. In C.I. Hovland & I.L. Janis, *Personality and persuasibility.* New Haven: Yale University Press.

Jenkins, C.D., Rosenman, R.H., & Friedman, M. (1967). Development of an objective psychological test for the determination of the coronary prone behavior pattern in employed men. *Journal of Chronic Diseases, 20,* 371–379.

Kaplan, H.B. & Pokorny, A.D. (1969). Self-derogation and psychosocial adjustment. *Journal of Nervous and Mental Disease, 149,* 421–434.

Kast, A.D. (1983). Sex differences in intrinsic motivation: A developmental analysis of the effects of social rewards. Unpublished doctoral dissertation, Fordham University.

Koch, S. (1956). Behavior as "intrinsically" regulated: Work notes toward a pre-theory of phenomena called "motivational." In M.R. Jones (Ed.), *Nebraska symposium on motivation* (Vol. 4). Lincoln, NB: University of Nebraska Press.

Koestner, R., Ryan, R.M., Bernieri, F., & Holt, K. (1984). Setting limits in children's behavior: The differential effects of controlling versus informational styles on intrinsic motivation and creativity. *Journal of Personality, 52,* 233–248.

Koestner, R., Zuckerman, M., & Koestner, J. (1987). Praise, involvement and intrinsic motivation. *Journal of Personality and Social Psychology, 53,* 383–390.

Lepper, M.R. & Greene, D. (1975). Turning play into work: Effects of adult surveillance and extrinsic rewards on children's intrinsic motivation. *Journal of Personality and Social Psychology, 31,* 479–486.

Lepper, M.R., Greene, D., & Nisbett, R.E. (1973). Undermining children's intrinsic interest with extrinsic rewards: A test of the "overjustification" hypothesis. *Journal of Personality and Social Psychology, 28,* 129–137.

Loevinger, J. (1976). *Ego development.* San Francisco: Jossey-Bass.

McGraw, K.O. & McCullers, J.C. (1979). Evidence of a detrimental effect of extrinsic incentives on breaking a mental set. *Journal of Experimental Social Psychology, 15,* 285–294.

Montessori, M. (1965). *Spontaneous activity in education.* (First published in English, 1917.) New York: Schocken.

Mossholder, K.W. (1980). Effects of externally mediated goal setting on intrinsic motivation: A laboratory experiment. *Journal of Applied Psychology, 65,* 202–210.

Olson, B.C. (1985). The effects of informational and controlling feedback on intrinsic motivation in competition. Unpublished doctoral dissertation, Texas Christian University.

Pittman, T.S., Davey, M.E., Alafat, K.A., Wetherill, K.V., & Kramer, N.A. (1980). Informational versus controlling verbal rewards. *Personality and Social Psychology Bulletin, 6,* 228–233.

Plant, R. & Ryan, R.M. (1985). Self-consciousness, self-awareness, ego-involvement, and intrinsic motivation: An investigation of internally-controlling styles. *Journal of Personality, 53,* 435–449.

Reeve, J., Olson, B.C., & Cole, S.G. (1985). Motivation and performance: Two consequences of winning and losing in competition. *Motivation and Emotion, 9,* 291–298.

Ross, M. (1975). Salience of reward and intrinsic motivation. *Journal of Personality and Social Psychology, 32,* 245–254.

Rotter, J.B. (1966). Generalized expectancies for internal versus external control of reinforcement. *Psychological Monographs, 80*(1), whole no. 609 (pp. 1–28).

Russell, J.C., Studstill, O.L., & Grant, R.M. (1979, September). The effect of expectancies on intrinsic motivation. Paper presented at the meeting of the American Psychological Association, New York.

Ryan, R.M. (1982). Control and information in the intrapersonal sphere: An extension of cognitive evaluation theory. *Journal of Personality and Social Psychology, 43,* 450–461.

Ryan, R.M. & Grolnick, W.S. (1986). Origins and pawns in the classroom: Self-report and projective assessments of individual differences in children's perceptions. *Journal of Personality and Social Psychology, 50,* 550–558.

Ryan, R.M., Koestner, R., & Deci, E.L. (in press). Ego involved persistence: When free choice behavior is not intrinsically motivated. *Motivation and Emotion.*

Ryan, R.M., Mims, V., & Koestner, R. (1983). Relation of reward contingency and interpersonal context to intrinsic motivation: A review and test using cognitive evaluation theory. *Journal of Personality and Social Psychology, 45,* 736–750.

Sansone, C. (1987). Task feedback, competence feedback and intrinsic interest: When choice makes a difference. Unpublished manuscript, University of Utah.

Shapira, Z. (1976). Expectancy determinants of intrinsically motivated behavior. *Journal of Personality and Social Psychology, 34,* 1235–1244.

Shostrom, E.L. (1966). *Manual for the Personal Orientation Inventory.* San Diego, CA: Educational and Industrial Testing Service.

Skinner, B.F. (1938). *The behavior of organisms: An experimental analysis.* New York: Appleton.

Smith, W.E. (1974). The effects of social and monetary rewards on intrinsic motivation. Unpublished doctoral dissertation, Cornell University.

Swann, W.B. & Pittman, T.S. (1977). Initiating play activity of children: The moderating influence of verbal cues on intrinsic motivation. *Child Development, 48,* 1128–1132.

Vallerand, R.J., & Reid, G. (1984). On the causal effects of perceived competence on intrinsic motivation: A test of cognitive evaluation theory. *Journal of Sport Psychology, 6,* 94–102.

White, R.W. (1959). Motivation reconsidered: The concept of competence. *Psychological Review, 66,* 297–333.

Yoshimura, M. (1979). The effects of verbal reinforcement and monetary reward on intrinsic motivation. Unpublished manuscript, Kyoto University Psychology Laboratory, Kyoto, Japan.

Zuckerman, M., Porac, J., Lathin, D., Smith, R., & Deci, E.L. (1978). On the importance of self-determination for intrinsically motivated behavior. *Personality and Social Psychology Bulletin, 4,* 443–446.

3 Intrinsic and extrinsic motivational orientations in peer interactions

Thane S. Pittman, Ann K. Boggiano, and Deborah S. Main

The effects of rewards and environmental constraints on the ways in which activities are categorized, approached, performed, and subsequently chosen have been the subject of a great deal of recent research, as several chapters in this volume amply demonstrate. In this chapter, we expand the intrinsic/extrinsic motivation analysis into the realm of interpersonal interactions. In so doing, a number of straightforward and interesting extrapolations from previous work to social interactions can be made. In addition, unique questions arise concerning both situational and developmental variables when interpersonal interactions are thought of as either intrinsically or extrinsically motivated.

Categories of interpersonal relationships

The exchange of reinforcements long has been recognized as a central aspect of human interpersonal relationships. Thibaut and Kelley (1959), for example, focused on various forms of interdependence stemming from the nature of each partner's control over the other's outcomes and on the stability of relationships by specifying the comparison of benefits available in current versus other available relationships. Equity theory (cf. Walster, Berscheid, & Walster, 1973) featured another aspect of reinforcement: the perceived fairness of the distribution of resources, based on the ratio of inputs and outcomes for various participants.

Consistent with this focus on reinforcement exchange as an important aspect of interactions, several analyses have categorized or classified interpersonal relationships according to the kinds of reinforcement exchange and distribution systems they employ. Deutsch (1976), for example, has argued that there are three principles of exchange on which relationships may be based: the principle of *equity,* which involves a system in which outcomes are proportional to inputs; the principle of *equality,* in which each member of a group receives an equal share regardless of his or her input;

and the principle of *need,* in which members receive available resources according to their need. Each of these principles was assumed to be associated with an emphasis on a particular aspect of interaction: equity with economic productivity, equality with solidarity, and need with nurturance. More recently, Clark and Mills (1979) have drawn a distinction between relationships based on differences in the operative norms concerning the receipt and delivery of benefits. In exchange relationships, benefits are given with the expectation that comparable benefits will be returned. In communal relationships, members follow the "norm of mutual responsiveness" (Pruitt, 1972), in which benefits are given out of concern for the needs of the other without the specific expectation of comparable return.

The point of this brief selective review simply is to illustrate that both the role of normative expectations concerning the allocation of resources and the empirical effects of reinforcement contingencies have proven to be useful in analyses of interpersonal interactions. In the past few years, social psychologists have studied a new and potent, yet very different, consequence of reinforcement practices – the sometimes detrimental effects of reward on subsequent intrinsic motivation. This work typically has involved activities with inanimate objects, including creative activities such as drawing and writing, scholastic activities such as math problems, as well as a variety of games. However, the implications of these findings for interpersonal relationships have not been fully considered. In this paper, we discuss some of these implications and demonstrate the feasibility of testing this analysis from a social-developmental perspective.

Intrinsic and extrinsic motivational orientation

When a person engages in an activity, he or she may do so from either an intrinsic or an extrinsic motivational orientation (Pittman, Boggiano, & Ruble, 1983). This distinction concerns the location of salient rewards – that is, whether reward (and, more generally, the reason for engagement in the activity) is seen to be inherent in the activity, or merely mediated by the activity. When a person adopts an intrinsic motivational orientation, the primary focus is on rewards inherent in the interaction with a target activity; the activity is approached as an "end in itself" (Kruglanski, 1975). Features such as novelty, entertainment value, satisfaction of curiosity, and opportunities for the exercise of skills and the attainment of mastery typically characterize the kinds of rewards sought from engagement in an activity when an intrinsic motivational orientation is taken. When a person adopts an extrinsic motivational orientation, the primary focus is on rewards that are mediated by, but are not part of, the target activity. The activity is approached as a "means to an end" (Kruglanski, 1975). Task features such as predictability, simplicity, and ease of completion typically are preferred when an extrinsic motivational orientation is adopted.

The most frequently demonstrated consequence of a person's shifting from an intrinsic to an extrinsic motivational orientation is a phenomenon often referred to as the overjustification effect (Lepper, Greene, & Nisbett, 1973). When subjects are rewarded for engaging in activities that initially are intrinsically interesting, they tend to lose interest in the tasks during subsequent free-choice periods (that is, they are less likely to engage in the activity) compared to subjects who were not rewarded (Deci, 1971). This effect has been replicated with a wide variety of activities, rewards, and populations (see Deci, 1975; Lepper & Greene, 1978; Deci & Ryan, 1985; Pittman & Heller, 1987; as well as several chapters in this volume). In our view, the overjustification phenomenon occurs because contingent reward provokes a shift in the individual from an intrinsic to an extrinsic motivational orientation (Pittman, Boggiano, & Ruble, 1983). Once an individual associates an activity with an extrinsic orientation, he or she is less likely to choose the activity in a free-choice period because the reason for engaging in the activity (the contingent reward) is no longer available.

Motivational orientations in interpersonal interactions

We propose that the activity of interacting with another person also may be approached from either an intrinsic or extrinsic motivational orientation (Pittman, 1982). In some interactions, including friendships or romance attachments, the salient rewards are part of the interaction itself, and are therefore intrinsically motivating. Other interactions, such as job interviews or sales transactions, would be characterized by an extrinsic motivational orientation, because they have as their main focus salient rewards that are mediated by, but are not inherent in, the relationship. It is worth noting here that most interactions may be approached with either an intrinsic or extrinsic motivational orientation.

In initial encounters, we would expect the kind of motivational orientation taken to be affected by this location of salient rewards, and by the presence or absence of external pressure to engage in the interaction. Initial encounters also are those for which the most direct extrapolation from the extant research can be made, since novel activities have been employed in most of that research. Because the most robust finding from this research is the overjustification effect, we chose first to test for this effect in interpersonal interactions.

Overjustification in interpersonal interaction

Several studies seem to demonstrate the effects of motivational orientation on interpersonal interactions. Garbarino (1975), for example, compared the performance of paid and unpaid tutors, and found that the paid tutors were more demanding and critical of their students than unpaid tutors. The students of paid tutors also learned less during the tutorial sessions than students of unpaid tutors. Seligman, Fazio, and Zanna (1980) had couples work through materials that emphasized either intrinsic or extrinsic aspects of relationships. Subsequently, those couples for whom extrinsic reasons had been made salient reported less love for each other than did couples for whom intrinsic reasons had been made salient. Finally, Kunda and Schwartz (1983) found that subjects who were paid for engaging in a moral act reported lower subsequent feelings of moral obligation than did subjects who had not been paid. Although all of these studies are consistent with the intrinsic-extrinsic motivational orientation analysis, none of them can be considered a clear demonstration of the overjustification effect. Such a demonstration requires showing that a procedure that would be expected to shift motivational orientation from intrinsic to extrinsic leads to a subsequent decrease in the likelihood of free-choice interaction.

As an initial test of the utility of the intrinsic-extrinsic motivational orientation analysis in the interpersonal realm, Pittman and Murphy (1987) either paid or did not pay pairs of naive, unacquainted college students for their first interactions with each other. In a subsequent free-choice period, all of the subjects were free to converse with their partners. We predicted that rewarded subjects would show an overjustification effect, that is, they would be less likely to converse with each other than subjects who had not been rewarded.

This prediction, however, had to be qualified in the specific experimental setting that we created. Intrinsic motivation researchers have identified several limiting conditions on the otherwise detrimental effects of reward on task interest. For example, if the task were of little interest initially (Calder & Staw, 1975), or if the task were either too simple or too difficult to be intrinsically interesting (Boggiano, Ruble, & Pittman, 1982), then rewards might either enhance or not affect subsequent task interest. Prior research has suggested, then, that contingent reward would attenuate subjects' inclination to converse only in subjects who initially enjoyed such conversations. In the Pittman and Murphy study, subjects conversed over an intercom system without seeing each other – a procedure primarily designed to minimize the effects of variables such as physical attractiveness and possible prior acquaintance, and to maximize the anonymity of the participants. However, pilot testing of the procedures indicated that not everyone found conversing with a stranger over an intercom to be a particularly engaging activity. Therefore, we divided the group of subjects on the individual-difference dimension of shyness (Zimbardo, 1977; Pilkonis, 1977), in the expectation that shy subjects would tend to avoid conversation in free-choice periods and that subjects who were not shy would not show such avoidance. The predicted decrease in the inclination to converse following a paid interaction, therefore, was expected to occur only with not-shy subjects.

The subjects were 72 female undergraduates who received credit for their introductory psychology classes for participation in the study. At the beginning of the semester, students completed a shortened version of the Stanford Shyness Survey (Zimbardo, 1977). The criteria used to classify respondents as shy or not-shy were similar to those used by Pilkonis (1977). Shy subjects were those who characterized themselves as moderately to extremely shy, "more" or "much more" shy than their peers, and shy in at least 50 percent of social situations. In addition to the criteria employed by Pilkonis, only those subjects who indicated that silence or a reluctance to talk was one manifestation of their shyness were included in the shy group. Not-shy subjects were those who reported themselves to be "not at all" or "slightly" shy, and less or much less shy than their peers. Thirty-six subjects were recruited from each of these two groups and were assigned randomly to the three experimental conditions. Not-shy subjects were paired, as were shy subjects, so that pairs could be used as the unit of analysis.

Subjects reported individually to separate rooms, connected via an intercom system to a control room. Subjects did not see each other during the study and did not know the identities of their partners.

In the conversation no-reward condition, pairs of unacquainted naive female subjects first conversed over the intercom. No rewards were made contingent on the initial conversation. Each subject was told that she should try to introduce into the conversation questions from a list provided by the experimenter. Each subject was led to think that her partner did not have such a list, and was asked not to mention the list to her partner. In reality, each subject was given a list of questions, ensuring that the conversation would flow smoothly. The experimenter remained in the control room during the initial conversation.

In the conversation reward condition, the procedure was the same except that each subject was told she would be paid one dollar for the conversation, and was given the money after the conversation.

A third no-conversation no-reward condition was included to check on

Table 3.1. *Mean number of seconds spent talking by pairs during the free-choice period*

	No conversation no reward	Conversation no reward	Conversation reward
Not shy	95.00	134.00	43.34
Shy	8.84	163.66	171.00

Note: The amount of time spent talking could range from a minimum of 0 seconds to a maximum of 300 seconds; 6 pairs (12 subjects) in each condition.

the expected differences in inclination to talk between shy and not-shy subjects, and to assess the effect of having the initial conversation in the conversation no-reward condition. No-conversation no-reward subjects first worked individually on a task (rating the physical attractiveness of photographs) that lasted as long as did the initial conversation in the other two conditions. The free-choice period thus was the first time subjects in this condition had the opportunity to converse.

To initiate the subsequent free-choice period, the experimenter explained over the intercom that she had to go to another suite of rooms to set up the next part of the study, and that she would leave the microphones on so that the subjects could talk if they wished. Several magazines also were left in each room to make an alternative activity available. During the five-minute period, the conversation, or lack thereof, was recorded, and this measure was the dependent variable (see Table 3.1). The number of seconds each pair conversed was subjected to a log transformation, and the transformed scores were entered into an analysis of variance. The main effect for the shyness variable was not significant, but the main effect for the conversation/reward variables was. This main effect was qualified by a significant interaction. The pattern of effects for the not-shy subjects was as predicted. The no-conversation no-reward and the conversation no-reward cells did not differ, but the introduction of reward, as predicted, caused a significant decrease in talking (i.e., an overjustification effect). For shy subjects, a different pattern emerged. In the no-conversation no-reward condition, shy subjects talked less than not-shy subjects, as expected. In fact, with the exception of one subject in one of the pairs, the shy subjects in the no-conversation no-reward condition did not talk at all. The addition of the initial conversation significantly increased free-choice talking for shy subjects, to a level comparable to that of not-shy subjects.

The addition of reward, however, had no effect for these shy subjects; they continued to talk at an equally high rate.

The findings for the not-shy subjects demonstrated clearly that overjustification effects could be produced in interpersonal interactions. There is good reason, then, to assess other implications that the intrinsic-extrinsic motivational orientation distinction might have for interpersonal interactions.

The effects for the shy subjects were somewhat different. Shy subjects talked very little in the baseline (no conversation) condition, but the addition of the structured conversation seemed to break the ice, and in both prior conversation conditions shy subjects talked quite a bit during the free-interaction period whether or not they previously had been rewarded. Why did reward have no effect on these subjects? We can speculate that the experience of engaging in the conversation successfully (something that was assured by the dovetailed sets of questions provided by the experimenter) gave shy subjects an unexpected experience of interpersonal competence. We know from a number of other studies in the intrinsic motivation literature that when competence feedback is coupled with reward, subsequent free-choice behavior does not decrease (e.g., Boggiano & Ruble, 1979; Chapter 6, this volume).

Contingency and motivation: The bonus effect

The process of shifting from one motivational orientation to another often involves the application of several of the basic attributional principles described by Kelley (1973). For example, the presence of extrinsic reward may lead to a shift from an intrinsic to an extrinsic motivational orientation through application of the discounting principle, which states that the presence of multiple reasons for engaging in a behavior tends to decrease confidence in any one causal explanation for the behavior. Since extrinsic reward provides a plausible alternative to any intrinsic motivational explanation, the discounting principle would predict decreased likelihood of maintaining an intrinsic motivational orientation.

Boggiano and Main (1986) have pointed out that a second basic attributional process, the augmentation principle, also has important implications for intrinsic motivation. The results of several studies suggest that simply placing two activities in an "*if* you do this, *then* you can do that" relationship leads to an increase of interest in the "then" activity and a decrease of interest in the "if" activity (Birch, Zimmerman, & Hind, 1980; Lepper, Sagotsky, Dafoe, & Greene, 1982). The augmentation principle states that if plausible inhibitory and facilitative causes for a given event both were present, then the role of the facilitative cause would be given more weight than it would have been given had the inhibitory cause not been present. This principle would lead us to expect such increased interest in the "then" activity, along with decreased interest in the "if" activity.

Boggiano and Main (1986) demonstrated this effect in two studies that showed that preschoolers' interest in playing with a puzzle or a maze depended on the activity's position in an if-then contingency. When the children were told that *if* they played with the maze, *then* they could play with the puzzle, they subsequently played more with the puzzle and less with the maze than did children for whom the two activities were not in any such contingent relationship. Similarly, when the children were told that *if* they played with the puzzle, *then* they could play with the maze, their preference for the maze increased and their preference for the puzzle decreased relative to the noncontingency control children.

If our general analysis were correct, we would expect similar responses, as predicted by the augmentation principle, in peer interactions. Boggiano and Main (1986) tested this prediction in a third experiment: Kindergarten and first grade boys either were shown one version of a block-building game that they were told they could play by themselves, or a similar block-building game that they were told they could play only with another child (named Ryan) by following along with Ryan on a television monitor (the "follow-me" game). Children in the "bonus" condition (in which play with Ryan was presented as a bonus) were told that *if* they played the game by themselves, *then* they could play the follow-me game with Ryan. Children in the "bribe" condition (in which an activity was used as a bribe to get the children to play the game along with Ryan) were told that *if* they played the follow-me game with Ryan, *then* they could play the other game by themselves. In the noncontingent condition, children simply were told that they first could play one game, then the other, with no contingency between the two games mentioned.

In a subsequent free-choice period, the experimenter left the child alone in the room with several activities, including the two block games; the amount of time the children spent playing the follow-me game and the individual block game was measured unobtrusively. Results indicated that children showed a strong preference for the *then* activity over the *if* activity. As can be seen in Table 3.2, when the follow-me game was the "bribe," interest in playing with Ryan later decreased, as compared with the children in the noncontingent control condition. However, the children for whom Ryan had been the "bonus" spent more time play-

Table 3.2. *Mean number of seconds spent playing with Ryan during the ten-minute free-choice period*

Ryan if-then contingency		
Bribe	Noncontingent	Bonus
109.22	144.10	258.00

ing the follow-me game than did children in the noncontingent control condition.

Further implications of the motivational orientation analysis in interpersonal interactions

Together, the Pittman & Murphy (1987) and Boggiano & Main (1986) studies demonstrate that overjustification phenomena do occur in the realm of interpersonal interactions. In addition to the effects shown in these studies, which have obvious implications for the stability and longevity of relationships, one also might expect changes in the quality of interactions. When a contingent reward is available, an extrinsic orientation theoretically would cause an individual to focus on expedient completion of an interaction in order to obtain the reward. We would expect persons in this situation to seek a path of least resistance, that is, to show a preference for simple, perhaps uncreative, ways of getting through the interaction. We would not expect characteristics such as unpredictability or task-irrelevant idiosyncrasy in the interaction partner to be as highly valued as they might be in a setting in which an intrinsic motivational orientation prevails (see Harter, 1978; Chapter 5, this volume). Some of these preferences also would be expected to carry over into subsequent unrewarded interactions (Pittman, Emery, & Boggiano, 1982).

How might individuals avoid or circumvent the potentially disruptive effects that extrinsic reward might have on intrinsically motivated interactions? There are some clues in the task-interest literature. We already have discussed the mitigating role that competence feedback or experience may have played for the shy subjects in the Pittman and Murphy study: When a primary aspect of an interaction is an experience of social competence, extrinsic rewards may have little effect on motivational orientation. Other tactics for maintaining an intrinsic motivational orientation might include minimizing the salience of extrinsic rewards or defining them as integral parts of the relationship, although the latter tactic might backfire when rewards were no longer available.

Clark and Mills (1979), Mills and Clark (1982), and Clark (1984) have found that the implicit rules for the exchange of benefits are very different in two types of relationships: communal and exchange. The rules for the exchange of benefits in communal relationships, such as friendships, may well exist for the purpose of maintaining an intrinsic motivational orientation even when extrinsic rewards are introduced.

Developmental aspects of motivational orientations in peer interactions

Interpersonal interactions, like most other psychological phenomena, undergo considerable developmental change. If we think about what is known concerning changes in children's approaches to and conceptions of others, it is possible to make predictions about the effects of rewards, constraints, and contingencies on peer interactions that take account of developmental changes.

One important aspect of social interactions that undergoes developmental change is person perception. We know that children six years old and younger tend to think of others in concrete, rather than abstract terms, focusing on external characteristics and overt behaviors rather than on internal qualities and enduring personality characteristics (Rholes & Ruble, 1984; Feldman & Ruble, 1981; Livesley & Bromley, 1973; Peevers & Secord, 1973). For these children, friendship is temporary and changeable (cf. Asher & Gottman, 1981), and the perceived characteristics of friends also tend to be concrete and external (e.g., "He lets me play with his toys"; "She gives me things").

In peer interaction, reward may be given by a third party (such as an experimenter or a parent), or by the interaction partner. In the latter case, although an offer of material reward from an acquaintance for interaction (e.g., "I'll give you ten dollars if you will hang around with me this afternoon") would seem incompatible with an intrinsic motivational orientation to an adult or an older child, a comparable offer from a potential playmate might seem quite reasonable to a child of six. If a reward for interaction came from the interaction partner, children age six or younger might find that this fit their notions of playmates and friends, and hence we would expect no decrease in subsequent interest in interaction with that partner. Older children, however, would be expected to show decreased interest. On the other hand, if the reward came from a third party (the experi-

Table 3.3. *Proportion of subjects choosing the confederate as a future playmate*

Age	Source of Reward: None	Experimenter	Peer
Six	.92	.59	.83
Nine	.75	.59	.59

menter), the extant intrinsic-extrinsic motivation literature would lead us to expect subsequent interest in the interaction to decline in both younger and older children.

Pittman and Dool (1985) tested these predictions with children who were attending day-care or after-school programs. Half of the subjects were age six, half age nine; there were equal numbers of males and females. In addition, six children from each combination of age and sex were recruited to act as experimental confederates.

There were three conditions: no reward, experimenter reward, and peer reward. The experimenter showed each subject-confederate pair several games, one of which could be played by the two children together, the others separately. In the no-reward condition, the experimenter simply asked if the children would like to play together. In the experimenter-reward condition, the experimenter offered the children cookies for playing together. In the peer-reward condition, the confederate offered the subject a cookie if he or she would play with the confederate. In all cases, the children then played a game together twice and then, depending on condition, received a cookie or not from the appropriate source. The experimenter then left the room for five minutes. During this free-choice period, the confederate always played with a game that could be played by one or several children. The amount of time the children spent talking was measured. After the free-choice period, the subject was asked privately whether he or she would like to play with the same partner or a new one if there were another session.

Analysis of variance of the arcsin-transformed proportions of subjects' choices of a future playmate revealed the predicted interaction of reward and age. As can be seen in Table 3.3, six-year-olds showed a decrease in interest in future interaction in the experimenter-reward condition, but showed no such decrease in interest in the peer-reward condition. Nine-year-old children, however, showed a decrease in interest in future interaction with their partner in both reward conditions. A similar pattern was obtained on the measure of amount of time spent talking during the free-choice period.

Motivational orientation and the development of scripts

The studies reviewed thus far seem to show clearly that young children's motivational orientations towards peer interaction were affected by the discounting and augmentation principles. A puzzling aspect of these findings, and of the findings with preschool children in the intrinsic motivation literature in general, is that other research seems to show that children of this age do not use such principles (Sedlak & Kurtz, 1981; Shultz, Butkowsky, Pearce, & Shanfield, 1975). One explanation for this apparent paradox is that young children do not employ attributional principles in a generalized and abstractly deductive manner (Lepper & Greene, 1978; Lepper et al., 1982). Instead, these children may employ well-differentiated and familiar scripts in concrete situations. Boggiano and Main (1986), using this line of reasoning, argued that young children have learned from specific experiences a script for all if-then situations, and assume that "then" activities are more enjoyable than "if" activities (e.g., *If* you eat your spinach, *then* you can have some ice cream). Use of this script by six- or seven-year-old children does not, however, constitute a grasp of the general principles of discounting and augmentation.

This script explanation for the apparent use of augmentation and discounting principles by young children in peer interactions was tested by Boggiano and Main (1986). Rather subtle "out of script" reasons for playing with another child, such as, "Do activity X, *because* you can do Y," theoretically would lead young children to employ the *additive schema* and to show increased interest in the bribe or X activity (Karniol & Ross, 1976; Sedlak & Kurtz, 1981). Older children, who are not reliant on simple generalization of well-known scripts, still would show discounting and augmentation even with the less common *because* statement, for they would be using the general principle instead of simply applying a script.

In this study, the children (six- and nine-year-old boys) all were told that another boy (Robby) had some Lego blocks. Children in the experimental condition were asked, "Do you want to play with Robby *because* you can play with his new Lego game?" For children in the control condition, the identical information was provided (i.e., that Robby had a Lego game); however, no reason was given regarding the purpose for interaction. All children then played along with a videotape of Robby for seven minutes.

In the subsequent free-choice period, the experimenter left the children alone with three activities: playing with a new block-building game along

Table 3.4. *Mean intrinsic interest shown in playing with Robby during the seven-minute free-choice period*

Age	Noncontingent	Because contingency
Younger	213.00	453.10
Older	355.67	175.22

with Robby on the videotape machine, playing with the Lego blocks by themselves, or playing with the new building blocks by themselves. By separating Robby from the original Lego game in the free-choice period, and providing a choice of a new game either with or without Robby, it was possible to get a clear assessment of interest in playing along with Robby.

As can be seen in Table 3.4, six-year-old children in the "because" condition showed an increased interest in playing with Robby compared to their noncontingent counterparts, and displayed use of the additive schema. In contrast, older children showed the expected decrease in playing with Robby in the because-contingency condition, reflecting their use of the more generalized augmentation principle.

Dispositional versus situational salience and peer interacation

Another means of explaining the performance of the children in Boggiano and Main's fourth study is to examine the nature of the suggested reason for playing with the peer ("because you can play with his new Lego game"). As we argued earlier, young children tend to view playmates in terms of the playmates' external, concrete characteristics and not in terms of traits or personality. In the Pittman and Dool (1985) study, interest in playing with a peer was not attenuated by the peer's offer of a cookie. In the Boggiano and Main study, young children's interest was increased by focusing their attention on a potential playmate's possessions. Presumably, the schema that young children employed in these two situations was something like, "Friends let me do things I like." Older children, however, in both studies reacted with decreased interest when external characteristics of the peer were made salient.

This line of reasoning led Boggiano, Klinger, and Main (1986) to predict that an emphasis on situational reasons for playing with a peer would enhance young children's interest in interaction, but attenuate the interest of older children. However, an emphasis on dispositional reasons for play-

Table 3.5. *Mean transformed proportion of time subjects spent playing with the peer*

	Age		
Condition	5½	7	9
Dispositional	.23	.54	.82
Situational	.45	.81	.14
Control	.20	.53	.58

ing with another child would be expected to have quite different effects. Older children, whose attention would be focused on internal characteristics of the interaction partner, would be expected to adopt an intrinsic motivational orientation and show increased subsequent interest in continued interaction. Younger children, however, theoretically would be relatively unaffected by dispositional information, since they tend not to think of peers in trait terms.

To test these predictions, Boggiano and her colleagues explained the follow-me game with Robby to five-and-one-half, seven, and nine-year-old boys. In the dispositional condition, each child was told that Robby, a new classmate at school, was very nice and had a new Lego game; these children then were asked if they wanted to play with Robby "because he's real nice." In the situational condition, children also were told that Robby was real nice and had a new Lego game, but then were asked if they wanted to play with Robby "because you can play with his new Lego game." In the control condition, each child was also told that Robby was real nice and had a new Lego game, but neither of these attributes was suggested as a reason for playing with him. All children then played along with a videotape of either a six- or a nine-year-old boy, depending on the subject's age, for seven minutes.

In the subsequent free-choice period, the same three activities used in Boggiano and Main's fourth study were available: playing the follow-me game with Robby and the new blocks, playing with the new blocks alone, or playing with the Lego blocks alone.

For the young children (five-and-one-half and seven years), the situational reason enhanced children's interest as predicted, whereas the dispositional reason had no effect (see Table 3.5). But for the older children, the dispositional reason augmented children's interest in playing with Robby, and the situational reason attenuated interest relative to the noncontingency control children.

Summary

The distinction between intrinsic and extrinsic motivational orientations has important theoretical and practical implications for analyses of human interaction. We have shown that the overjustification effect may impact human interactions: Given the circumstances specified by our theoretical analyses, children who are offered external rewards tend to lose interest in continued interaction with a partner after those rewards are no longer present. Furthermore, the complex predictions that may be generated by combining our knowledge about these processes with recent findings in developmental psychology have been accurate in the tests to which they have been subjected. In addition to these empirical confirmations, the intrinsic/extrinsic motivational orientation analysis has heuristic value. For example, predictions concerning the quality of interactions and the nature of desired interaction partners, which might not otherwise be considered, can be generated using this analysis. Finally, the insights provided by further research on this topic might shed light on the more problematic practical aspects of human interaction.

References

Asher, S. R., & Gottman, J. M. (1981). *The development of children's friendships.* New York: Cambridge University Press.

Birch, L. L., Zimmerman, S., & Hind, H. (1980). The influence of social-affective context on preschool children's food preferences. *Child Development, 51,* 856–861.

Boggiano, A. K., Klinger, C., & Main, D.S. (1986). Enhancing interest in peer interaction: A developmental analysis. *Child Development, 57,* 852–861.

Boggiano, A. K., & Main, D. S. (1986). Enhancing children's interest in activities used as rewards: The bonus effect. *Journal of Personality and Social Psychology, 51,* 1116–1126.

Boggiano, A. K., & Ruble, D. N. (1979). Competence and the overjustification effect: A developmental study. *Journal of Personality and Social Psychology, 37,* 1462–1468.

Boggiano, A. K., Ruble, D.N., & Pittman, T.S. (1982). The mastery hypothesis and the overjustification effect. *Social Cognition, 1,* 38–49.

Calder, B. J., & Staw, B. M. (1975). Self-perception of intrinsic and extrinsic motivation. *Journal of Personality and Social Psychology, 31,* 599–605.

Clark, M. S. (1984). Record keeping in two types of relationships. *Journal of Personality and Social Psychology, 47,* 549–557.

Clark, M. S., & Mills, J. (1979). Interpersonal attraction in exchange and communal relationships. *Journal of Personality and Social Psychology, 37,* 12–24.

Deci, E. L. (1971). Effects of externally mediated rewards on intrinsic motivation. *Journal of Personality and Social Psychology, 18,* 105–115.

Deci, E. L. (1975). *Intrinsic motivation.* New York: Plenum.

Deci, E. L., & Ryan, R. M. (1980). The empirical exploration of intrinsic motivational processes. In L. Berkowitz (Ed.), *Advances in Experimental Social Psychology* (Vol. 13). New York: Academic Press.

Deci, E. L., & Ryan, R. M. (1985). *Intrinsic motivation and self-determination in human behavior.* New York: Plenum.

Deutsch, M. (1976). Theorizing in social psychology. *Personality and Social Psychology Bulletin, 2,* 134–141.

Feldman, N. S., & Ruble, D. N. (1981). The development of person perception: Cognitive and social factors. In S. Brehm & S. Kassin (Eds.), *Developmental social psychology.* New York: Oxford University Press.

Garbarino, J. (1975). The impact of anticipated reward upon cross-age tutoring. *Journal of Personality and Social Psychology, 32,* 421–428.

Harter, S. (1978). Pleasure derived from challenge and the effects of receiving grades on children's difficulty level choices. *Child Development, 49,* 788–799.

Karniol, R., & Ross, M. (1976). The development of causal attributions in social perception. *Journal of Personality and Social Psychology, 34,* 455–464.

Kruglanski, A. W. (1975). The endogenous-exogenous partition in attribution theory. *Psychological Review, 83,* 387–406.

Kunda, Z., & Schwartz, S. H. (1983). Undermining intrinsic moral motivation: External reward and self-presentation. *Journal of Personality and Social Psychology, 45,* 763–771.

Lepper, M. R., & Greene, D. (1978). *The hidden costs of reward.* Hillsdale, NJ: Erlbaum.

Lepper, M.R., Greene, D., & Nisbett, R. E. (1973). Undermining children's intrinsic interest with extrinsic reward: A test of the overjustification hypothesis. *Journal of Personality and Social Psychology, 28,* 129–137.

Lepper, M. R., Sagotsky, G., Dafoe, J. L., & Greene, D. (1982). Consequences of superfluous social constraints: Effects on young children's social inferences and subsequent intrinsic interest. *Journal of Personality and Social Psychology, 42,* 51–65.

Livesley, W., & Bromley, D. (1973). *Person perception in childhood and adolescence.* London: Wiley.

Mills, J., & Clark, M. S. (1982). Communal and exchange relationships. *Review of Personality and Social Psychology, 3,* 121–144.

Peevers, B. H., & Secord, P. F. (1973). Developmental changes in attribution of descriptive concepts to persons. *Journal of Personality and Social Psychology, 27,* 120–128.

Pilkonis, P. A. (1977). The behavioral consequences of shyness. *Journal of Personality, 45,* 596–611.

Pittman, T. S. (1982). *Intrinsic and extrinsic motivational orientation toward others.* Paper presented at the meeting of the American Psychological Association, Washington, D.C.

Pittman, T. S., Boggiano, A. K., & Ruble, D. N. (1983). Intrinsic and extrinsic motivational orientations: limiting conditions on the undermining and enhancing effects of reward on intrinsic motivation. In J. Levine & M. Wang (Eds.), *Teacher and student perceptions: Implications for learning.* Hillsdale, NJ: Erlbaum.

Pittman, T. S., & Dool, C. (1985). Age, source of reward, and intrinsic motivation in peer interaction. Paper presented to the Society for Research in Child Development, Toronto.

Pittman, T. S., Emery, J., & Boggiano, A. K. (1982). Intrinsic and extrinsic motivational orientations: Reward induced changes in preference for complexity. *Journal of Personality and Social Psychology, 42,* 789–797.

Pittman, T. S., & Heller, J.F. (1987). Social motivation. In M. Rosenzweig & L. Porter (Eds.), *Annual Review of Psychology,* Vol. 38. Palo Alto, CA: Annual Reviews, Inc.

Pittman, T. S., & Murphy, E. (1987). Effects of reward and shyness on interest in future interactions. Unpublished manuscript.

Pruitt, D. G. (1972). Methods for resolving differences of interest: A theoretical analysis. *Journal of Social Issues, 28,* 133–154.

Rholes, W. S., & Ruble, D. N. (1984). Children's understanding of dispositional characteristics of others. *Child Development, 55,* 550–560.

Sedlak, A. J., & Kurtz, S. T. (1981). A review of children's use of causal inference principles. *Child Development, 52,* 759–784.

Seligman, C., Fazio, R. H., & Zanna, M. P. (1980). Effects of salience of extrinsic rewards on liking and loving. *Journal of Personality and Social Psychology, 38,* 453–460.

Shultz, T. R., Butkowsky, I., Pearce, J.W., & Shanfield, H. (1975). Development of schemata for the attribution of multiple psychological causes. *Developmental Psychology, 11,* 502–510.

Thibaut, J. W., & Kelley, H. H. (1959). *The social psychology of groups.* New York: Wiley.

Walster, E., Berscheid, E., & Walster, G. W. (1973). New directions in equity research. *Journal of Personality and Social Psychology, 25,* 151–176.

Zimbardo, P. G. (1977). *Shyness: What it is, what to do about it.* Reading, MA: Addison-Wesley.

4 The motivation for creativity in children

Teresa M. Amabile and Beth A. Hennessey

Slow and shy as a child, Albert Einstein did so poorly in school that when his father asked the headmaster what profession his son should adopt, the answer was simply, "It doesn't matter. He'll never make a success of anything."

The German school over which this headmaster presided was regimented and highly militaristic. Einstein complained bitterly about it in his autobiography:

> It is nothing short of a miracle that the modern methods of instruction have not yet entirely strangled the holy curiosity of inquiry; for this delicate little plant, aside from stimulation, stands mainly in need of freedom; without this it goes to wreck and ruin without fail. It is a very grave mistake to think that the enjoyment of seeing and searching can be promoted by means of coercion and sense of duty. . . . This coercion had such a deterring effect upon me that, after I had passed the final examination, I found the consideration of any scientific problem distasteful to me for an entire year. (Einstein, 1949, pp. 16–17)

Partly in an attempt to escape from such a regimented learning environment, Einstein left Munich for Zurich when he was fifteen, hoping to enroll in the Polytechnic Institute there. To his dismay, however, he failed the entrance examination and was required to enroll in a Swiss school for remedial coursework. According to one Einstein scholar (Holton, 1972), this episode represented a turning point in Einstein's schooling, and perhaps in his scientific thinking as well. In sharp contrast to Einstein's previous experiences, this school was humanistic and focused on the individual's unencumbered search for knowledge. This social atmosphere was suited ideally to Einstein's independent style of thinking and working. There was little emphasis on memorization, much emphasis on individual laboratory work and student-initiated investigation, and a concentration on the development of relaxed, democratic exchanges between students and teachers. To the end of his life, Einstein remembered this school fondly: "It made an unforgettable impression on me, thanks to its liberal spirit and the simple earnestness of the teachers who based themselves on no external authority" (Holton, 1972, p. 106). At this school, Einstein devised the first *Gedankenexperiment* that would lead him to the theory of relativity.

Einstein's experience was not unique. In first-person accounts of their lives and work, many celebrated creative individuals have reported that their creativity and their interest in their work were greatest when they concentrated on the work itself, rather than on externally imposed directives (Amabile, 1983a). Many of these reports include accounts of childhood experiences, as did Einstein's. They suggest that, throughout life, people are most creative when they are intrinsically motivated – that is, motivated primarily by interest in the task itself – and least creative when they are extrinsically motivated – that is, motivated primarily by socially imposed goals that are external to the task itself.

Such consistent anecdotal evidence, combined with the program of experimental research that we and our colleagues have conducted during the past fifteen years, has led to the *Intrinsic Motivation Principle of Creativity:*

> People will be most creative when they feel motivated primarily by the interest, enjoyment, satisfaction, and challenge of the work itself – rather than by external pressures.

Social and developmental psychologists have studied intrinsic and extrinsic motivation intensively for the past twenty years. The insights from their theories and research can help us understand the motivation for creative behavior in children. Lepper and Greene and their colleagues (1973; 1978) operationally defined intrinsic motivation as the presumed motivation behind any behavior that occurs in the apparent absence of extrinsic incentives. They focused primarily on the undermining of intrinsic motivation by the imposition of extrinsic constraints, a phenomenon that they called the *overjustification effect.* Lepper and Greene discovered that children who were initially intrinsically interested in an activity lost that intrinsic motivation if they came to see themselves as engaging in the activity to achieve an extrinsic goal.

Other theorists have conceptualized intrinsic motivation more organismically. White (1959) and Harter (1978) asserted that intrinsic motivation was based on the innate human need for competence in meeting optimal challenges. DeCharms (1968) proposed that intrinsically motivated behaviors arose from a desire to experience personal causation (self-determination). Deci and Ryan and their colleagues (1971; 1975; 1978; 1985) included both competence and self-determination as primary. They stated that "it is important to emphasize that it is not the need for competence alone that underlies intrinsic motivation; it is the need for *self-determined competence*" (Deci & Ryan, 1985, p. 50).

This feeling of self-determination seems to be what Einstein and many other creative people saw as central to their best work. Self-determination, then, is the core of the Intrinsic Motivation Principle of Creativity, and the focus of our research and theorizing on creativity. Other psychological theorists have suggested that creativity would most likely be demonstrated by individuals who were intrinsically motivated to perform a task. Crutchfield (1962) postulated that there was a basic antipathy between creativity and the extrinsic "ego-involved" motivation that might be aroused by external constraints such as the pressure to conform. He wrote, "In being concerned with goals extrinsic to the task itself, and particularly as rendered anxious about potential threats in the situation, [the problem solver's] cognitive processes become less flexible, his insights less sensitive" (p. 125). Lepper and Greene (1978) clearly suggested that the intrinsically motivated state would be more conducive to creativity. They hypothesized that the intrinsically motivated person, in contrast to the extrinsically motivated person, would feel freer to take risks because those risks carried no liabilities – save self-imposed ones. Finally, Deci and Ryan (1985) stated that, when people were intrinsically motivated (by the needs for competence and self-determination), they would seek situations that interested them and that required the use of their creativity and resourcefulness.

Conceptual framework

What do we mean by creativity? Definitions of creativity offered by psychologists have focused variously on characteristics of the creative person, features of the creative process, or aspects of the creative product. Like most creativity researchers, we have used a product definition: A product or idea is creative when it is a novel and appropriate response to an open-ended task. However, we have found this conceptual definition to be unsuited for direct application to research. For this reason, we have formulated a more specific operational definition that relies on the consensus of experts: A product or idea is creative to the extent that expert observers agree that it is creative (Amabile, 1982a; Hennessey & Amabile, in press). In our research, then, we ask subjects to perform a task in a specific domain (such as art) and then ask experts in that domain (e.g., artists) to independently assess the creativity of the products.

The theory of creativity on which we have been working does not propose that intrinsic motivation is all that is required for the production of a truly creative work. Instead, our componential model of creativity (Amabile, 1983b) proposes that three components are necessary and equally important, and that creativity will be determined by the relative strength of each of these. The first component is domain-relevant skills, which include knowledge, experience, and talent in a particular domain. The second component is creativity-relevant skills, which include cognitive styles (such as independent, flexible, risk-oriented thinking), working styles (such as high energy and persistence), and the ability to view problems from new perspectives. Task motivation is the third component; we propose that people are more likely to produce creative work when they are intrinsically, rather than extrinsically, motivated toward a task.

In our research, we have set out to match subjects on domain-relevant and creativity-relevant skills so that we could more closely examine the role of individual differences in the third component of our model – task motivation. We suggested that even talented people who had produced very creative work in the past would not work at their most creative levels if they were extrinsically motivated toward a particular task. We further thought that, to a large extent, environmental factors would determine this motivational orientation. In one respect, the task-motivation component of our model may be the most important: It appears to be most subject to immediate influence, and therefore more readily altered by practical interventions.

From these notions about intrinsic motivation and creativity, we derived a specific hypothesis: The extrinsic constraints that undermined intrinsic motivation in children also would undermine their creativity. This hypothesis is supported by studies of the effects of constraint both on children's intrinsic motivation and on their creativity.

The negative approach: undermining creativity by undermining intrinsic motivation

The basic research paradigm

Each of the studies reviewed in this chapter relied on a modified version of the standard overjustification paradigm (e.g., Lepper, Greene, & Nisbett, 1973; Amabile, DeJong, & Lepper, 1976). In this paradigm, subjects are assigned randomly to constraint or no-constraint conditions and are given an intrinsically interesting task. Qualitative aspects of their performance then are measured. In a number of these studies, subsequent interest to engage in the target activity under free play conditions also is assessed. To be considered a valid investigation of the proposed link between intrinsic motivation and aspects of performance, a study of this type must meet a number of criteria.

First, the experimental task must be intrinsically interesting. Second, a control group of children not performing under constraints must be included in the experimental design. Also, in constraint conditions, a clear contingency between task participation and the extrinsic goal must be established during the main experimental session. And finally, when surveillance or choice restrictions are imposed, these constraints must be made salient to subjects at the time of task engagement.

Many overjustification studies have demonstrated that the imposition of extrinsic constraints could undermine children's subsequent intrinsic interest in a task. For example, a number of researchers (Greene & Lepper, 1974; Lepper & Greene, 1975; Lepper, Greene, & Nisbett, 1973; Loveland & Olley, 1979) have reported that children who initially displayed a high level of interest in drawing lost interest in the task after working for an expected reward. Similarly, Karniol and Ross (1977) found that nonevaluative, noninformative rewards significantly undermined children's intrinsic interest. Lepper, Sagotsky, Dafoe, and Greene (1982) devised an experiment to determine whether presenting one activity as a means for earning an opportunity to engage in another activity would undermine subsequent intrinsic motivation, regardless of which activity was the means and which was the end. They found that intrinsic motivation consistently was undermined for a task that was suggested as the means.

These studies, and many others like them, illustrated how extrinsic constraints could undermine children's motivation toward and enjoyment of an activity. The fundamental question that guides our research is whether these same constraints also would affect children's creativity. Although only a few investigators have addressed this problem directly, some research has investigated aspects of children's performance related to creativity.

Effects of constraints on creativity-relevant aspects of performance

In a study of the effect of reward on children's artistic creativity, Lepper, Greene, and Nisbett (1973) found that preschoolers who initially displayed a high level of intrinsic interest in drawing with Magic Markers lost interest in drawing after working for an expected Good Player Award. Compared with a group of children who were given an unexpected reward after drawing and a control group that received no reward, the subjects who had played with the Magic Markers to receive a Good Player Award spent significantly less time using the markers during free-play periods. This decrement in interest persisted for at least a week beyond the initial experimental session. Furthermore, the globally assessed "quality" of the drawings made by children expecting a reward was lower than that of the drawings made by the two comparison groups.

Taking a similar approach, Greene and Lepper (1974) offered rewards to preschoolers under one of two conditions: for one group of children, receipt of the Good Player Award was contingent upon task performance; for the second group, the reward was contingent upon the "quality" of their work. Children in both reward conditions produced drawings of poorer "quality" than their non-rewarded counterparts. A reduction in intrinsic interest again was observed in children who received the rewards. Loveland and Olley (1979) also examined the effect of expected reward on preschoolers' drawings. Subjects were first observed during free-play periods and rated on their interest in the target activity. During the main experimental session, half of the children were promised a reward for their participation; children in the control group expected no reward. Measures of children's time spent drawing during subsequent free periods and of the quality of their drawings in those periods were collected one and seven weeks later. Results indicated that children with a high level of initial motivation for the drawing task lost interest when rewarded, but the same reward contingency caused children with initially low levels of motivation to gain interest in the task. Further, during the initial session, high-interest rewarded subjects drew more pictures than did their high-interest non-rewarded peers: the pictures drawn by rewarded children, however, were judged to be of poorer quality. Low-interest subjects, when rewarded, also drew more pictures than did their low-interest non-rewarded counterparts, but for this group, the quality of performance was not affected by condition.

Finally, employing a very different experimental task, Garbarino (1975) asked fifth- and sixth-grade girls to teach a matching task to girls in the first and second grades. The older children either were promised a reward (a free movie ticket) or were told nothing of a reward. Two raters then observed the tutoring sessions and independently rated a broad range of qualitative performance dimensions. These dependent variables included the following: the tutors' use of evaluation, hints, and demands; the learners' performance; the emotional tone of the interaction, including instances of laughter between the children; and the efficiency of the tutoring (learning per unit of time spent).

Overall, rewarded tutors conducted sessions that were high-pressure and businesslike, and non-rewarded tutors held sessions that were relaxed, yet highly efficient. The subjective ratings made by the two observers characterized the rewarded sessions as tense and hostile, and the nonrewarded sessions as warm and relaxed. In addition, the rewarded sessions were marked by more demands and more negative evaluative statements by the tutors, less laughter between subjects, and poorer learning by the younger students. Each of these investigations pointed to the same conclusions as the original findings of Lepper and his colleagues (1973): For children who initially displayed a high level of interest in a task, working for an expected reward decreased their motivation and undermined the globally assessed quality of their performance.

A few intrinsic motivation studies have focused on the creative aspects of performance, most using adult subjects. One study, however, used a younger subject population of high school students. In this study (Kruglanski, Friedman, & Zeevi, 1971), Israeli high school students who either had or had not been promised a reward (a tour of the Tel Aviv University psychology department) were given two open-ended creativity tasks. These tasks, adapted from Barron (1968), required subjects to list as many titles as possible for a literary paragraph, and to use as many words as possible from a fifty-word list in writing a story.

Originality ratings of these products were made by two independent judges, who displayed good interjudge reliability. These ratings revealed a clear and statistically significant superiority of non-rewarded subjects. In addition, nearly significant differences were found between the two groups on two intrinsic motivation measures: non-rewarded subjects expressed greater enjoyment of the activities and were more likely to volunteer for further participation.

Effects of constraint on children's creativity

Because so little systematic work has been done on the effects of extrinsic constraints on children's creativity, we have designed a research program to answer two simple questions: First, do the extrinsic constraints that appear to undermine children's subsequent intrinsic motivation also undermine the creativity of their immediate performance? And second, to what extrinsic constraints and to what creative tasks might these effects apply? In a series of studies, we examined children's verbal and artistic creativity under extrinsic constraints ranging from reward and evaluation to competition and restricted choice. Our results consistently demonstrated that a wide range of extrinsic constraints undermined both verbal and artistic creativity.

In one study prototypical of our research (Amabile, Hennessey, & Grossman, 1986, Study 1), we set out to examine the impact of reward expectation on children's verbal creativity. Elementary school children, ages five to ten, were asked to tell a story to accompany a set of illustrations in a book without words. Children were asked to say "one thing" about each page into a tape recorder. Like all the creativity tasks used in our research, this story-telling activity was designed with two goals in mind. First, we sought to minimize individual differences in domain-relevant and creativity-relevant skills, because these differences might cause variability in baseline performance. In the story-telling task, for example, differences in children's verbal fluency were controlled by restricting children to one sentence per page. Second, we sought to use tasks for which a wide variety of responses was appropriate in order to accurately test hypotheses about creativity. In other words, the target activity had to be open-ended (see Amabile, 1982a; Hennessey & Amabile, 1988; Hennessey & Amabile, in press; McGraw, 1978).

At the beginning of the experimental session, children in grades one through five were given an opportunity to take two pictures with an instant camera. To be allowed to use the camera, subjects in the reward condition were asked to promise to later tell a story. So that this contingency would be salient, these children wrote their names on a piece of paper, a contract also signed by the experimenter. Subjects in the no-reward condition simply took two pictures and then told a story; there was no contingency established between the two tasks. Elementary school teachers familiar with children's writing later rated the stories for creativity. Results indicated that children in the no-reward condition told stories that were significantly more creative than the ones told by children in the reward condition.

It is significant that this effect occurred even when non-rewarded subjects experienced the "reward" and even when the reward was delivered *before* the target activity. The only difference in the experiences of rewarded and non-rewarded children in this paradigm was their *perception* of the reward activity (i.e., the picture taking) as contingent or not contingent upon the target activity. It appears that the perception of a task as the means to an end was the crucial element.

Another of our investigations (Amabile, 1982b) examined the effect of expected reward. In this case, however, the experimental task involved artistic creativity, and the reward was introduced in a competitive setting that incorporated an evaluative element. Girls aged seven to eleven years made paper collages during one of two parties held in the common room of their apartment complex. Subjects in the experimental group competed for prizes, whereas those in the control group expected that the prizes would be raffled off.

Artist-judges later rated each collage on creativity, and their judgments reflected a high level of interjudge reliability. Collages made by the control group were judged as significantly more creative than the collages made by the experimental group. Once again, the results were consistent with the proposition that intrinsic motivation would be conducive, and extrinsic motivation detrimental, to creativity.

Each of these studies tested the effects of rewards delivered by experimenters in classrooms or similar settings. One of our more recent investigations (Hennessey, 1989, Study 1) expanded upon this paradigm by exploring the impact of task-contingent rewards administered by a computer. Because many electronic educational programs have been based on operant conditioning techniques, we thought it essential to determine whether reinforcement provided by software would have the same detrimental effects as rewards delivered by an experimenter, teacher, or parent.

Participants, children aged seven to thirteen years, were assigned randomly to one of three conditions. All then performed an open-ended creativity task with the aid of a computer. In this activity, children created geometric designs by using the computer to draw colored lines within the confines of a sixteen-point grid. Subjects in the reward-experimenter condition were told that the experimenter would give them a Good Computer User Award when they completed their drawings. Subjects in the reward-computer condition also expected a reward, but they were told that the computer controlled access to a special box that contained the awards. To subjects in the control condition, no mention was made of a Good User Award or reward contingency.

Judges' ratings of the creativity of the designs revealed that children working under constraint conditions produced designs that were somewhat less creative than those produced by children who did not expect a reward. When older subjects (ages ten to thirteen years) were considered separately, the deleterious impact of reward was particularly apparent. The expectation of reward significantly undermined creativity, and this effect was observed regardless of whether the source of the reward was a human being or a computer. In fact, designs made by children assigned to the reward-computer condition were judged to be significantly less creative than those produced by children in either of the other two experimental groups.

In a related investigation (Hennessey, 1989, Study 2), we wanted to determine whether the expectation of evaluation might also have a negative impact upon creativity. Participants in this phase of the research again were children ranging in age from seven to thirteen years, and the target creativity task was identical to that employed in Study 1. Subjects in the evaluation-experimenter condition were told that upon completion of their design, they would receive a report card indicating how well the experimenter thought they had performed. Subjects assigned to the evaluation-computer group also expected to be evaluated, but they were told that the computer would determine how well they had performed and register their grades on the screen. For children assigned to the non-evaluation-control condition, no mention was made of a report card or evaluation contingency.

Creativity scores revealed that children who had been assigned to constraint conditions produced designs that were judged somewhat less creative than designs produced by children who did not expect an evaluation. Again, when only older subjects (ages ten to thirteen) were considered separately, the deleterious impact of evaluation was especially evident. The anticipation of evaluation significantly undermined creativity, and this effect was observed regardless of whether the report card was expected to come from a human being or a computer.

In another study (Berglas, Amabile, & Handel, 1979), we also wanted to examine the impact of evaluation on children's creativity. Here, however, our focus was on the effect that *prior* evaluation would have on subsequent performance. We predicted that highly salient evaluation on one task would lead children to expect evaluation on a later target task with the same experimenter, and that the expectation would undermine their creativity on that later task. All subjects, boys and girls in grades two through six, made two art works. The first involved painting with a spinning disk and the second – which was the target task – involved making a paper collage. Experimental-group children were evaluated positively by the experimenter on their "spin-art" before they made their collages. Control-group subjects simply made the two art works and were not evaluated. Results indicated a clear superiority of the control group over the experimental group on measures of creativity. In other words, we observed a negative impact of prior evaluation on creativity of performance.

Another focus of our research has been the role of choice. Although we expected that choice would influence motivation and creativity in a manner similar to that of other social-environmental factors, there are important differences between choice and these other variables, such as expectation of reward or evaluation. With reward and evaluation, there are some goals external to the target task, some goals for which the task is the means to an end. However, when choice is the independent variable, there is no such external goal; instead, subjects' perceptions of self-determination in task engagement are manipulated directly.

In a preliminary test of the effects of choice on creativity (Amabile & Gitomer, 1984), we asked nursery school children to make a paper collage. Children who were assigned to the choice condition were allowed to choose any five out of ten boxes of materials to use in their collage. For children in the no-choice condition, however, the experimenter made the box selections – yoking the two conditions in a matched-pairs design. All subjects then completed their collages, which later were rated for creativity by artists.

Two weeks after the initial sessions had ended, a behavioral measure of subsequent interest in making collages was obtained. Over a three-day span, leftover materials were made available, and each child's engagement in the activity during free-choice periods was timed. As predicted, there was a substantial difference in collage creativity between conditions. Subjects in the choice condition made collages that were rated significantly more creative than those made by subjects in the no-choice condition. In addition, children in the choice condition spent somewhat more time with collage materials during free-play than did children in the no-choice condition.

There are some circumstances, however, under which choice may be expected to undermine creativity. If children perceive themselves as choosing to participate in an activity in order to obtain a reward, then their intrinsic motivation theoretically would shift to extrinsic motivation, and their creativity would decline. To test this hypothesis, we employed a 2 × 2 factorial design in which the presence or absence of choice was crossed completely with the presence or absence of reward (Amabile, Hennessey, & Grossman, 1986, Study 2). We predicted that creativity would be undermined only in those children who explicitly contracted with the experimenter to perform the target activities in order to obtain a reward – in other words, in those children who were given a choice about performing the activities for reward.

Subjects in this investigation were eighty students in grades three, four, and five. All children participated in the experimental session individually. Subjects in the choice reward condition were told that they could either go back to their classrooms, or if they signed a contract promising to make a collage and tell a story, first could take two pictures with an instant camera as a reward. It was made clear that some children did, in fact, decide to leave.

In the choice no-reward condition, the children were told that they could make collages and tell stories or go back to their classroom; again, it was made clear that the decision to return to class was acceptable. In the no-choice reward condition, subjects were told that because they were going to make collages and tell stories for the experimenter, their reward would be to first take two pictures with the camera. And in the no-choice no-reward condition, the picture-taking was introduced as simply one of a series of tasks to be completed. In all four conditions, picture-taking was the first activity introduced. The two target tasks that followed, collage-making and story-telling, were counterbalanced.

A 2 × 2 ANOVA on the creativity scores for both the stories and the collages revealed the predicted interaction between reward and choice. Subjects in the choice reward condition told less creative stories than did the other three groups. The creativity of children who had been given a choice about their participation had been undermined seriously by the reward manipulation. However, for children who did not perceive that the decision to complete the tasks was under their control, no such deleterious effects of reward were observed. Thus, this study demonstrated that it might not be reward per se that undermined creativity, but the functional significance of reward as controlling performance.

A study by Koestner and his colleagues (1984) supported our findings. These researchers set out to determine whether another extrinsic constraint – behavioral limits – affected children's motivation and creativity. In this study, six- and seven-year-old children were asked to engage in an intrinsically interesting painting activity under three limit-setting conditions that varied along information and control dimensions. In the controlling-limits group, restrictions pertaining to task neatness were stated in terms of "shoulds" and "musts." The informational group received a verbal communication conveying the same behavioral constraints but without expressed external pressure, and with an acknowledgment of subjects' possible conflicting feelings about the limits. For the control (no-limits) group, no mention was made of these constraints. After the children painted, they were left alone for a free-play session. The amount of time they spent painting during this session was used as a measure of intrinsic motivation. Finally, the children were asked to rate how much they enjoyed the activity. Paintings made during the main session were rated by artist-judges on creativity, using our consensual assessment technique (Amabile, 1982a; Hennessey and Amabile, in press). Results indicated a main effect for condition: subjects in the no-limits and informational-limits groups spent more free-choice time painting than did controlling-limits subjects. Thus, intrinsic motivation was significantly lower for children in the controlling-limits condition. In addition, a marginal effect for limit-setting style emerges on the self-report measure of enjoyment: controlling-limits children expressed less enjoyment than did informational-limits subjects. Most importantly for our purposes, effects for limit-setting style also were found for creativity. The no-limits group produced pictures that were significantly more creative than did the controlling-limits group; the informational-limits group was intermediate.

Questions about mechanism

These studies offer consistently strong evidence of the undermining of children's creativity by extrinsic constraints. However, many questions about mechanism remain unanswered. Lepper and Greene (1978) suggest a cognitive mechanism that incorporates use of an attributional framework. They prupose that subjects cognitively analyze the reasons for engagement in a task. Under conditions of salient extrinsic constraint, this cognitive analysis would lead subjects to use the discounting principle (Kelley, 1973). That is, they would discount their intrinsic interest as a cause of their task engagement because a more salient and plausible cause (the extrinsic constraint) also was present (see also Bem, 1972).

The problem with this analysis, as Lepper and Greene (1978) have acknowledged, is that very young children are incapable of performing standard "discounting" tasks. Indeed, in one study in which we closely examined children's cognitive abilities (Amabile, Hennessey, & Grossman, 1986, Study 1), we found that young children could not apply the discounting principle to stories even when these children were the subjects of the stories. Lepper and Greene have suggested an alternative cognitive explanation: Perhaps children used cognitively simple "scripts," in which an activity always was undesirable if the child was offered inducements to pursue it.

It is possible, of course, that the mechanism is more affective than cognitive – that, as Deci and Ryan (1985) might suggest, people feel less positively toward an activity if their engagement in that activity is not self-determined, but rather constrained by others. Unfortunately, we have not found evidence of an affective mechanism. In none of our studies did we find a significantly lower level of positive affect among children who had experienced extrinsic constraint during task engagement. Only one study – that by Koestner and colleagues (1984) – found a weak link between decrements in intrinsic motivation, creativity, and positive affect.

The difficulties we have encountered in investigating these mechanisms are even more profound. Not only have we been unable to determine whether affect or cognition mediated the undermining of intrinsic motivation, the studies reported in this chapter did not show consistently that an undermining of intrinsic motivation accompanied the demonstrated decline in creativity. The proposed link between creativity and intrinsic motivation was not found to be nearly as strong as we had expected. Our reasoning had been this: If the intrinsically motivated state were more conductive to creativity than the extrinsically motivated state, and if extrinsic constraints undermined intrinsic motivation, then an imposition of extrinsic constraints on children's performance of creativity tasks would lead to both lower levels of intrinsic motivation *and* lower levels of creativity. We almost always found the latter, but only sometimes the former.

The reasons for this paradox are unclear. It is true that we never found a *reversal* of the expected effect; that is, we never found that constrained children showed *higher* levels of intrinsic motivation. More often, we simply found no difference. Perhaps our behavioral and self-report measures of intrinsic motivation were inadequate. Perhaps a more comprehensive and valid battery of measures could be devised.

It *is* clear, from the extensive list of overjustification studies, that extrinsic constraint undermines intrinsic motivation in children. It is also clear, from the creativity studies just reported, that extrinsic constraint undermines creativity in children. Why our extrinsic constraint studies did not consistently show decrements in intrinsic motivation *along with* decrements in creativity is a puzzle. But it is a puzzle that we have begun to solve from a different angle.

The positive approach: maintaining creativity by maintaining intrinsic motivation

When attempting to demonstrate a definitive link between creativity and intrinsic motivation, it is just as important conceptually to demonstrate that creativity will be maintained when intrinsic motivation is maintained as it is to demonstrate that creativity will be undermined when intrinsic motivation is undermined. Practically, it is *more* important to do so (Hennessey & Amabile, 1987). In a series of recent studies we endeavored to "immunize" children against the negative effects of extrinsic constraint on their creativity by bolstering the salience of intrinsic motivational factors.

In the first of these investigations (Hennessey, Amabile, & Martinage, 1989, Study 1), children ages seven to eleven participated in two group-training sessions on two consecutive days. During each session, groups of two or three children (randomly assigned to condition and group) watched a videotape and discussed the content of the videotape with an experimenter. In the crucial intrinsic-motivation training, the videotapes depicted two eleven-year-old children talking with an adult about various aspects of their schoolwork. The scripts for these tapes had been written so that the children on the tape would serve as models of highly intrinsically motivated individuals.

The intrinsic-motivation training tapes were intended to communicate two points. The first was the importance of finding intrinsically enjoyable aspects to whatever one has to do, and concentrating on them for maximal enjoyment. Here is an example of a tape segment that addresses this issue:

Adult: Tommy, of all the things your teacher gives you to do in school, think about the one thing you like to do best and tell me about it.

Tommy: Well, I like social studies the best. I like learning about how other people live in different parts of the world. It's also fun because you get to do lots of projects and reports. I like doing projects because you can learn a lot about something on your own. I work hard on my projects and when I come up with good ideas, I feel good. When you are working on something that you thought of, and that's interesting to you, it's more fun to do.

Adult: So, one of the reasons you like social studies so much is because you get to learn about things on your own. And it makes you feel good when you do things for yourself; it makes it more interesting. That's great.

The second point addressed in the training tapes was the benefits of cognitively distancing oneself from socially imposed extrinsic constraints and maintaining a focus on the intrinsically enjoyable aspects of a task. Here is an example:

Adult: It sounds like both of you do the work in school because you like it, but what about getting good grades from your teacher or presents from your parents for doing well? Do you think about those things?

Tommy: Well, I like to get good grades, and when I bring home a good report card, my parents always give me money. But that's not what's really important. I like to learn a lot. There are a lot of things that interest me, and I want to learn about them, so I work hard because I enjoy it.

Sarah: Sometimes when I know my teacher is going to give me a grade on something I am doing, I think about that. But then I remember that it's more important that I like what I'm doing, that I really enjoy it, and then I don't think about grades as much.

Adult: That's good. Both of you like to get good grades, but you both know that what is really important is how you feel about your work, and that you enjoy what you are doing.

In each intrinsic-motivation training session, the experimenter showed segments of the videotape and conducted discussions. During these discussions, the experimenter asked the children to describe what they had seen on the tape, to answer for themselves the questions the adult on the tape had posed, and to voice their opinions about the content of the tape. Throughout, she offered interpretations of the tape and of the subjects' comments, all with the aim of making the children more aware of behaviors associated with intrinsic motivation and of ways of coping with extrinsic constraint.

Children in a control condition also participated in two group training sessions with the same experimenter, but the videotapes these children viewed had nothing to do with intrinsic motivation. On these tapes, the same adult as on the training tape asked the same child actors to discuss their favorite foods, rock groups, seasons of the year, and so on. These topics guided the discussions that the experimenter had with children in the control condition.

The day after their second training session, all children participated in an individual testing session with a second experimenter in a different room. The children's teachers and the experimenters were careful to avoid mentioning any connection between the training and testing sessions, and denied a connection if the children asked. The testing session was aimed at obtaining two main measures: (1) a measure of the child's intrinsic/extrinsic motivational orientation, as assessed by Harter's (1981) test of Intrinsic vs. Extrinsic Motivation in the Classroom (only intrinsic interest and mastery scales were administered because of time limitations); and (2) a measure of creativity in the presence or absence of a salient extrinsic constraint – our standard paradigm. In this case, the creativity task was storytelling, and the extrinsic constraint was a reward of using a Polaroid camera. Thus, this testing session (after the completion of Harter's test by each child) followed a 2 × 2 experimental design. Half of the children had experienced the intrinsic motivation training, and half had been in the control group. As a cross dimension, half explicitly contracted with the experimenter to tell a story in exchange for permission to take some pictures with the camera, and half simply took pictures as an activity preceding the storytelling.

Our results were striking. First, the children who had been trained scored significantly higher on Harter's intrinsic interest scale than the children who had not been trained. Considering the brevity of our training sessions, and the stability that Harter reports for scores on her test, this finding was remarkable. Even more remarkable, however, was our second finding: Although the children in the control group showed the usual decrement in creativity under contracted-for reward (a marginally significant effect here), the children in the intrinsic-motivation training group showed no such decrement. In fact, they scored significantly *higher* on creativity under conditions of contracted-for reward! It appears that we succeeded not only in immunizing these children (at least temporarily) against the negative effects of extrinsic constraint on their creativity, but in training them to interpret extrinsic incentives in a way that contributed to, rather than undermined, creativity.

Two subsequent investigations (Hennessey, Amabile, & Martinage, 1989, Study 2; Hennessey & Zbikowski, in press) have replicated these most encouraging initial findings. Together these studies establish a real link between intrinsic motivation and creativity and strengthen the contention that directed discussion sessions focused on intrinsic reasons for working in school and explicit methods for distancing oneself from reward contingencies could play a significant role in counteracting the overjustification effect.

Another look at mechanism

Even when we assume that intrinsic motivation is conducive to creativity and that extrinsic motivation is detrimental, we still are left wondering about the mechanism by which a motivational state affects creative behavior.

Simon (1967) suggested that the control of attention is the most important function of motivation. McGraw (1978) proposed that extrinsic motivation improved performance on algorithmic tasks (those with clear and straightforward paths to solution) but undermined performance on heuristic tasks (those for which some search is required). Using these notions, we have developed a metaphor for guiding thought and future research on the question of mechanism.

Imagine that a task is like a maze that must be solved. Say that there is only one entrance to the maze, and that there is one clear and straight path leading to an exit. The direct path is an algorithm for this task – a solution that is familiar and well-practiced. It leads to an exit, which is an acceptable solution to the problem. Although the solution is acceptable, however, it is uncreative. It is neither novel nor elegant; it engenders no insight.

There might well be other ways out of the maze – more creative solutions. However, these cannot be discovered by following the algorithmic pathway. They can be discovered only by deviating from the path, by exploring the maze, and by developing heuristic approaches to the task. This requires not only exploration, but risk-taking too. Any maze contains more dead-ends than exits, and the probability of getting caught in the former is high. The exploration must be flexible enough to permit retracing of steps and reformulation of plans.

The point is this: If you were extrinsically motivated, your motivation would come primarily from something outside the maze, such as a promised reward or an external evaluation. Under these circumstances, the most reasonable thing to do would be to follow the familiar algorithm. The usual exit would be reached with a minimum amount of fuss; the task would be satisfactorily completed, the extrinsic goal would be achieved. If you were intrinsically motivated, however, you would *enjoy being in the maze;* you would find the exploration and risk-taking to be, in themselves, rewarding. Only if you had an intrinsic interest in the activity itself, *and* only if your social environment allowed you to retain that intrinsic focus, would you be able to discover a truly creative solution.

Practical implications

In much of our research, we have been the bearers of bad news. We have discovered a number of ways to destroy creativity in children: make them understand that they are doing something to obtain a reward; encourage them to compete with each other; lead them to focus on an external evaluation of their work; restrict their choices in how they may perform a task. Obviously, many current educational systems and methods of childrearing have implemented each of these techniques. What is the good news in all of this? What may be done in classrooms and in homes to maintain and stimulate children's creativity?

According to our componential model of creativity, strengthening each of the three components – domain-relevant skills, creativity-relevant skills, and task motivation – would enhance children's creativity in any domain. Thus one method for fostering children's creativity would be to improve their domain-relevant and creativity-relevant skills. In other words, we could teach children the basic knowledge and skills for particular domains, which is what traditional education is all about, and teach them creative-thinking skills, which has been the emphasis of creativity training programs during the past twenty-five years or so (e.g., Torrance, 1972).

There should be other methods for improving children's creativity, however. These methods may be even more effective in producing immediate gains than teaching domain-relevant or creativity-relevant skills. Unfortunately, these methods virtually have been ignored by both teachers and creativity researchers. They involve task motivation, which is the third component of our model of creativity. According to the model, methods that maintain or increase children's intrinsic motivation toward their work in general should lead to a maintenance or an increase of their creativity in many work domains, and methods that maintain or increase children's intrinsic motivation toward a specific task should have similar effects on that task.

Here, the good news comes from our training study. The intrinsic-motivation training incorporated two basic principles that, according to the componential model and the intrinsic-motivation principle derived from that model, would lead to the maintenance and stimulation of creativity: (1) take the focus off extrinsic goals and constraints; and (2) concentrate on intrinsic motives. The first of these could be implemented in two ways by parents and teachers. One way would be to structure the child's work environment so that competition, external rewards, external evaluation, and other constraints were deemphasized. Children could be taught to rely more on self-evaluation and self-reward. Rewards and evaluations certainly could be used, but in ways that did not cause children to focus on external inducements. For example, rewards could be presented as "bonuses" after completion of some particularly good work, rather than as initial inducements – especially when children seemed initially intrinsically interested in an activity.

Another method for taking the focus off extrinsic goals and constraints is the one we used in our intrinsic-motivation training study: teach children ways to cognitively distance themselves from, but not to ignore, extrinsic constraints. The point would be to teach children to cognitively keep reward, competition, evaluation, and other constraints in their place, so that these factors did not overwhelm intrinsic enjoyment of their work.

The training sessions also attempted to teach children to concentrate on intrinsic motives. Clearly, this is something that parents and teachers could do easily in the normal course of interacting with children. These adults could ask children to think and talk about the most fun, interesting, and challenging aspects of their activities. Parents and teachers also could help children to explore enjoyable activities and to make the less enjoyable ones more interesting. Throughout, adults could ask children to focus on the interest, enjoyment, and satisfaction of a task.

The results of the training study suggested that we were successful in teaching children to take the focus off external goals and constraints and to concentrate on intrinsic motives. If two brief training sessions were successful in even temporarily enhancing children's intrinsic motivation and immunizing them against the negative effects of constraint on their creativity, how much more effective would such training be if it came from parents and teachers as part of the normal course of child-rearing? Then, we might run less risk of stifling the creativity of today's young Einsteins.

References

Amabile, T. M. (1982a). Social psychology of creativity: A consensual assessment technique. *Journal of Personality and Social Psychology, 43,* 997–1013.

Amabile, T. M. (1982b). Children's artistic creativity: Detrimental effects of competition in a field setting. *Personality and Social Psychology Bulletin, 8,* 573–578.

Amabile, T. M. (1983a). *The social psychology of creativity.* New York: Springer-Verlag.

Amabile, T. M. (1983b). Social psychology of creativity: a componential conceptualization. *Journal of Personality and Social Psychology, 45,* 357–377.

Amabile, T. M., DeJong, W., & Lepper, M. R. (1976). Effects of externally-imposed deadlines on subsequent intrinsic motivation. *Journal of Personality and Social Psychology, 34,* 92–98.

Amabile, T. M., & Gitomer, J. (1984). Children's artistic creativity: Effects of choice in task materials. *Personality and Social Psychology Bulletin, 10,* 209–215.

Amabile, T. M., Hennessey, B. A., & Grossman, B. S. (1986). Social influences on creativity: The effects of contracted-for reward. *Journal of Personality and Social Psychology, 50,* 14–23.

Barron, F. (1968). *Creativity and personal freedom.* New York: Van Nostrand.

Bem, D. (1972). Self-perception theory. In L. Berkowitz (Ed.), *Advances in experimental social psychology* (Vol. 6). New York: Academic Press.

Berglas, S., Amabile, T. M., & Handel, M. (1979). *Effects of evaluation on children's artistic creativity.* Paper presented at the meeting of the American Psychological Association, New York.

Crutchfield, R. S. (1962). Conformity and creative thinking. In H. Gruber, G. Terrell, & M. Wertheimer (Eds.), *Contemporary approaches to creative thinking.* New York: Atherton Press.

DeCharms, R. (1968). *Personal causation.* New York: Academic Press.

Deci, E. (1971). Effects of externally mediated rewards on intrinsic motivation. *Journal of Personality and Social Psychology, 18,* 105–115.

Deci, E. (1975). *Intrinsic motivation.* New York: Plenum.

Deci, E. L., & Porac, J. (1978). Cognitive evaluation theory and the study of human motivation. In M. Lepper & D. Greene (Eds.), *The hidden costs of reward.* Hillsdale, NJ: Erlbaum.

Deci, E. L., & Ryan, R. M. (1985). *Intrinsic motivation and self-determination in human behavior.* New York: Plenum.

Einstein, A. (1949). Autobiography. In P. Schilpp (Ed.), *Albert Einstein: Philosopher-scientist.* Evanston, IL: Library of Living Philosophers.

Garbarino, J. (1975). The impact of anticipated reward upon cross-age tutoring. *Journal of Personality and Social Psychology, 32,* 421–428.

Greene, D., & Lepper, M. R. (1974). Effects of extrinsic rewards on children's subsequent intrinsic interest. *Child Development, 45,* 1141–1145.

Harter, S. (1978). Effectance motivation reconsidered: Toward a developmental model. *Human Development, 21,* 34–64.

Harter, S. (1981). A new self-report scale of intrinsic versus extrinsic orientation in the classroom. *Development Psychology, 17,* 300–312.

Hennessey, B. (1989). The effect of extrinsic constraints on children's creativity while using a computer. *Creativity Research Journal, 2,* 151–168.

Hennessey, B. & Zbikowski, S. (in press). Immunizing children against the negative effects of reward: A further examination of intrinsic motivation training techniques. *Creativity Research Journal.*

Hennessey, B., & Amabile, T. (1987). *Creativity and learning: What research says to the teacher.* Washington, DC: National Education Association Professional Library.

Hennessey, B., & Amabile, T. (1988). Story-telling: A method for assessing children's creativity. *Journal of Creative Behavior, 22,* 235–246.

Hennessey, B., & Amabile, T. (in press). Product creativity: The consensual assessment technique. *Journal of the American Creativity Association.*

Hennessey, B., Amabile, T., & Martinage, M. (1989). Immunizing children against the negative effects of reward. *Contemporary Educational Psychology, 14,* 212–227.

Holton, G. (1972). On trying to understand scientific genius. *American Scholar, 41,* 95–110.

Karniol, R., & Ross, M. (1977). The effects of performance irrelevant rewards on children's intrinsic motivation. *Child Development, 48,* 482–487.

Kelley, H. H. (1973). The processes of causal attribution. *American Psychologist, 28,* 107–128.

Koestner, R., Ryan, R., Bernieri, F., & Holt, K. (1984). Setting limits on children's behavior: The differential effects of controlling vs. informational styles on intrinsic motivation and creativity. *Journal of Personality, 52,* 233–248.

Kruglanski, A. W., Friedman, I., & Zeevi, G. (1971). The effects of extrinsic incentive on some qualitative aspects of task performance. *Journal of Personality, 39,* 606–617.

Lepper, M. R., & Greene, D. (1975). Turning play into work: Effects of adult surveillance and extrinsic rewards on children's intrinsic motivation. *Journal of Personality and Social Psychology, 31,* 479–486.

Lepper, M. R., & Greene, D. (1978). *The hidden costs of reward: New perspectives on the psychology of human motivation.* Hillsdale, NJ: Lawrence Erlbaum Associates.

Lepper, M., Greene, D., & Nisbett, R. (1973). Undermining children's intrinsic interest with extrinsic rewards: A test of the "overjustification" hypothesis. *Journal of Personality and Social Psychology, 28,* 129–137.

Lepper, M. R., Sagotsky, G., Dafoe, J. L., & Greene, D. (1982). Consequences of superfluous social constraints: Effects on young children's social inferences and subsequent intrinsic interest. *Journal of Personality and Social Psychology, 42,* 51–65.

Loveland, K. K., & Olley, J. G. (1979). The effect of external reward on interest and quality of task performance in children of high and low interest motivation. *Child Development, 50,* 1207–1210.

McGraw, K. (1978). The detrimental effects of reward on performance: A literature review and a prediction model. In M. Lepper & D. Greene, (Eds.), *The hidden cost of reward.* Hillsdale, NJ: Erlbaum.

Simon, H. (1967). Motivational and emotional controls of cognition. *Psychological Review, 74,* 29–39.

Torrance, E. P. (1972). Can we teach children to think creatively? *Journal of Creative Behavior, 6,* 114–143.

White, R. (1959). Motivation reconsidered: The concept of competence. *Psychological Review, 66,* 297–323.

Part II

Competence and motivation

The chapters in this section focus on the antecedents and consequences of perceived competence. In Chapter 5, Susan Harter presents a comprehensive model of the relationship among perceived competence, affect, and motivational orientation. In her model, mastery urges are directed by an individual's success or failure experiences and by perceived level of control, along with the feedback he/she receives from socializing agents, such as teachers and parents. Each of these experiences engenders an important affective reaction, and the interaction of these factors influences the child's perception of his/her competence, which in turn and over time leads to a particular motivational orientation. Harter documents and analyzes the changes in components of extrinsic motivation as children progress through school. In discussing the distinction between intrinsic and extrinsic orientations on the one hand, and internalized motives on the other, the author makes a distinction very relevant to the theoretical position taken by Ryan, Connell, and Grolnick in Chapter 8.

Judith Harackiewicz, George Manderlink, and Carol Sansone (Chapter 6) employ an elegant model to examine how information about competence, communicated verbally rather than through rewards, influences intrinsic motivation. Competence cues are shown to affect intrinsic motivation through four intervening processes: an individual's perceived competence, the value the individual places on being competent, his or her level of anxiety over performance, and his or her level of perceived control. Individual differences in achievement motivation also are studied, linking this chapter with those in the third group.

In Chapter 7, Diane Ruble and colleagues (Ellen Grosovsky, Karin Frey, and Renae Cohen) offer a theoretically rich description of the development of competence assessment processes. Although children at all ages clearly show individual differences in assessments of their competence, the process by which children generate these self-judgments may well depend on developmental level. The authors review developmental differences in the use of social-comparison information and report two interesting studies on differences between self- and other-evaluation. Several additional studies assessing developmental changes in the use of individual versus social standards of assessment are reported, and the authors discuss the implications of their more recent findings, indicating that even kindergartners may use social comparison information in their competence judgments.

5 The relationship between perceived competence, affect, and motivational orientation within the classroom: Processes and patterns of change

Susan Harter

The field of psychology during the 1960s and early 1970s witnessed an intense focus on cognitive processes and their implications for behavior. More recently, two general trends have been noteworthy. Constructs involving motivation, affect, and the self have come into vogue. Moreover, these systems are not being studied in isolation. Rather, models emphasizing the relationships among these systems characterize much recent theorizing and research. The present chapter represents one such effort. Specifically, we will address the domain of children's scholastic performance, demonstrating how perceptions of competence, affective reactions, and motivational orientation toward classroom learning are all intimately linked.

The initial impetus for the work described here can be traced to White's (1959; 1963) concept of effectance motivation. In part to counter the singular focus on extrinsic motivational factors touted by learning and drive theorists during the 1940s and 1950s, White placed heavy emphasis on the intrinsic motivational forces that impelled the child toward mastery. Our efforts have addressed both intrinsic and extrinsic motivational factors in the context of classroom learning. That is, we have been interested in the relative strength of both intrinsic and extrinsic motivation, as they relate to one of the most important preoccupations of childhood: performance in school.

Several questions are addressed within this general framework:

1. Do self-perceptions, in the form of judgments about one's scholastic competence, bear any relationship to one's motivational orientation along a continuum from an intrinsic interest in learning to an extrinsic motivation to perform in order to meet external standards and win rewards? Is the more competent pupil more likely to manifest an intrinsic orientation, in

Preparation of this chapter was facilitated by a grant from N.I.C.H.D.

contrast to the less competent pupil, who is more likely to be extrinsically oriented?

2. What role do children's affective reactions to their competence play in mediating the relationship between self-judgments and motivational orientation? Do more competent children have much more positive affective reactions to their performance, which in turn impel them toward a more intrinsic interest in learning? Conversely, does the less competent child experience negative affective reactions that attenuate his or her intrinsic interest? Are there differences also in the discrete affects reported by children displaying high and low levels of competence in response to their academic successes and failures?

3. Are there developmental differences – that is, grade-related changes – in children's motivational orientations as they progress through school? Does intrinsic interest in learning decline, and, if so, what factors within the school environment contribute to this waning intrinsic motivation?

4. As children progress through school, are they equally affected by the environmental changes that are postulated to attenuate intrinsic motivation? How do we explain the fact that although many children's intrinsic interest in learning seems to decline as they move from grade to grade, other children show no such effect, and a small number of students actually show increases in intrinsic motivation?

5. Is our dichotomy between intrinsic and extrinsic motivation too restrictive? Might there be other motivational orientations that are equally powerful in the classroom? Specifically, we refer to the child's internalized motivation to perform well, an orientation that need not involve an intrinsic interest in challenge, curiosity, or learning, despite the fact that school performance appears self-motivated. Might there be different kinds of self-motivated behavior, intrinsic versus internalized, that have different origins as well as different patterns of correlates? Can we identify typologies representing different combinations of intrinsic, internalized, and extrinsic motivation? If so, which type of child perceives himself or herself to be most competent? Moreover, do children who manifest different types of motivational patterns have different affective experiences with regard to their school performances, and do they report different discrete affects?

These are the questions that will be addressed in this chapter. Our initial questions were guided by theory, but in the course of investigating them, serendipitous findings emerged. We can only speculate about these findings at present. Still, we offer interpretations that introduce hypotheses for further research, particularly with regard to the interaction between school environment variables and the individual pupil.

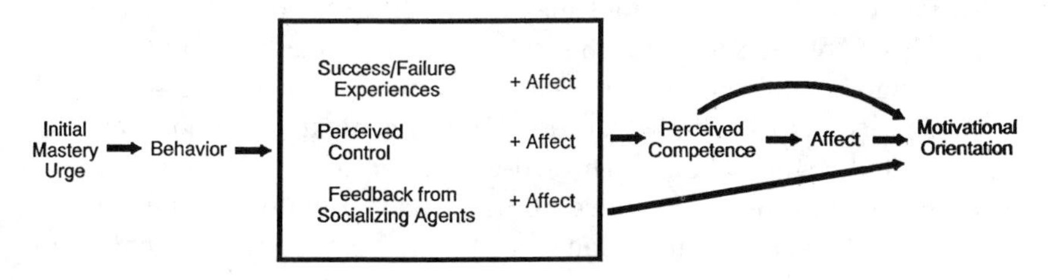

Figure 5.1. Chain of factors influencing motivational orientation.

The theoretical model

Our original model (Harter, 1978) was all-encompassing, in the sense that we postulated a number of antecedents and correlates of a child's motivational orientation. In this model it was suggested that the responses of socializing agents to the very young child's initial effectance urges, as well his or her successes or failures at these attempts to master the environment, undoubtedly would have a major impact on the child's self-perceptions of competence, affect, and motivational orientation. Figure 5.1 presents a number of the relationships postulated in the initial model, with certain modifications.

Developmentally, the child's initial mastery urges provoke behaviors from which effectance motivation is inferred. These behaviors result in some degree of success or failure. In addition, these successes or failures are accompanied by perceptions of control over the outcomes. Moreover, these behaviors meet with feedback from the significant socializing agents in the child's life. It is likely that each such consequence of the child's behavior is accompanied by an affective reaction. These affects conceivably would differ depending upon a number of factors. For example, a child may be excited about his or her success, happy that he or she was able to control the outcome, and proud that the parents observed his or her success and responded positively. Conversely, a child may be frustrated over a failure experience, angry that he or she could not exercise control over the outcome, and anxious or ashamed about the parents' negative response.

This model postulates that the combination of these factors would have a direct impact on the child's perceived competence. These self-perceptions also would provoke an affective reaction, which in turn would affect the child's motivational orientation. Perceptions of competence also might contribute directly to motivation. The motivational orientation that results from this chain of influences would, in turn, modify the initial mastery urges and provoke a new set of behaviors and consequences.

An interest in these questions may be traced to William James (1892), whose theory of the self states that self-evaluation gives rise to feelings or emotions about the self. These feelings, in turn, motivate the individual to engage in acts of self-preservation. In the context of school learning, we predicted a similar chain: The self-evaluation of one's scholastic competence would produce associated affects; these evaluative judgments and related affects would, in turn, lead to a particular motivational orientation.

In our model, we suggest that the causes of the affect produced by one's perceptions of competence might well differ from the causes of the affects preceding perceived competence. This is because competence-related affect involves an evaluation of the self. In contrast, the preceding affects relate more directly to the outcome of an event, one's sense of control, and feedback from others. According to the model, these factors eventually would influence the affect prompted by perceptions of competence; however, these affects theoretically would be mediated by the self-evaluative component. The need to postulate different affective reactions at various points in the chain has been underscored by other theorists as well. Weiner and his colleagues (Weiner, 1985; Weiner, Russell, & Lerman 1978), for example, have urged that we distinguish between affects related to outcome and those linked to the individual's perceptions of control. Dweck and Elliott (1983) also have postulated a number of different affective reactions in their model of achievement behavior, distinguishing between affects associated with the activity itself, with the means, and with the outcome in relation to one's goal.

In Figure 5.1, three components of the model are in boldface type – perceived competence, affect, and motivational orientation – because the relationships between these components are the primary topics of this chapter. Direct evidence on the postulated links will be presented here. At present, however, we have limited evidence on the preceding components of the model, although a few findings and speculations will be addressed. The consequences of behavior that are postulated as antecedents of perceived competence are organized in one box in the figure, because we do not understand yet their complex interactions and the specific impact each factor has on perceived competence and motivational orientation. In future refinements of this model, these critical issues must be considered.

The relationships postulated among the three boldfaced components are consistent with a variety of sequential models in the literature (Bandura, 1978; Kanfer, 1980; Wicklund, 1978). In each of these models, self-evaluative reactions to one's own performance are thought to produce an affective reaction that, in turn, affects one's tendency to engage in a given behavior. It is interesting that the models vary in terms of which emotions are expected to be provoked – for example, general positive or negative reactions versus affects directed toward oneself, such as pride or shame. We will return later to the issue of individual differences in the discrete affects that accompany judgments of competence.

Operational definitions and initial correlational findings

To test such relationships empirically, it first was necessary to operationally define constructs such as perceived competence, intrinsic versus extrinsic motivation, and affect. Our measurement construction efforts have been described in detail elsewhere (Harter, 1981; 1982). We began with self-report measures, using a questionnaire format designed to offset children's tendency to give socially desirable responses. We also adopted a domain-specific approach, designing measures to tap children's self-perceptions within such domains as academic competence, athletic competence, and social acceptance. It was our assumption, substantiated by subsequent findings, that perceptions of competence and motivational orientation might well differ across the various domains of a child's experience. In the domain of scholastic performance, perceived cognitive competence was assessed by items tapping perceptions of how well one was doing in class, how smart one thought one was, how well one understood one's classwork, how easy it was to figure out one's assignments, and how quickly one was able to perform academic tasks.

In assessing the child's motivational orientation (Harter, 1981), we opted for a measurement strategy that pitted an intrinsic orientation against an extrinsic orientation in a series of forced-choice questions. We were interested in the degree to which a child was curious and intrinsically interested in learning, and the degree to which he or she sought challenges and opportunities to master material independently. This intrinsic pattern was contrasted to a more extrinsic orientation in which a child tended to avoid challenge and independent mastery; his or her primary motivation was to please the teacher and to obtain good grades. We identified three motivational dimensions, each defined by a separate subscale: (1) preference for challenge versus preference for easy work; (2) incentive to work to satisfy one's interest and curiosity versus incentive to work to please the teacher and obtain good grades; (3) tendency to engage in independent mastery attempts versus a tendency to depend upon the teacher. Each subscale yielded a separate score.

With these measures in hand, we were in a position to test predictions derived from our model. We first focused on the hypothesis that a child's motivational orientation in the classroom (intrinsic versus extrinsic) would be related intimately to his or her sense of scholastic competence. In our earliest studies, we examined merely the correlations between perceived scholastic competence and each of the three motivational dimensions. Our predictions were supported by findings (see Harter, 1981) revealing that perceived scholastic competence was related strongly to preference for challenge ($r = .57$), to curiosity ($r = .33$), and to a desire for independent mastery ($r = .54$). Moreover, higher-order factoring indicated that perceived cognitive competence, challenge, curiosity, and mastery formed a distinct factor with extremely high loadings of .76, .87, .70, and .80, respectively. The high intercorrelations among the motivational components led us to combine these three motivational subscales in subsequent studies (Harter & Connell, 1984) to attain one mastery motivation score, which has correlated quite highly with perceived scholastic competence for both elementary school ($r = .52$) and junior high school ($r = .58$) students. Thus, among normative samples, we found evidence that students who perceived themselves to be scholastically competent manifested more intrinsic motivation compared to students who perceived themselves to be less competent. Students in this latter group also opted for a more extrinsic orientation.

The robustness of this relationship between perceived scholastic competence and motivational orientation more recently has been demonstrated among learning disabled children and gifted pupils. Among mainstreamed learning disabled pupils (Renick, 1986), perceived scholastic competence was found to be correlated highly with motivational orientation ($r = .53$). In our research, we also have divided a group of gifted elementary school pupils (Harter & Zumpf, 1986) into two groups – those who scored above the group's motivational orientation mean (and thereby demonstrated a more intrinsic orientation) and those who scored below the mean. We discovered that even within this intellectually select group, the perceived scholastic competence of those who scored above the mean was 3.6, compared to 3.0 for those below – quite a substantial difference. Thus, across a range of grades from our normative sample (third through ninth) and among certain special educational populations, we found ample evidence that perceptions of scholastic competence were related directly to one's self-reported motivational orientation in the classroom.

The directionality of this relationship and the mediating role of affect

Next, we became interested in the directionality of these relationships among elementary and junior high school students. Does one's perceived competence lead one to adopt a particular motivational orientation, or, conversely, does one's motivational orientation precede one's evaluation of one's cognitive competence? Moreover, might one's affective reactions serve as a mediating link?

Our first evidence bearing on the directionality of these relationships relied on causal modeling or path-analytic techniques (Connell, 1981; Harter & Connell, 1984). As described earlier, perceived competence was measured by the child's responses to items asking how well the child thought he or she performed in his or her schoolwork, how quickly he or she could complete assignments, how good his or her grades were, and so on. Here the focus was on relatively objective criteria. Competence-related affect, on the other hand, was tapped by items referring to feeling good or bad about one's work, worrying about completing schoolwork, and so forth. Motivational orientation was defined as a composite of the three motivational subscales from our scale of Intrinsic versus Extrinsic Orientation in the Classroom (Harter, 1981) – specifically, Preference for Challenge, Curiosity/Interest, and Independent Mastery.

With regard to the three primary components of the model, the findings revealed a chain by which the evaluation of one's scholastic competence influenced one's affective reaction to one's competence, which, in turn, had an impact on one's motivational orientation. In addition, there was a direct path from competence evaluation to motivation. Thus the more competent the child perceived himself or herself to be, the more positive were his or her affective reactions, and the more likely the child was to manifest an intrinsic motivational orientation. Conversely, the less competent child was more likely to report a negative emotional reaction which, in turn, was related to a more extrinsic motivational orientation. Interestingly, the path from affect to motivation was stronger for young adolescents than for elementary school pupils. Evidence for additional relationships in the overall model also was found: both the success/failure component, in the form of achievement level, and perceptions of control were found to impact the child's perceived scholastic competence.

In a follow-up study (Kowalski, 1985) we found corroborating evidence for the postulated relationships among perceived competence, affect, and motivational orientation. Kowalski, also employing path-analytic techniques, found that the best-fitting model for data obtained from sixth graders was one in which paths from perceived competence to both affect and motivational orientation were substantial. Moreover, the link between affect and motivational orientation improved the fit, suggesting that a portion of one's motivational orientation is mediated by the affective reaction to one's competence.

Behavioral evidence

The findings just cited were based on self-report measures; in subsequent studies (Guzman, 1983; Harter & Guzman, 1986) we investigated whether these relationships would be manifest in a behavioral setting. We were interested specifically in one motivational component: preference for challenge. Fifth and sixth grade students were selected to represent a range of perceived competence, including the extremes of high and low perceived competence. These children were brought into our laboratory in groups (from seven to ten in a group), where they were given an anagram task in a classroom setting designed to simulate their typical school environment.

Five levels of anagram difficulty, as defined by the number of letters in the anagram (three to seven letters), were included. During a practice phase, students were asked to attempt to solve anagrams from all difficulty levels. They then were told that a choice phase would follow, during which they were to pick eight anagrams to solve; they were told that in this phase, they could select any level of difficulty. They also were informed that they would be given letter grades for their performance: they needed to solve all eight correctly to obtain an A, six for a B, four for a C, and so on.

In this situation the primary affect of interest to us was state anxiety. Thus, after the practice phase, but before the choice phase, we asked students to complete a series of ratings so we could determine their level of anxiety in this problem-solving situation. Two types of items were included: those referring to emotional states (jittery, tense, nervous, shaky, worried) and those referring to specific cognitions ("I am worried that I'm not solving the anagrams quickly enough, worried that I'm not doing as well as the others, worried that I might get the wrong answer, worried that the other kids will think I am dumb, worried that I won't get a good grade").

The findings revealed that children's level of perceived cognitive competence was highly predictive of their choice of difficulty level, as was the worry/thought component. The more competent the child perceived himself or herself to be, and the lower his or her worry level, the more likely the child was to select more difficult anagrams. Children who perceived themselves as less competent and who expressed the most anxiety tended to pick the easiest anagrams.

These relationships suggested to us that the worry component may have mediated the relationship between perceived cognitive competence and difficulty-level choice. To examine this possibility, we partialled out the effects of the worry component; the findings revealed that the relationship between perceived competence and difficulty-level choice no longer was significant. Although this statistical procedure did not test directly our proposed causal links, it strongly suggested that perceived competence influenced one's level of worry, which, in turn, determined the level of difficulty that a child was willing to attempt in a problem-solving situation. The fact that the measure of state anxiety was specific to this situation further bolstered this interpretation.

It was of particular interest that the worry/thought component, but not the measure of specific emotional reactions (e.g., tense, nervous), was related to perceived competence and predicted difficulty-level choice. Thus, if children perceived themselves to be competent, they expressed fewer worries about their performance and about the reactions of the other children, which in turn led them to pick the more difficult anagrams to solve. Children whose perceived competence was low reported more worries about their task performance, which, in turn, led them to select easy anagrams. In contrast to the relationships found to the worry component, the correlation between ratings of one's emotional state, per se, and both perceived competence ($r = -.09$) and difficulty-level choice ($r = -.06$) were negligible.

This finding that the cognitive worry component had a greater impact on difficulty-level choice than the judgments of one's emotionality was consistent with previous studies (Morris & Liebert, 1969, 1970). As mentioned above, our worry statements were directly related to the children's performance on the anagram task. In contrast to these more focused worry statements, the one-word emotion labels (e.g., nervous, tense) were not task-specific. It also may be that children can less accurately judge their emotional states than they can their specific worries about performing a specific task. It would thus seem plausible that the cognitive component would have more of an impact on their actual choice behavior.

These findings also have more far-reaching implications for our use of terms such as affect. They suggest that we cannot be content to make general references to affect or to emotion without specifying to what such a construct refers. In each of the three studies discussed, the predictive affect component has been defined as self-reported judgment of how one felt about one's performance. Performance-related judgments of this type were related closely to both perceived competence and motivational orientation. It may well be that observations of a child's emotional state, by others or by the child himself or herself, are less predictive of the other components in this particular model. However, the evidence to date has supported strongly the postulated links between the child's perceived competence, affective judgments about performance, and motivational orientation. Furthermore, this evidence is founded on both self-report and behavioral measures of motivation.

The developmental decline of intrinsic motivation

In addition to the study of individual differences in motivation and their determinants, we also have been interested in developmental shifts associated with grade level. These findings, which have been reported elsewhere (Harter, 1981), reveal a systematic change from grades three through nine, from a predominantly intrinsic motivational orientation in third grade to a more extrinsic motivational orientation in junior high school. Although the change is gradual during this period, the most dramatic shift occurs between the sixth grade in elementary school, and the seventh grade in junior high. As children progress through school, they tend to express less interest in intellectual challenge and independent mastery of material, and less frequently name curiosity as a motivation for learning. We have speculated that children may be adapting to the demands of the school culture, which increasingly reinforces an extrinsic motivational orientation. As their focus narrows on the products of their learning, evaluated by grades, children show increasing disinterest in the learning process itself, as revealed by their waning intrinsic motivation.

That children are systematically mastering these standards is suggested by dramatic developmental changes on two additional subscales embedded in our measure of intrinsic versus extrinsic orientation. We have labelled these Internal Criteria for success and failure and Independent Judgment. Independent Judgment taps the extent to which students understand what they should be doing in the classroom. Internal Criteria taps the extent to which they know how well they are doing, indicating that they have internalized the performance standards and can evaluate themselves accordingly. We have colloquially referred to these two subscales as "knowledge of the rules of the game called school." Our findings have revealed a dramatic developmental increase in scores on these two subscales, which combine to form one higher-order factor that we have labelled Informational (in contrast to the higher-order factor defined by the three motivational subscales). As children advance from grade to grade, they seem to acquire more and more information about how the school system operates and about the standards and practices governing their performance in school. We would submit, by way of interpretation, that this increasing understanding is related intimately to the developmental decline in intrinsic motivation; as children learn that the higher their grade level, the more likely they are to be rewarded for the products of their efforts, rather than for an intrinsic interest in learning, intrinsic motivation wanes.

Eccles, Midgley, and Adler (1984) have provided an extensive summary of findings documenting similar trends, and have offered a much more comprehensive analysis of the possible reasons why students' attitudes toward school learning and achievement become increasingly negative as they progress through the school system. These authors have cited changes in the school environment as the presumed cause. That is, as students progress through the grades, the school environment becomes more impersonal, more formal, more evaluative, and more competitive. The educational focus shifts from the process of learning to an evaluation of products or outcomes. There is an increasing emphasis on social comparison, as students tend to be graded in terms of their relative performance on standardized tests and assignments, and as information on individuals' performance levels becomes more public. Eccles and his colleagues think that these changes are particularly dramatic in the transition from elementary school to junior high school.

These changes in the school environment have several implications with regard to the motivational changes associated with grade level. For example, as Brush (1980) has demonstrated, students have expressed negative attitudes about drills, testing, grading on the curve, competition, and a teacher's emphasis on right and wrong rather than on the learning process. These teaching styles, in turn, theoretically would influence motivation. Nicholls' (1979) analysis of such effects has focused on implications for the self. He has suggested that when a student's attention is focused on the assessment of his or her ability rather than on the learning task itself, the child's interest and motivation is attenuated. He has noted that school environments that rely heavily on social comparison cause students to focus their attention on the question "How smart am I?" which, in turn, has a negative impact on motivation.

Eccles and colleagues have reviewed further evidence indicating that student self-perceptions of their academic ability decline as students make the transition to junior high school (Simmons, Blyth, & Carleton-Ford, 1982; Simmons, Rosenberg, & Rosenberg, 1973). Moreover, anxiety over one's scholastic performance has been found to increase from grade to grade, and particularly during the transition from elementary school to junior high school (Burhmester, 1980). Thus, there would appear to be a constellation of grade-related changes in the school environment that affect self-evaluation and affective reactions, which in turn influence children's motivation and attitudes toward learning. These factors are summarized in Figure 5.2; we have adapted them to our original model and included their hypothesized effects on perceived competence, affect, and motivation.

The analysis by Eccles and colleagues is compelling. However, as those authors have pointed out, none of the studies they reviewed tested directly

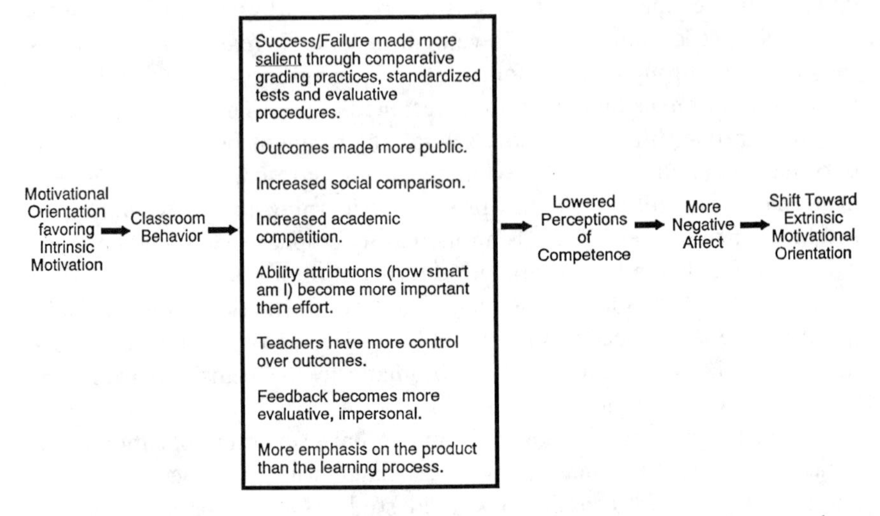

Figure 5.2. Hypothesized model of how changes in the school environment (particularly upon entrance to junior high school) influence competence, affect, and motivation.

the causal relationship between changes in the school environment and children's motivational patterns and attitudes. There are, however, numerous laboratory studies that bear indirectly on this question. The groundbreaking studies of Lepper and his colleagues (Lepper & Greene, 1975), as well as of Deci and his colleagues (Deci, 1975), clearly demonstrated that external rewards would undermine subjects' intrinsic motivation to engage in activities that, before the reward was offered, had been found intrinsically interesting. A spate of studies have ensued, illuminating the nature of the processes underlying such effects (see Deci & Ryan, 1981; Lepper & Gilovich, 1981). For example, it has been demonstrated that tangible rewards are more likely to undermine intrinsic interest than are verbal rewards such as praise. However, as Deci and his colleagues have demonstrated, verbal rewards and teaching practices that subjects perceive as controlling also attenuate intrinsic motivation. Thus, the function of the reward was found to be critical. It also has been demonstrated (Lepper & Gilovich, 1981) that surveillance, as well as social comparison, would undermine intrinsic interest. Thus the experimental literature has suggested that a constellation of factors, many of which can be observed within the school system, leads children to abandon their intrinsic interest in learning and to adopt a more extrinsic motivational orientation.

Further experimental studies

In our experiments, because we have been interested in the educational implications of this type of extrinsic reward, we have examined the effects of grading practices on children's behavioral preference for challenge. In one study (Harter, 1978) children were given an anagram task under two conditions. In the first condition, subjects were told simply that the task was a word game that it was thought children would enjoy. Subjects in the second condition were given the same anagrams, but were graded on their performance in an effort to focus their attention on an evaluation of whether they were able to solve the anagrams. We found differences between the game and grades conditions on several converging measures: Children in the grades condition avoided challenge by selecting the easier anagrams; they manifested less pleasure as assessed by smiling; they considered comparable anagrams to be more difficult; and they verbally expressed that they preferred easier anagrams so they could avoid getting a bad grade. Many subjects in the grades condition also spontaneously commented that the potential threat of a bad grade made them nervous or anxious.

Thus, the findings revealed that grades have a combination of behavioral, affective, and attitudinal consequences. A similar pattern of findings was reported by Maehr and Nicholls (1972), who gave eighth-grade subjects both easy and hard tasks under either an external or internal evaluative situation. In their internal condition, social comparison was deemphasized and emphasis was placed on performing the task for its own sake. Subjects in the external condition expressed greater preference for easy tasks and were less motivated to continue the task.

In a follow-up of our earlier anagram study, we sought to examine the effect of a constellation of factors that we postulated would undermine intrinsic motivation on the dimension of children's preference for challenge (Harter & Guzman, 1986). Children in small groups were given the anagrams in a simulated classroom situation; they were graded on their performance, timed on each problem, and given direct and public feedback by an impersonal teacher figure on whether their answers were correct. The group situation also fostered social comparison because children were asked to raise their hands when they thought they had correctly solved each anagram.

In this study we were interested primarily in children's preference for challenge relative to their problem-solving ability. Before introducing fifth and sixth graders to the grading procedure, we allowed them to practice anagrams at all levels of difficulty (three to seven letters). The practice phase allowed us to determine each subject's ability at this problem-solving task. We then explained the grading criteria and allowed the children to select a difficulty level for each of eight trials.

The findings were quite clear. During this choice phase, children systematically selected anagrams that were easier than the most difficult ones they could master, that is, anagrams that had one less letter than the most difficult anagrams they were able to solve correctly during the practice phase. For example, subjects who had solved six-letter anagrams in the practice phase selected five-letter anagrams during the choice phase; children who had solved five-letter anagrams in the practice phase selected four-letter anagrams under the graded condition, and so forth. Thus children in these conditions systematically avoided challenges commensurate with their demonstrated ability.

These studies have revealed that when a number of the factors implicated in the developmental decline of intrinsic motivation were manipulated in a laboratory-classroom situation, direct effects were obtained. The combination of the grades imposed by an impersonal evaluator, a focus on the correct solution, and the salience of social comparison served to attenuate children's interest in and enjoyment of the learning process and moderated their preference for challenge. In addition, these factors caused performance anxiety, which may mediate the effects. We still do not know what the relative importance of each of these factors might be, either in the experimental situation or in the classroom. However, it seems likely that these factors interact to produce the detrimental motivational effects observed in the naturalistic as well as in the simulated school environment.

Grade-related changes in learning-disabled pupils

Of particular interest is the fact that these effects are not limited to the regular classroom pupil, but extend to one special educational population we have examined: learning-disabled students. In one study with Mari Jo Renick (Renick, 1986), we compared our cross-sectional normative data on grade-related changes in both the motivational and informational factors with findings on mainstreamed learning-disabled children. These learning-disabled pupils spent the majority of their school day in the regular classroom setting, although they also were assigned to a Learning Disabilities Resource Room for special remedial help in school subjects in which they were particularly deficient.

Figure 5.3 presents a comparison of the trends for normal and learning-disabled students in grades three through seven. Two findings are noteworthy – one highlighting similarities between the two groups, the other

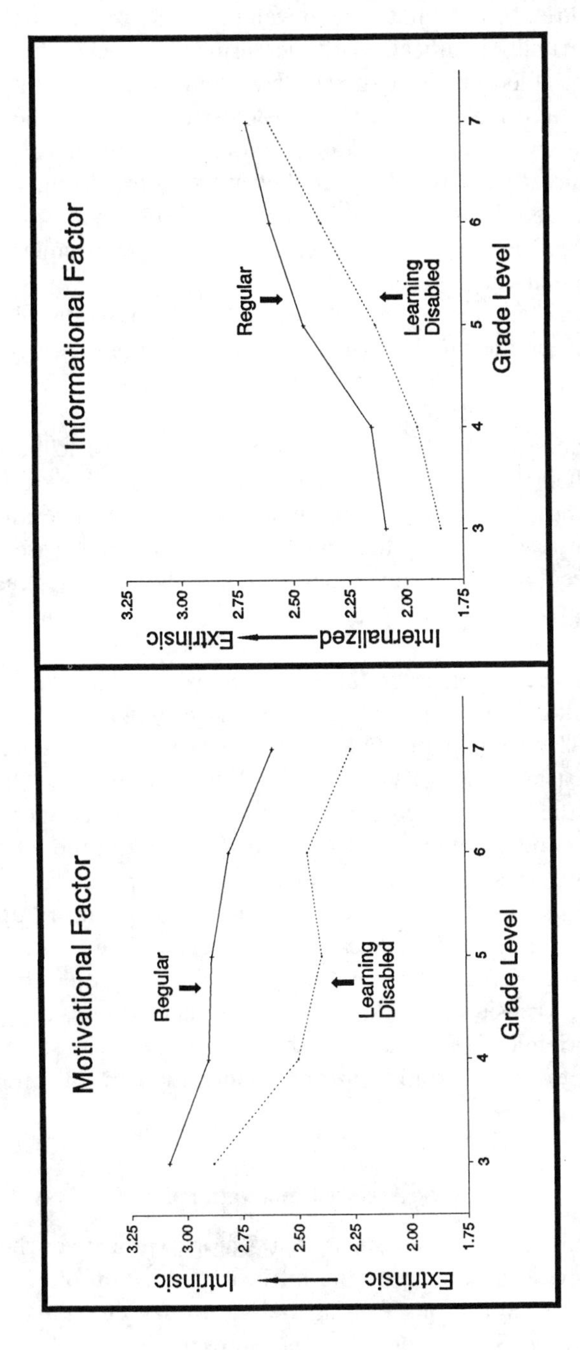

Figure 5.3. Grade-related shifts in the motivational and informational factors for regular and learning-disabled students.

emphasizing differences. First, the developmental trends of these two groups were virtually identical. With increasing grade level, both normal and learning-disabled children showed a systematic decrease in intrinsic motivation; their orientations shifted progressively toward the extrinsic pole of the scale. On the informational factor, these students also showed a systematic increase, revealing that they were internalizing the school system's standards. Thus we would appear to be observing processes in the mainstreamed learning-disabled child that are very similar to those revealed in regular classroom pupils.

The primary difference between the regular and learning-disabled groups was found between their mean scores. As can be seen in Figure 5.3, scores on both factors for the learning-disabled children were systematically lower than for the regular pupils at every grade level. This greater extrinsic orientation among the learning-disabled pupils appeared to be quite realistic, given their intellectual limitations. Greater avoidance of challenge, more dependence on the teacher for help in mastering material, greater reliance on the teacher's judgment about what to do, and a greater need for external feedback about one's performance all would appear to represent an adaptive response by these children, in light of their learning disabilities.

Overall, this pattern suggested that with increasing grade level, the mainstreamed learning-disabled child heard a message similar to the one heard by the regular classroom pupil – a message signaling the need to curb one's intrinsic interest in learning. The primary difference between the groups was that, from the outset, the learning-disabled child adopted a less intrinsic orientation, commensurate with his or her disabilities and the related need for additional extrinsic motivation, guidance, and structure. These findings also cautioned us against categorical value judgments concerning the desirability of an intrinsic orientation. For children with certain intellectual deficits, the most adaptive strategy for maximizing performance may well entail a more extrinsic orientation. Thus we need to consider a child's motivational orientation in relation to his or her particular strengths and weaknesses, rather than touting intrinsic motivation as the optimal orientation for all pupils.

Individual differences in grade-related motivational shifts

The implication of this discussion is that factors within the school environment systematically attenuate the intrinsic motivation of *all* students, particularly during transitions such as the one from elementary school to junior high school. Such is not the case, however. A small number of students actually has shown increased intrinsic motivation, and a large subgroup has shown no major change in its level or type of motivational orientation (Harter, Whitesell, & Kowalski, 1986; Riddle, 1986).

Eccles and her colleagues have suggested that the explanation for such individual differences can be found in the interaction between the student's ability level and changes in the school environment. These authors have pointed out that school changes that heighten the salience of ability and cause increased anxiety over one's performance relative to that of other students are more likely to moderate the motivation of students who are not especially able or who do not perceive themselves as very capable. These researchers cited findings suggesting that environmental settings that focus an individual's attention on the self rather than on the task itself have debilitating effects on the motivation of all but the most competent and confident individuals (Brophy, 1983; Doyle, 1979).

We have begun to examine this hypothesis in our work (Harter, Whitesell, & Kowalski, in press; Riddle, 1986). To do so, we employed a longitudinal design, testing students in the spring of their sixth-grade year in elementary school and six months later in late fall of their seventh-grade year, after the transition to junior high. The junior high school we selected drew students from four different elementary schools. As a result, the seventh graders were confronted with a changing social-reference group; approximately three-fourths of the students were new to them. To capitalize on the potential role of feedback in the form of grades, the seventh graders were tested after they had received their first report cards.

We were particularly interested in the hypothesis that changes in motivational orientation (intrinsic to extrinsic) would be related to changes in students' perceptions of competence. Thus we first identified three subgroups of subjects: those whose perceptions of scholastic competence (1) increased, (2) decreased, or (3) remained the same across the two grade levels. In identifying these three groups, we employed a procedure that controlled for regression to the mean. We first determined the relationship between scores at the sixth grade and seventh grade levels, calculating the degree of perceived competence that would be predicted in each individual in the seventh grade, based on the regression line determined for the group as a whole. Increasers were defined as those whose scores increased .40 above the predicted value; decreasers were those whose scores decreased by this amount; and those whose perceived competence in the seventh grade was consistent with the prediction equation were considered not to have changed. Since the standard error of measurement was approximately .35, changes of .40 or greater were considered to be real or meaningful. This procedure controlled for regression to the mean because increases or decreases in the seventh grade were independent of the student's level of competence in the sixth grade.

The perceived scholastic-competence scores of these three groups at the two grade levels are presented in Figure 5.4. As can be seen in this figure, the changes of those whose perceptions either increased or decreased were marked. Although we did not know the precise factors responsible for these changes, we speculated that the enhanced salience of performance feedback and social comparison in junior high school, within the context of a new reference group, caused pupils to reevaluate their scholastic competence. As a result, a sizeable number altered their conceptions of their academic ability.

To test the hypothesis that changes in motivational orientation paralleled these shifts in perceived scholastic ability, we examined a composite mastery motivation score composed of three subscales – preference for challenge, curiosity, and independent mastery. As can be seen in Figure 5.4, the composite score was related to perceived scholastic ability, in the sense that students whose perceptions of competence increased also manifested increases in their preference for challenge, curiosity, and independent mastery. By contrast, students whose perceptions of scholastic competence decreased showed a corresponding shift toward preference for easy schoolwork and a greater dependence on the teacher. Thus the pattern provided strong support for the hypothesis that changes in motivational orientation were related intimately to changes in perceptions of scholastic competence. Moreover, affect was implicated strongly as a mediator of this relationship; it was correlated with both perceptions of competence and with motivational orientation.

These findings indicate that the transition to junior high school does not have a universally debilitating effect on perceived competence, affect, or motivational orientation. We have inferred that this transition enhances the salience of ability-related information, which in turn may cause students to alter their perceptions of their academic competence. Changes in self-evaluation, provoked by grade-related changes in the school system, then produce individual differences in motivational orientation.

Students' perceptions of changes in educational practices

It should be noted that the previous interpretation relied heavily on inferences about changes in the school environment. However, we had no direct evidence that educational practices increasingly focused on an external evaluation of the products of students' performance, or that teachers highlighted the importance of grades rather than an intrinsic interest in

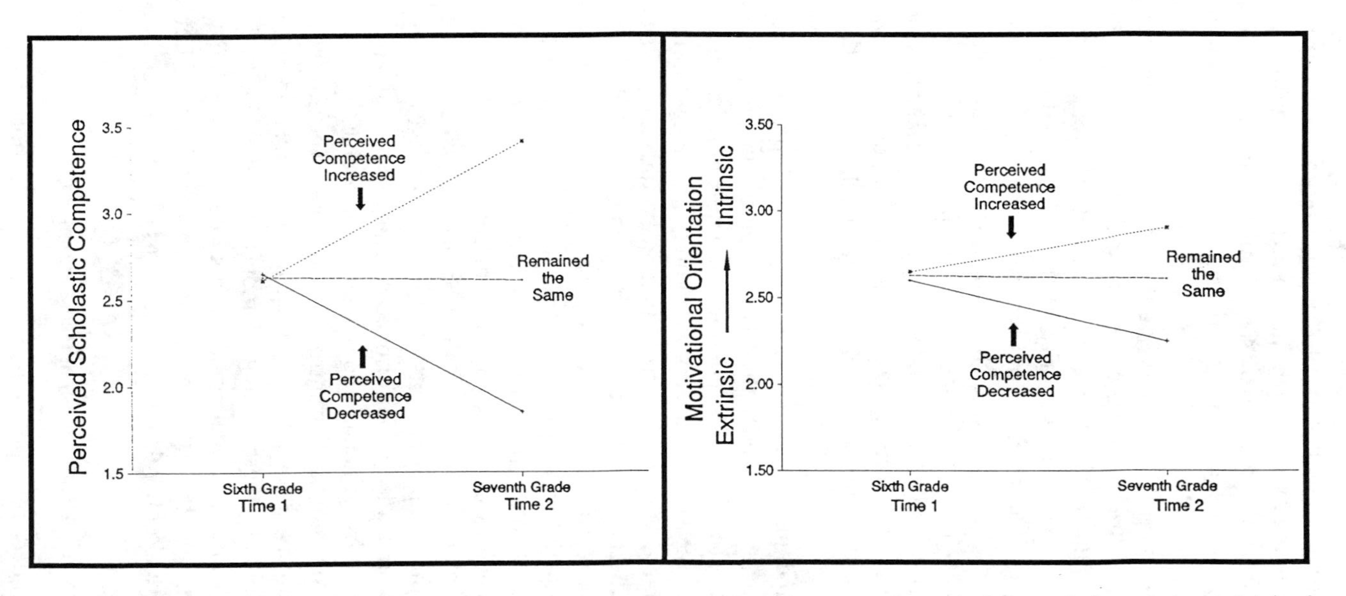

Figure 5.4. Changes in perceived scholastic competence and motivational orientation among those who increased, decreased or maintained their level of perceived scholastic competence between sixth and seven grade.

learning. We therefore conducted a follow-up study in which we asked students to evaluate their school environment on these dimensions. Middle school students were asked to compare school practices during their current academic year with the educational practices they experienced during the preceding year on the following dimensions: importance of grades, scholastic competition, importance of knowing the correct answer, perceptions of teachers' control, use of social comparison, and the extent to which one's scholastic competence became more salient (Harter, Whitesell & Kowalski, in press). The vast majority of these students indicated that educational practices had changed and that there was a greater emphasis on these dimensions. Thus we were able to demonstrate that a number of the inferred changes do indeed appear to occur in the school setting, at least as perceived by middle school students. That is, these students thought that more emphasis was placed on competence evaluation, academic performance, and social comparison, which in turn made their ability more salient.

There was a small minority of students that did not report such changes in educational practices. Although the basis for these students' perceptions was not clear, the existence of this subgroup was interesting, and it allowed us to test the hypothesis that students who perceived changes in the educational environment would differ from those who did not. Specifically, we documented the fact that those children who perceived changes were more likely to be extrinsically motivated and more anxious about their schoolwork. Such children also reported that scholastic success was more important to them than did those who perceived no changes.

However, the findings also documented an interaction between perceived competence and motivational orientation, consistent with our previous analysis. Among the group of students who perceived changes and reported greater emphasis on academic performance, competence evaluation, and social comparison, those students who perceived themselves as being competent were able to maintain their intrinsic motivation, whereas those who scored low on perceived competence opted for a more extrinsic motivational orientation. Thus these findings demonstrated that, in the face of perceived changes in educational practices, not all students would opt for an extrinsic motivational orientation, and that such individual differences in motivation were closely related to perceptions of competence.

Implications of program changes for gifted students

Recently we extended this type of analysis to an evaluation of a program for gifted children (Harter & Zumpf, 1986). One of our local public schools recently initiated an experimental program for gifted pupils in the third and fourth grades. The program involved segregating these pupils in self-contained classrooms where the curriculum was tailored to their intellectual level as well as to their special interests. School officials hoped that such a program might help sustain gifted pupils' intrinsic interest in learning and offset the normative decline that our previous findings documented. Ideally, the program would enhance students' intrinsic motivation. As part of our evaluation, we tested pupils on several measures at the beginning of the program in September and at the end of the school year eight months later. Among the measures administered were perceptions of scholastic competence and intrinsic versus extrinsic orientation.

Contrary to the hopes of the school administrators, we found no systematic increases in intrinsic motivation. Rather, we discovered three subgroups of gifted children: those whose intrinsic motivation increased, those whose motivation showed no change, and those whose motivation shifted toward a more extrinsic orientation. To aid in our understanding of these patterns of motivational change, we sought to determine whether there were any parallel changes in children's perceptions of scholastic competence. Thus we employed a strategy similar to the one we used in our junior high transition study. We looked for subgroups of gifted pupils, namely those showing significant increases or decreases in perceptions of scholastic competence during their year in the self-contained program.

We reasoned that students who enrolled in a special program for the gifted would face new academic expectations, new criteria for the evaluation of their competence, and a new social comparison group – namely peers who had been selected because of intellectual promise. Since the program drew from several neighborhoods in the district, many of these pupils did not know one another. This combination of factors undoubtedly would cause the issue of academic competence to become quite salient, and would lead pupils to reevaluate their competence within their new environment.

When we examined the changes in motivational orientation in each of these subgroups, the pattern of findings was quite clear. Those gifted pupils whose perceptions of competence increased during the program showed corresponding increases in intrinsic motivation. Conversely, students whose perceptions of competence decreased showed a parallel shift toward a more extrinsic motivational orientation. Thus, even within this intellectually select group, the processes we had identified earlier appeared to be operative. Changes in the academic environment appeared to provoke a reevaluation of one's scholastic competence which, in turn, led to changes in motivational orientation.

This pattern was illuminating because it bolstered our conviction that even within select educational populations, such as the gifted, we must be sensitive to individual differences. Moreover, we need to identify the underlying processes involved in the adoption of a motivational orientation. For example, social comparison processes among gifted children would appear to have some of the same effects as they do among more diverse, normative groups. Thus a gifted pupil who feels less competent than his or her gifted peers would tend to adopt a more extrinsic motivational orientation. The desired shift toward a more intrinsic orientation, on the other hand, is likely to occur among only those gifted pupils who think they are excelling relative to their select new reference group.

A refinement in our typology of motivation

In the preceding discussion, our primary motivational construct has been described along a continuum from intrinsic to extrinsic motivation, in which "intrinsic" implies self-motivation and "extrinsic" implies a response to external factors. However, any thoughtful analysis of child behavior would reveal that these were not the only motivational forces at work, particularly with regard to behaviors that appear to be self-motivated. Consider the child who, in the absence of surveillance, appears self-motivated to clean his or her room, to take out the garbage, to share a favorite toy with a not-so-favorite cousin, to study for a test in a school subject he or she enjoyed least, or to refrain from retaliating despite the provocations of a sibling. It would be very unlikely that these apparently self-motivated behaviors were driven by intrinsic interest or enjoyment of the process.

A more plausible interpretation would be that these behaviors represent the internalization of rewards, information, attitudes, and so forth, that initially were external and had been introduced by the socializing agents in the child's environment. That is, behaviors that initially are controlled by extrinsically established contingencies come to be performed spontaneously because the child has learned that these behaviors are important. The child becomes capable of engaging in self-reward and no longer is dependent upon external rewards or sanctions. This notion of an internalization process is not new, by any means, to students of child development. There is ample historical precedent in the writings of psychoanalysts, building upon Freud's notion of the super-ego and the ego-ideal, as well as in the theorizing and empirical work of social learning theorists (see Aronfreed, 1969; 1976). For the most part, these analyses have focused on the cultural shaping necessary to motivate children to perform acts that are not intrinsically interesting or rewarding, in the absence of surveillance or intervention by socializing agents (see Harter, 1982b, 1983, for a more complete discussion of these issues in the context of motivational development). Moreover, theorists and investigators have charted the developmental course of internalized motivation (see Chandler, 1981). Other theorists and investigators have examined the particular child-rearing practices on the part of care-givers that foster internalization (see Maccoby & Martin, 1983).

Investigators recently have begun to apply these constructs to classroom learning, and it has become apparent that seemingly self-motivated behaviors may have very different determinants (Harter, 1982b; Ryan, Connell & Grolnick, this volume). Consider two children who appear equally self-motivated to complete a science project. Child A may complete this assignment because he or she finds the project interesting and the process enjoyable and challenging, and because he or she is curious to answer the questions raised. Child B, on the other hand, may work diligently on the project because he or she knows that it is important to complete lessons and that such projects, in the long run, will enhance his or her education – a very desirable goal. Child A would appear to be demonstrating intrinsic motivation, in the sense that White intended when he introduced the term "effectance motivation"; whereas Child B would appear to be demonstrating internalized motivation to perform those behaviors that initially were encouraged or rewarded by socializing agents.

Within our work, we previously had introduced this distinction (Harter, 1978, 1982b); however, until recently, we had not tested this construct empirically. Certain of our findings seemed to support this distinction between intrinsic and internalized motivation, suggesting that it would be fruitful to operationalize each of these dimensions independently. For example, in our interpretation of the developmental or grade-related shifts documented in Figure 5.3, we suggested that the motivational changes reflected a shift from intrinsic to extrinsic motivation, whereas the increases in the informational factor reflected the internalization of the standards and values put forth by the school culture. However, this was a post hoc analysis that merely pointed out the need for a more precise operationalization of such constructs.

We therefore sought to examine the distinction between intrinsic and internalized motivation, incorporating both in a new measure that also tapped extrinsic motivation. This self-report instrument differed from our previous questionnaire in that the new measure did not employ a forced-choice format. We opted instead for a format in which each of these three dimensions could be measured independently. Such a procedure allowed the child respondent to indicate that more than one source of motivation was operative – an outcome that was not possible in our previous measure, in which intrinsic and extrinsic motivation represented opposite ends of a continuum. It would appear plausible, for example, that some of children's classroom performances may be determined by a combination of two or possibly all three sources of motivation. Conversely, there may be children for whom none of these sources was powerful, that is, children who were relatively unmotivated to engage in classroom learning. A measure that assessed each source independently allowed us to look for various combinations of motivational influences, as well as to examine a child's overall level of motivation.

The questionnaire we constructed consisted of three subscales: Intrinsic, Internalized, and Extrinsic motivation, with eight items on each. Items were worded as statements to which the child could respond on a four-point scale: Very True, Pretty True, Only Sort of True, Not Very True. The scale was introduced to the children as a questionnaire asking them about the reasons why they do their schoolwork. The Intrinsic subscale included such reasons as "I do my schoolwork because what we learn is really interesting; because I enjoy figuring things out; because it is challenging; because it makes me think hard and I really enjoy that; because I like to solve hard problems; and because I enjoy trying to understand things I do not already know." Thus it tapped the features represented by the intrinsic pole of our earlier scale – namely, preference for challenge, independent mastery, and enjoyment of the learning process.

The Internalized subscale included such reasons as "I do my schoolwork because I've learned for myself that it's important for me to do it; because I just know, without having to be told, that I should do my schoolwork; because it's important to get a good education; because it means a lot to me to do well; and because it's important to know as much as you can." The emphasis here was on values that the child had internalized; this scale focused on the outcomes of school performance.

The Extrinsic motivation subscale focused on performance either to obtain rewards and approval or to avoid sanctions and disapproval. Both parents and teachers were included as sources of extrinsic motivation. Items included, "I do my schoolwork because my teacher will be pleased with me if I do; because I will get something extra or special privileges from the teacher for getting the work done; because my parents will be mad or annoyed with me if I don't; because my teacher will give me a bad grade if I don't; because my parents will be happy with me if I do; and because I'll get in trouble with my parents if I don't." (Half of the extrinsic items were positive, involving approval and rewards, and half were negative, involving disapproval and sanctions. Half of each positive and negative set referred to the teacher and half of each set referred to the parents.)

We first administered this instrument to sixth, seventh, and eighth graders, and the measure revealed excellent psychometric properties. There was considerable within-subject variability in subscale scores; the internal consistencies of the three subscales were all greater than .85; and the factor-analysis, for which we employed an oblique rotation, revealed a clear, three-factor structure in which each subscale defined its own factor. Thus, we were confident that these constructs represented meaningful motivational dimensions for children in this age range and that this measure might reveal interesting individual differences.

A major goal in constructing this instrument was to determine whether different types of children, displaying different combinations of these three motivational dimensions, existed, and if so, what correlates of these styles might be identified. We began this search by looking for students whose scores represented combinations of high (top third) or low (bottom third) values across the three dimensions. Given three dimensions, there were eight possible combinations of high and low scores. At one extreme, a student would score high on all three components – Intrinsic, Internalized, and Extrinsic – whereas at the other extreme a student would score low on all three components. There were six other possible combinations of high and low scores across the three dimensions.

Our analysis revealed that of the possible eight combinations, four patterns stood out with sufficient frequency to suggest that they were the primary combinations that defined our population of middle school students. These were as follows:

	Intrinsic	*Internalized*	*Extrinsic*
(A)	High	High	Low
(B)	High	High	High
(C)	Low	Low	High
(D)	Low	Low	Low

The Type A student was one who claimed to be both intrinsically interested in learning and motivated for internalized reasons. This type of child scored quite low on extrinsic motivation, the implication being that he or she no longer needed extrinsic rewards and sanctions as motivation to do schoolwork.

The Type B student was one who appeared to need all three sources of motivation. Unlike the Type A student, this student appeared to need external rewards and sanctions to maximize his or her performance. One may speculate that for such a child, the internalization process was neither as complete nor as intense as for the Type A child; the Type B child, therefore, could not perform well without external support.

The Type C student displayed a pattern that was the opposite of the one found in the Type A student. Neither intrinsic nor internalized motivation played a primary role for Type Cs. The only source of motivation for such students appeared to be external rewards and privileges, in combination with the desire to avoid sanctions and disapproval, from teachers and parents.

The Type D student represented a motivational nadir, as it were. None of the sources we included appeared to motivate him or her. Although it was possible that unidentified sources might be operative, a more plausible interpretation was that such students showed little, if any, motivation for classroom learning.

Having established that these were the most prevalent motivational patterns, we next were interested in how these patterns were related to children's perceptions of scholastic competence, as well as to their affective reactions to their school performance. The affect measure asked students to rate whether they felt Very Good, Pretty Good, Not So Good, or Pretty Bad about three aspects of their performance: how they did at schoolwork, how smart they were in school, and the grades they received. A composite score was calculated across these three items. In addition to these indices of perceived competence and affect, we also wanted a measure of students' perceptions of whether they were accepted by their teachers, which we thought might be an interesting correlate of these typologies. The pattern of findings, presented in Figure 5.5, was quite consistent across the measures of competence, affect, and teacher acceptance.

The Type A students, who scored high on both intrinsic and internalized motivation, but low on extrinsic motivation, also scored highest on the scales tapping perceptions of teacher acceptance and of scholastic competence, and reported the most positive affect about their school performance. The Type B students, who had high scores on all three motivational sources, followed closely behind, although their scores were lower on all three variables.

The Type C student, motivated predominantly by external rewards and sanctions, showed quite a different pattern, particularly with regard to perceived competence and affect. On perceived competence, the Type C students scored almost an entire scale point lower than the Type Bs. Another large difference was observed in the affective reactions the Type C students reported about their schoolwork. These differences between the Type B and Type C students were consistent with our earlier analysis that highlighted the relationships among perceived scholastic competence, af-

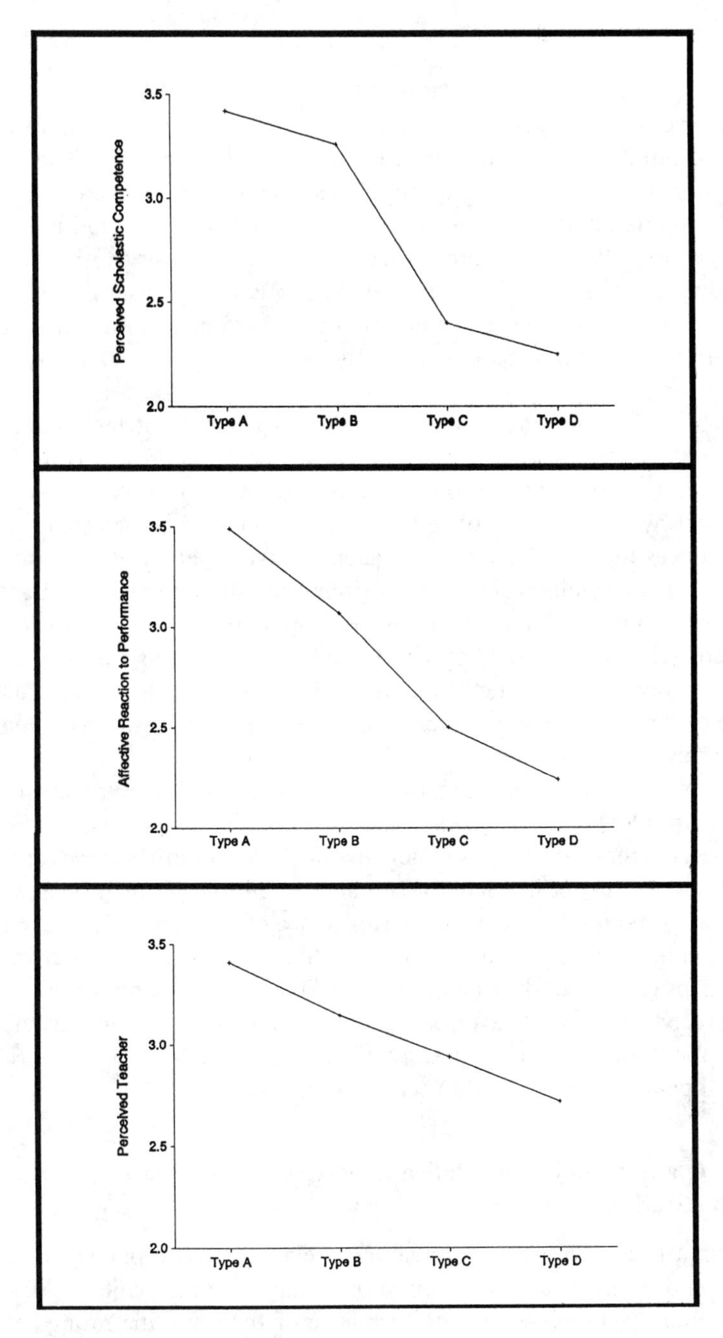

Figure 5.5. Perceived competence, affect, and teacher acceptance for combination of internalized, intrinsic and extrinsic motivation.

fect, and motivational orientation. Those students who did not perceive themselves to be very competent felt relatively bad about their performance and appeared to opt for an extrinsic motivational orientation. The findings from our newest scale, which tapped each source of motivation independently, illuminated this pattern: These extrinsically motivated individuals showed virtually no self-motivation of either form, intrinsic or internalized. Although they reported relatively high levels of extrinsic motivation, it would appear that such an orientation sustained only marginal academic performance, assuming that these students' perceptions of their competence were realistic.

Such extrinsically motivated Type C students did not feel shunned by teachers, although their perceived teacher acceptance was considerably less than that reported by the Type B and Type A students, who were impelled by both sources of self-motivation. These findings may speak to preferences teachers have for particular motivational styles. It is plausible that teachers would react more positively to students who thought that school learning was important and who appeared to be intrinsically motivated. Acceptance would appear to be less forthcoming for children who required rewards and sanctions to motivate them to perform. The fact that these extrinsic students also were less competent also might make teachers less likely to accept them.

The most extreme, negative perceptions were held by Type D students, who scored low on all sources of motivation. These students felt the least competent, reported the most negative feelings about their performance, and reported the least teacher acceptance of all four motivational profiles. It is highly likely that the actual performance of such unmotivated students was relatively poor, given that no incentives or sanctions, either intrinsic or extrinsic, appeared to be operative. That such students would receive or perceive the lowest level of teacher support also was understandable, given the difficulty teachers must have in responding positively to students who appeared uninterested in school learning.

Discrete affects and their relation to perceived competence and motivation

The measures of affect that have been related to both perceived competence and motivational orientation have tapped either children's general emotional reactions to their performance or their specific ratings of their anxiety levels. Although the relationships revealed by these measures appeared to be quite meaningful, they did not speak to the issue of which affects were most naturally experienced by children at different levels of competence and motivation. Thus, in our more recent studies, we have asked students to specify which affects they experienced as a result of both scholastic success and failure.

Our procedure involved giving children lists of both "good feelings" and "bad feelings," from which they were to choose the most salient positive emotion and the most salient negative emotion they might feel in response to success and failure, respectively. In constructing this list, we relied on earlier studies in which children named the emotions they were most likely to feel in both situations. Of particular interest in these lists was the distinction between affects that were related to the self and those that were more outcome-related or externally directed. Both Cooley (1902) and James (1892), in their early writings on the self, emphasized the fact that self-judgments typically produced affective reactions directed toward the self as an object or target. Pride and shame were prototypes of these self-affects.

In our assessment of the discrete affects experienced by children, therefore, we were sensitive particularly to possible distinctions between self-affects and those that could be interpreted as externally directed (Kowalski, 1985). Among the positive feelings, pride was the single self-affect that we included. We included five other positive affects – happy, excited, surprised, relieved, and grateful – that related more directly to either outcomes or attributions for success and failure (see Weiner & Graham, 1983). Among our list of negative emotions, three self-affects were included: ashamed, mad at oneself, and guilty. The other negative emotions included worried, frustrated, sad, and mad.

The most interesting findings involved the relationship between perceived scholastic competence and the combinations of emotions children reported for success and for failure. By combinations we refer to three possibilities: (1) self-emotions for both success and failure (e.g., proud over success and ashamed over failure); (2) a self-affect for one but not both events, (e.g., proud over success and frustrated over failure, or happy over success and mad at oneself over failure); and (3) externally directed emotions in response to both success and failure (e.g., happy over success and mad over failure, or relieved over success and frustrated over failure).

The results (Kowalski, 1985) indicated that children who reported self-emotions for both success and failure had the highest perceived-competence scores (3.10); those who reported only one self-affect scored lower on perceived competence (2.90); and those who reported no self-affects, whose emotions for success and failure both were externally directed, had the lowest perceived-competence scores (2.70). Thus, the more likely one was to respond with self-affects, the greater one's perceptions of competence.

Although it makes intuitive sense that the self-affect of pride in response to one's successes would be associated with perceived competence, we wondered why students who regarded themselves as more competent also experienced a negative self-affect in response to failure. One could turn to Cooley (1902) for an analysis that provides certain insights into such a pattern. For Cooley, the most desirable combination was found in the competent individual who not only felt pride in his or her accomplishments but who also took responsibility for his or her failures and constructively criticized the self. Such a pattern would be associated with greater competence, to the extent that taking personal responsibility for one's failures may impel one to improve one's performance. According to Cooley, individuals who experienced self-affects in response to both success and failure were those who had internalized standards of behavior; therefore, outcomes would have direct implications for the self. In contrast, individuals who experienced emotions that were more externally directed would appear to be taking less personal responsibility for outcomes, and would have fewer internalized standards to guide their behavior.

Affect and motivational orientation

Cooley's analysis has direct implications for the relationship that one's type of affect might bear to one's motivational orientation. One would predict that individuals who experienced self-affects in response to success, as well as to failure, would manifest higher levels of self-motivation than those who reported externally directed affects. The latter individuals theoretically would manifest lower levels of self-motivation and higher levels of extrinsic motivation. Among those students who reported self-affects for both success and failure, self-motivation, particularly in the form of internalized motivation, would be found at higher levels than would extrinsic motivational factors.

To examine these predictions, we turned to data obtained from our study that distinguished among internalized, intrinsic, and extrinsic motivation. In this study, we had asked students to identify the emotions they experienced when they did their schoolwork, and those they experienced when they did not do their schoolwork. These emotions, selected from our checklist, were directed toward the activity itself, rather than toward the outcomes of performing one's schoolwork.

For the purpose of contrast, we have presented the findings for two

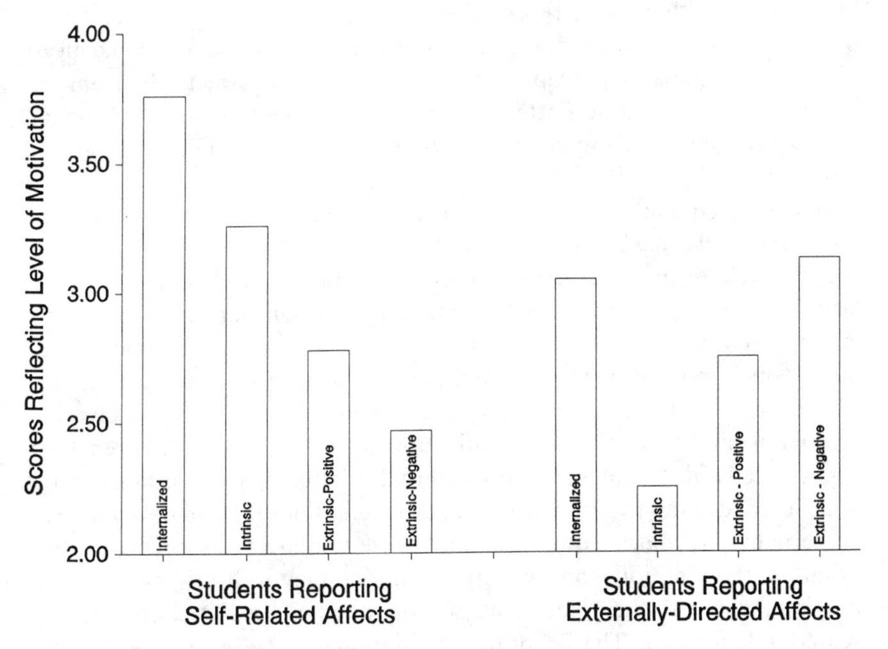

Figure 5.6. Motivational orientation scores for students reporting self-affects compared to those reporting externally-directed affects.

groups: (1) students who experienced self-affects both when they did, and when they did not, do their schoolwork, and (2) students who experienced externally related affects both when they did, and when they did not, do their schoolwork. Among the first group were students who reported feeling proud when they did their schoolwork and mad at themselves when they did not. Among the second group, a typical pattern involved relief when they did their schoolwork and worry when they did not.

The pattern of results is presented in Figure 5.6 in which it can be seen that this study strongly supported predictions derived from Cooley's analysis. Among those students who reported self-affects, internalized motivation represented the strongest source of motivation, followed by the intrinsic form of self-motivation. Extrinsic motivation, particularly negative extrinsic motivation in the form of the avoidance of disapproval and sanctions, was less important for this group. Individuals who experienced self-affects were those who reported high levels of self-motivation, particularly internalized motivation, in keeping with Cooley's contention.

Among those students who reacted with externally related affects, we found, as predicted, that both sources of self-motivation were markedly lower than for those who reported self-affects. In addition, extrinsic motivation, in the form of avoiding disapproval and sanctions, was much more likely among those who reported externally related affects than among those who expressed self-affects. (Extrinsic motivation, in the form of working for approval and positive rewards, did not differ between the two groups.)

When we combine the two sets of findings regarding the correlates of affect types, we have a pattern in which self-affects are associated with higher levels of both perceived competence and self-motivation, particularly internalized motivation. Thus, to expand upon our initial model, it is not only the valence of one's emotional reaction that is critical in mediating one's motivational orientation, but the specific affect itself. Students who experienced self-affects were more likely to perceive themselves as competent and to exhibit self-motivation than were those children who experienced affects that were more externally directed. There is much more to be learned about the antecedents of those emotions that we have labelled "externally directed," as well as about those that are "self-directed." For example, the emotions that we have identified may well originate in children's reactions to the antecedents we identified in our initial model, presented in Figure 5.1. That is, different emotional reactions may well relate to particular outcomes – that is, to success or failure – and to perceptions of control, as well as to feedback from socializing agents. There is a growing body of work, for example, by Weiner and his colleagues (Weiner, 1985; Weiner & Graham, 1983) indicating that the nature of the attributions one makes for success or failure will influence the particular affects that one experiences. As we noted at the outset, much more needs to be known about the interaction of these variables, and about how affects attached to these earlier events impact the three components of the model addressed in this chapter. It is clear that in such endeavors we need to attend to the discrete affects experienced by children, as well as to the antecedents of these affects.

Summary and conclusions

We have provided evidence for a model that hypothesized strong relationships between a child's perceived scholastic competence, affect about school performance, and motivational orientation. In addition to demonstrating that these variables were correlated, path-analytic techniques demonstrated the predicted sequentiality. Consistent with numerous sequential models in the literature, it was hypothesized that individual differences in perceived competence would predict individual differences in affective reactions to school performance, which in turn would impact a student's motivational orientation. The evidence clearly indicated that children who perceived themselves to be competent felt better about, and showed less anxiety about, their school performance, which in turn led them to adopt or maintain an intrinsic motivational orientation. Conversely, the student with low levels of perceived competence felt badly about his or her performance, was more anxious, and opted for an extrinsic motivational orientation.

In addition to demonstrating this pattern of individual differences, we also sought to further examine developmental changes in motivational orientation. The general pattern revealed that with increasing grade level (grades three through nine), intrinsic motivation decreased as children gradually adopted a more extrinsic orientation. This shift was dramatic particularly between the sixth grade, a child's final year in elementary school, and the seventh grade, the child's first year in junior high school. It is interesting that this pattern was observed not only in regular classroom pupils, but in mainstreamed learning-disabled students as well. A variety of factors involving changes in the school environment were postulated to be responsible for this systematic shift, factors that made one's academic successes and failures more salient. As students passed through the grade levels, it would appear that the school environment became more impersonal, more evaluative, and more competitive as the emphasis was placed on the products of one's efforts, rather than on the process of learning itself. In the higher grades, there was more focus on one's ability, as manifested in grades, and on social comparison, as students tend to be graded in terms of their relative performance on standardized tests. The outcomes of one's performance also tended to become more public.

It was hypothesized that these environmental changes would lead to lowered perceptions of competence and heightened anxiety over one's performance, which in turn would cause students to adopt a more extrinsic motivational orientation. Although the postulated antecedents have not been documented directly within the naturalistic school setting, experimental studies manipulating these hypothesized causal factors revealed that they serve to attenuate the child's intrinsic interest in learning.

A major goal of this chapter was to document the fact that changes in the school environment did not systematically attenuate the motivation of all students. Certain students actually showed developmental increases in intrinsic motivation, and there was a large subgroup that showed no major changes in motivational orientation. It was hypothesized that these effects would be predicted by changes in students' perceived scholastic competence during educational transitions, specifically during the shift to junior high school. For those students who showed increases in their perceptions of their scholastic competence within their new seventh-grade reference group, there was a parallel shift toward enhanced intrinsic motivation. Students whose perceptions of competence decreased during this transition showed a corresponding shift toward extrinsic motivation. Those who showed no changes in their perceived competence showed no motivational shifts, as predicted. In addition, both competence and motivational orientation were correlated with students' affective reactions to their performance, suggesting that affect may function as a mediator of these motivational effects.

We initially inferred that factors in the school environment were responsible for these changes. Educational transitions, it was hypothesized, impelled students to reevaluate their scholastic competence; the resultant changes in students' self-perceptions of competence were thought to provoke corresponding changes in affective responses and motivational orientation. In a subsequent study, we documented these changes: Middle school students reported that their school environment changed from year to year, with increasing emphasis on academic performance, competence evaluation, social comparison, and ability. These processes also appear to affect special populations – for example, the gifted – when such pupils undergo changes in educational placement that place them in a new comparison group.

It also was suggested that our initial conception of classroom motivation, dimensionalized along a single continuum of intrinsic to extrinsic motivation, could be broadened. Intrinsic motivation represents but one type of self-motivation. Another type is internalized motivation, in which behaviors that initially were under the control of externally established contingencies came to be performed because the child had learned from socializing agents that these behaviors were important. The motivation became internalized when the child no longer needed rewards, sanctions, or surveillance to perform these behaviors. It was hypothesized that this type of internalized motivation may be responsible for the school performance of certain children.

A new measure that tapped individually these three sources of motivation (intrinsic, internalized, and extrinsic) was developed. With this measure, we identified four types of students representing different combinations of these motivational dimensions. These groups were as follows: (A) students who scored high on intrinsic, high on internalized, and low on extrinsic subscales; (B) students who scored high on all three sources of motivation; (C) students who scored low on both intrinsic and internalized, but high on extrinsic, subscales; (D) and students who scored low on all three sources of motivation. Our examination of the correlates of these four types revealed that Type A students perceived themselves to be the most scholastically competent, reported the most positive emotional reactions to their school performance, and reported the highest levels of perceived teacher acceptance. The Type D students scored lowest on perceived competence and teacher acceptance, and reported more negative affective reactions to their schoolwork. Types B and C fell systematically in between. This typological approach allowed us to broaden our understanding of students' motivational patterns and to demonstrate that perceived scholastic competence, affective reactions, and motivational orientation were intimately linked – a conclusion that was in keeping with our model.

Finally, we suggested that it would be fruitful to examine the discrete affects reported by students, in addition to students' general ratings of their emotions and/or anxiety. Of particular interest was the distinction between self-affects, for example, pride over one's accomplishments and shame over one's failures, and emotions that were more externally directed, for example, happiness, relief, anger, worry, frustration, and sadness. Our findings revealed that the experience of self-affects was associated with higher levels of perceived scholastic competence; pupils who perceived themselves as being less competent were more likely to report externally directed emotions. Furthermore, there was a strong relationship between type of affect and motivational orientation. Students who reported self-affects were much more likely to manifest self-motivation, particularly internalized motivation; both internalized motivation and intrinsic motivation were much less prevalent among children who reported externally directed affects. Extrinsic motivation was much more prevalent in this latter group of students. The implications of these findings were examined along with the need to further explore these constructs from the perspectives of individual differences, the school environment, and developmental change.

References

Aronfreed, J. (1969). The concept of internalization. In D. A. Goslin (Ed.), *Handbook of socialization theory and research.* New York: Rand-McNally.

Aronfreed, J. (1976). Moral development from the standpoint of a general psychological theory. In T. Lickona (Ed.), *Moral development and behavior.* New York: Holt, Rinehart and Winston.

Bandura, A. (1978). The self system in reciprocal determinism. *American Psychologist, 33,* 344–358.

Brophy, J. (1983). Motivation in the classroom. In S.G. Paris, G.M. Olson & H.W. Stevenson (Eds.), *Learning and motivation in the classroom.* Hillsdale, NJ: Erlbaum.

Brush, L. (1980). *Encouraging girls in mathematics: The problem and the solution.* Cambridge, MA: Abt Books.

Buhrmester, D. (1980). Assessing elementary-aged children's anxieties: Rationale, development, and correlates of the school concerns scale. Unpublished masters thesis, University of Denver.

Chandler, C. (1981). The effects of parenting techniques on the development of motivational orientations in children. Unpublished doctoral dissertation, University of Denver.

Connell, J.P. (1981). A model of the relationships among children's self-related cognitions, affects and academic achievement. Unpublished doctoral dissertation, University of Denver.

Cooley, C.H. (1902). *Human nature and the social order.* New York: Charles Scribner & Sons.

Dweck, C. & Elliott, E.S. (1983). Achievement motivation. In E.M. Hetherington (Ed.), *Handbook of child psychology: Socialization, personality, and social development* (Vol. 4). New York: Wiley.

Deci, E.L. (1975). *Intrinsic motivation.* New York: Plenum Press.

Deci, E.L. & Ryan, R.M. (1981). The empirical exploration of intrinsic motivational processes. In L. Berkowitz (Ed.), *Advances in experimental social psychology* (Vol. 13). New York: Academic Press.

Doyle, W. (1979). Classroom tasks and students' abilities. In P.L. Peterson & H.J. Walberg (Eds.), *Research on teaching: Concepts, findings, and implications.* Berkeley, CA: McCutchan.

Eccles (Parsons), J., Midgley, C. & Adler, T.F. (1984). Grade-related changes in the school environment: Effects on achievement motivation. In J.G. Nicholls (Ed.), *The development of achievement motivation.* Greenwich, CT.: JAI Press.

Guzman, M.E. (1983). The effects of competence and anxiety levels on problem-solving performance and preference for challenge. Unpublished Masters thesis, University of Denver.

Harter, S. (1978). Effectuance motivation reconsidered: Toward a developmental model. *Human Development, 1,* 34–64.

Harter, S. (1981). A new self-report scale of intrinsic versus extrinsic orientation in the classroom: Motivational and informational components. *Developmental Psychology, 17,* 300–312.

Harter, S. (1982a). The perceived competence scale for children. *Child Development, 53,* 87–97.

Harter, S. (1982b). A developmental perspective on some parameters of the self-regulation process in children. In F. Kanfer & P. Karoly (Eds.), *The Psychology of self-management: From theory to practice.* New York: Pergamon Press.

Harter, S. (1983). Developmental perspectives on the self-system. In E.M. Hetherington (Ed.), *Handbook of child psychology: Vol. 4. Socialization, personality, and social development.* New York: John Wiley & Sons.

Harter, S. & Connell, J.P. (1984). A comparison of alternative models of the relationships between academic achievement and children's perceptions of competence, control, and motivational orientation. In J. Nicholls (Ed.), *The development of achievement-related cognitions and behaviors.* Greenwich, CN.: JAI Press.

Harter, S. & Guzman, M.E. (1986). The effects of perceived cognitive competence and anxiety on children's problem-solving performance, difficulty level choices, and preference for challenge. Unpublished manuscript, University of Denver.

Harter, S., Whitesell, N. & Kowalski, P. (1986). The effect of transitions to new academic environments on children's perceptions of competence, control, and motivational orientation. Unpublished manuscript, University of Denver.

Harter, S. & Zumpf, C. (1986). The effect of segregated programs for the gifted on their perception of competence, social support, and motivational orientation. Unpublished manuscript, University of Denver.

James, W. (1892). *Psychology: The briefer course.* New York: Holt, Rinehart & Winston.

Kanfer, F.H. (1980). Self-management methods. In F.H. Kanfer & A.P. Goldstein (Eds.), *Helping people change: A textbook of methods,* 2nd edition. New York: Pergamon Press.

Kowalski, P.S. (1985). The role of affective experience in early adolescents' networks of self-perceptions. Unpublished doctoral dissertation, University of Denver.

Lepper, M.R. & Gilovich, T.J. (1981). The multiple functions of reward: A social-developmental perspective. In S.S. Brehm, S.M. Kassin, & F.X. Gibbons (Eds.), *Developmental social psychology.* New York: Oxford University Press.

Lepper, M.R. & Greene, D. (1975). Turning play into work: Effects of adult surveillance and extrinsic rewards on children's intrinsic motivation. *Journal of Personality and Social Psychology, 31,* 479–486.

Maccoby, E.E. & Martin, J.A. (1983). Socialization in the context of the family: parent-child interaction. In E.M. Hetherington (Ed.), *Handbook of child psychology: Vol. 4. Socialization, personality, and social development.* New York: Wiley.

Maehr, M.L. & Nicholls, J.G. (1972). Freedom from external evaluation. *Child Development, 43,* 177–185.

Morris, L.W. & Liebert, R.M. (1969). Effects of anxiety on timed and untimed intelligence tests: Another look. *Journal of Consulting and Clinical Psychology, 33,* 240–244.

Morris, L.W. & Liebert, R.M. (1970). Relationships of cognitive and emotional components of test anxiety to physiological arousal and academic performance. *Journal of Consulting and Clinical Psychology, 35,* 332–337.

Morris, L.W. & Liebert, R.M. (1973). Effects of negative feedback, threat of shock, and level of trait anxiety on the arousal of two components of anxiety. *Journal of Consulting Psychology, 20,* 321–326.

Nicholls, J.G. (1979). Quality and equality in intellectual development: The role of motivation in education. *American Psychologist, 34,* 1071–1084.

Riddle, M. (1986). The effects of the transition to seventh grade on students' perceived competence, anxiety, motivational orientation, and sense of control. Unpublished doctoral dissertation, University of Denver.

Renick, M.J. (1986). Intrinsic versus extrinsic classroom orientation among learning disabled children and its relationship to perceptions of competence. Unpublished manuscript, University of Denver.

Simmons, R.G., Blyth, O.A., & Carleton-Ford, M.A. (1982). The adjustment of early adolescents to school transitions. Paper presented at the American Research Association Annual Meeting, New York.

Simmons, R.G., Rosenberg, F., & Rosenberg, M. (1973). Disturbance in the self-image at adolescence. *American Sociological Review, 38,* 553–568.

Weiner, B. (1985). An attributional theory of achievement motivation and emotion. *Psychological Review, 92,* 548–573.

Weiner, B., Russell, D., & Lerman, D. (1978). Affective consequences of causal ascriptions. In J.H. Harvey, W.J. Ickes, & R.F. Kidd (Eds.), *New directions in attribution research* (Vol. 2). Hillsdale, NJ: Lawrence Erlbaum.

Weiner, B. & Graham, S. (1983). An attributional approach to emotional development. In C.E. Izard, J. Kagan, & R. Zajonc (Eds.), *Emotion, cognition, and behavior.* Hillsdale, NJ: Lawrence Erlbaum.

White, R.W. (1959). Motivation reconsidered: The concept of competence. *Psychological Review, 66,* 297–333.

White, R.W. (1963). Ego and reality in psychoanalytic theory. *Psychological Issues, Monograph 3.*

Wicklund, R.A. (1978). Self-awareness theory: Three years later. In L. Berkowitz (Ed.), *Cognitive theories in social psychology.* New York: Academic Press.

6 Competence processes and achievement motivation: Implications for intrinsic motivation

Judith M. Harackiewicz, George Manderlink, and Carol Sansone

A core assumption in many theories of intrinsic motivation is that individuals are motivated to feel competent (Deci & Ryan, 1980, 1985; Lepper, 1980; White, 1959). Perceptions of competence are assumed to be intrinsically rewarding, and are hypothesized to be direct determinants of subsequent intrinsic interest. When people are made to feel more competent at some activity, they are expected to enjoy it more. In a classic paper, White (1959) argued that intrinsic motivation was related to the feelings of efficacy that resulted when a person successfully performed an action and caused a desired change in the environment. From this perspective, intrinsic interest can be seen to emerge in an individual from his or her ongoing exchange with the outer world. Perceptions of competence are inferred to result from one's successes over time in mastering task challenges.

What is the basis for judging successful task mastery? Research and theory concerning the nature of ability and achievement behavior have suggested two primary sources of information relevant to this process of self-assessment. Perceived competence may develop as a result of task-intrinsic feedback, in which an individual judges his or her performance and progress relative to individual experience and personal standards. Alternatively, it may result from social feedback, in which an individual judges his or her performance relative to that of others. Although young children first learn to evaluate themselves with respect to personal mastery, adolescents and adults rarely evaluate their abilities in a social vacuum (Nicholls, 1984; Ruble, Boggiano, Feldman & Loebl, 1980). Although adults are capable of judging their competence with respect to individual progress and standards, we would argue that most self-evaluation involves a social component.

Although a certain amount of feedback may come from the task itself (e.g., assembling a puzzle), direct experience alone does not always provide an adequate sense of one's overall performance. In fact, individuals frequently are dependent on social input to know how well they are doing, and

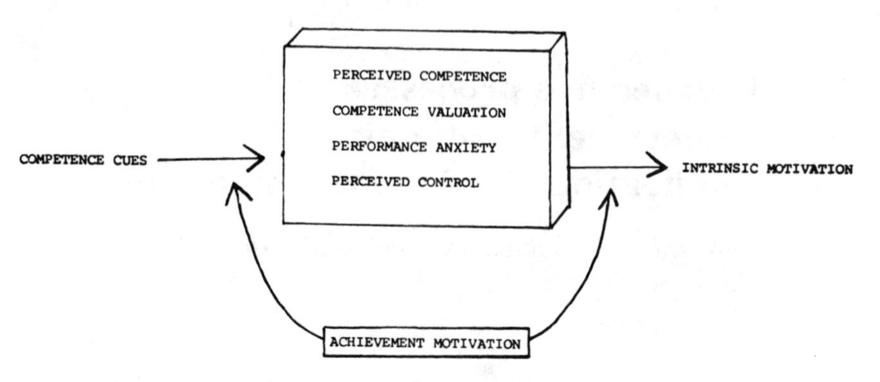

Figure 6.1. A process model of intrinsic motivation.

to develop their standards for the future. People often evaluate their own performance with respect to that of relevant others (Festinger, 1954), and they may learn how to judge the quality of their performance from external agents, such as teachers and employers. Clearly, an individual's sense of competence is, in large part, a consequence of his or her social interactions.

In this chapter, we will discuss how information about competence, provided in a social context, influences intrinsic motivation. To be informative about competence, communications (which may be given before or after task engagement) should enable individuals to evaluate their performance with respect to external standards. Performance information may be supplied in many forms, including social norms, performance goals, and feedback about the quality of performance. Although tangible rewards also may provide important information about performance (Harackiewicz, Manderlink & Sansone, 1984; Ryan, Mims & Koestner, 1983), verbal communications will be the focus of this chapter. We will use the term "competence cue" to refer to a communication from an external source that contains specific performance information, and, therefore, has the potential to influence perceived competence. We will examine the processes by which competence cues may influence subsequent intrinsic interest in an activity, and discuss how individual differences in achievement motivation moderate these processes (cf. Harackiewicz & Sansone, 1991). Figure 6.1 presents a schematic model of the critical variables.

Effects of competence cues on internal processes

Information relevant to self-assessment does not affect an individual's internal state unless he or she cognitively appraises task performance and the associated competence cues (Bandura, 1977). Individuals may differ in how they interpret and process competence cues, so in different people identical communications might have dissimilar effects on perceived competence and other processes. Our model suggests that individual differences in achievement motivation are particularly important in this regard. Most theoretical formulations have suggested that achievement-oriented individuals prefer situations that facilitate their self-assessment of competence (Atkinson, 1974; McClelland, 1961; Murray, 1938; Spence & Helmreich, 1983). This preference, typically measured in terms of task choice and persistence, also might be a determining factor in the processing of competence information.

Competence cues, by definition, theoretically would influence an individual's perceptions of his or her competence. According to Bandura (1977; 1982a), individuals judge their performance through an internal process of efficacy judgment. Positive outcomes of their comparisons of their performance with relevant standards contribute to perceptions of self-efficacy (i.e., perceived competence) and feelings of satisfaction. The outcome, however, depends on whether there is a discrepancy between the goal and performance. When standards are met, perceptions of competence are enhanced; when standards are not met, dissatisfaction and perceptions of inefficacy are fostered.

Communications about competence may affect other internal states in addition to perceived competence, including attitudes about performance, interest in doing well at an activity, and the value placed on being competent at an activity (Harackiewicz & Manderlink, 1984). Competence valuation reflects an affective involvement with attaining competence or an interest in task mastery. Competence cues may define an otherwise ordinary situation as an achievement episode, in which competence becomes salient or important (Harackiewicz, Sansone, & Manderlink, 1985; Nicholls, 1984). When external cues suggest that a task offers an opportunity to test personal skills, that task may be experienced by an individual as more meaningful (Hackman & Oldham, 1980). In such situations, the attainment of excellence may take on added significance.

To the extent that external competence cues focus an individual's attention on the evaluation of his or her performance, they may arouse performance anxiety (Harackiewicz, Sansone & Manderlink, 1985; Kanouse, Gumpert, & Canavan-Gumpert, 1981). Competence cues may lead individuals to worry about the implications of present performance for assessment of their ability level. Individuals may experience test anxiety (Sarason, 1980), evaluation apprehension (Rosenberg, 1969), or social anxiety (Schlenker & Leary, 1982). This performance anxiety may interfere with their attention to the task at hand (Geen, 1980; Wine, 1971).

Finally, competence cues may influence perceptions of external control, causing individuals to feel pressured, or to think that the communicator is trying to direct their behavior (Deci & Ryan, 1980). Individuals may come to feel less personal control over their task performance when external agents set standards, assign goals, or impose deadlines (Boggiano & Ruble, 1986; Lepper, 1980). These individuals may perceive that their task performance is instrumental in satisfying external contingencies, and their feelings of self-determination may be undermined. These externally mediated motivational techniques may induce performance pressure and feelings of constraint.

Achievement orientation

Individual differences in achievement orientation may moderate the effects of competence cues on the internal states discussed above, as suggested in Figure 6.1. Although all competence cues potentially may enhance self-efficacy, high and low achievers may interpret these cues differently. Achievement-oriented individuals have been shown to be interested in diagnostic ability assessment (Trope, 1975), to value competence (Harackiewicz & Manderlink, 1984; Heckhausen, 1968), and to desire objective ability feedback (McClelland, 1961). They hold high expectations for their performance (Kukla, 1978), and they are particularly likely to become involved in activities that afford self-evaluation (Greenwald, 1982). Consequently, they may benefit from available competence cues, and should welcome opportunities for self-assessment, perceive themselves as competent, and care about doing well.

Those who are not oriented towards achievement, on the other hand, may avoid ability assessment when possible, have lower performance expectations, and are more likely to experience test anxiety (Atkinson, 1974; Geen, 1980; Kukla, 1978). When a focus on ability assessment is unavoidable, the negative aspects of performance evaluation typically may be more salient for low achievers. They may begin an activity with lower expectations for performance or worry about their performance, and they are unlikely to value competence as much as high achievers. If they do not expect to perform well, or if they experience performance anxiety, they may not benefit from positive feedback.

Implications for intrinsic motivation

Clearly, competence cues can influence important internal processes in addition to enhancing perceptions of competence. They may increase the value of competence while initiating other processes that have negative implications for intrinsic motivation. What is needed then is a consideration of how these internal states combine to influence intrinsic motivation. A basic tenet of Deci and Ryan's cognitive evaluation theory (Deci & Ryan, 1980, 1985) is that competence cues should enhance intrinsic motivation only in a context of self-determination. Their positive effects will be reduced if they are directive and coercive or if they imply performance pressure. In fact, such controlling cues can undermine task interest, even when they provide positive information about performance (Pittman, Davey, Alafat, Wetherill & Kramer, 1980; Ryan, 1982).

Even if the cues indicated competence, and were communicated in a style that emphasized their informational content rather than the directive or coercive intentions of the communicator, a high level of intrinsic motivation still might not be achieved; individuals also must care about attaining competence at the activity. If they did not care about doing well, competence cues might be irrelevant to task enjoyment. When competence is highly valued, however, positive performance information should have a greater impact on subsequent interest (Harackiewicz & Manderlink, 1984). Finally, individuals who worry about ability assessment may become distracted from their ongoing task performance and the activity itself, with negative implications for their subsequent interest in the activity (Harackiewicz, Manderlink & Sansone, 1984). Even if the outcome of evaluation were positive, the experience of performance anxiety might detract from task involvement and enjoyment.

The processes that mediate the effects of competence cues on intrinsic motivation may differ according to individual differences in achievement orientation. When competence cues provide positive information about task performance in a context of self-determination, achievement-oriented individuals may care about doing well and perceive themselves as competent. To the extent that they do, their intrinsic interest theoretically would be enhanced. Low achievers, on the other hand, may experience performance anxiety and perceive themselves as less competent, suggesting that their intrinsic interest may not always be enhanced by positive performance information. Thus, competence cues may enhance or reduce interest, depending on an individual's achievement orientation.

In sum, the availability of competence information, the style in which it is communicated, and individual differences in achievement motivation all may influence intrinsic motivation through the four internal processes discussed above. We are not suggesting, however, that these are the only variables that will affect these processes. In fact, the task itself and the context in which it is performed may also influence intrinsic motivation. For example, competence evaluation may become more salient to an individual who is performing a task with others, than to one who is performing the task alone. In addition, some activities may be inherently more meaningful or important to an individual because of personal experience or cultural norms. The primary focus of the research to be reported here, however, is on how competence cues affect these internal processes and intrinsic motivation.

Overview of our research program

Our research has examined the effects of the different kinds of competence cues discussed above on intrinsic motivation, within a framework that directs attention to the processes that mediate their effects. More specifically, we have focused on two dimensions that we consider to be basic characteristics of all competence cues: their timing in the process of task engagement, and the extent to which they emphasize ability assessment versus task performance. Because competence information is conveyed within the context of a larger social interaction, however, other dimensions are likely to be relevant as well (Bandura, 1982a; Deci & Ryan, 1985).

The timing of competence cues may be especially important with respect to perceived competence. Objective cues, particularly those that facilitate the development of self-efficacy during task involvement, should be most effective in enhancing mastery and perceived competence (Bandura, 1982a). Performance information supplied before or during task engagement enables individuals to monitor their progress as they work and provides ongoing feedback. When feedback is not given until task conclusion, individuals may miss the opportunity to experience mastery while engaged in the task. In contrast, other effects associated with the availability of competence cues during task engagement may have a negative effect on intrinsic motivation. If an external agent must continually monitor an individual's performance to provide ongoing competence information, the individual may experience feelings of external control and pressure that might interfere with intrinsic motivation.

Although all competence cues involve some degree of performance evaluation, the effect of these cues may vary depending upon the context in which they are embedded in task performance. The evaluation of competence may be integrated into the activity, so that the focus is on task performance, or the evaluation may be centered on the assessment of individual ability level. For example, before task engagement subjects might be informed of the average score of others, thus providing them with a standard with which to evaluate their performance. This social-comparison cue enables subjects to compare their performance to an external standard without placing an explicit emphasis on ability assessment. Alternatively, an evaluation may be centered on an assessment of individual ability, such as when an external agent communicates an expectancy based on an individual's prior performance of similar tasks. In this case, the information the individual receives emphasizes his or her ability at the activity. When competence cues emphasize individual ability rather than task performance, they may be particularly likely to arouse evaluative concerns. Although some individuals (e.g., high achievers) may welcome the opportunity to evaluate their abilities, others (e.g., low achievers) may worry about their performance and become distracted from the task. Cues that focus on task performance rather than ability assessment may be optimal for minimizing performance anxiety and maintaining task involvement. On the other hand, cues that emphasize ability assessment may lead achievement-oriented individuals to care more about doing well, and these individuals may become more involved in an activity when it affords the opportunity to demonstrate competence.

General paradigm

We will describe three lines of research that are relevant to our model. In the studies discussed here, we manipulated competence cues along the dimensions of task performance and ability assessment and offered them to subjects engaged in enjoyable activities, and then measured subsequent intrinsic interest in the activities. Competence cues always were provided in an informational manner, without external pressure, so that relative competence always was attained in a context of self-determination. The studies also shared a common methodology. High school or college students worked on an interesting puzzle or game for several trials in two sessions. In the first session, subjects worked a few puzzles, then completed a self-report measure of achievement motivation. In the experimental session, which was conducted a few weeks later, competence cues were manipulated before subjects began working the puzzles, and others were manipulated at the conclusion. To provide believable positive information about competence, we used novel activities for which subjects would not have well-formed expectations about their abilities. We identified a level of performance that could be attained by nearly all subjects, and used it to set ostensible performance norms. Intrinsic interest was measured at the end of the experimental session.

We typically measured several process variables during the experimental sessions. Before starting the puzzles, subjects rated how well they expected to perform (anticipated performance), and indicated how important it was to them to do well (importance). We also measured how well subjects actually did (performance), and collected their judgments of performance at task completion (perceived performance). Finally, subjects completed a questionnaire concerning their task enjoyment. This six-item enjoyment scale constituted our dependent measure of intrinsic interest. Several studies have reported correlations of approximately .40 between similar self-report scales and behavioral measures in a free-choice situation, and have found comparable patterns of effects on the two measures of intrinsic motivation (Harackiewicz, 1979; Harackiewicz et al., 1984; Ryan et al., 1983).

The achievement measure that we have used in our research is derived from the Personality Research Form (PRF) (Jackson, 1974). This sixteen-point scale measures individual differences in achievement orientation. The PRF has theoretical roots in Murray's (1938) theory of needs and is an unusually well developed personality inventory (Anastasi, 1982). This achievement scale has proven reliable (Jackson, 1974) and valid (Fiske, 1973; Harper, 1975).

A process analysis of the effects of competence cues

In an initial study relevant to our theoretical framework (Harackiewicz, Sansone & Manderlink, 1985), we varied the availability of three competence cues and measured their effects on two mediating variables: perceived competence and competence valuation. High school males played an enjoyable word game, which involved forming as many words as possible from contiguous letters in a matrix. Although the experiment was conducted in a group setting, subjects worked individually. The three competence cues were presented as written communications, and the crossing of their availability resulted in an eight-cell experimental design. Subjects were informed of a normative standard before they began a set of puzzles; this standard was the average number of words purportedly found by other students in their school. Because students could monitor their own performance, the standard allowed objective self-evaluation during task engagement.

The feedback manipulation was identical to the standard, except for the timing of informing students of the norm, which was at the conclusion of the activity. This allowed students to determine whether they had attained the norm once they had finished. Because the norm was set artificially low, all subjects surpassed it; subjects who received either the standard or feedback manipulation therefore learned that their task performance was better than average.

An expectancy manipulation, given before the puzzles, informed students that based on their prior performance, it was predicted that they would do better than average. This manipulation provided personalized information about earlier performance, with explicit implications for the task they were about to begin. Individuals thus received a prediction about their future performance based on an evaluation of their ability. No objective information was given about the task at hand.

Both the standard and expectancy manipulations were intended to enhance feelings of competence, and both made competence assessment salient before the puzzles were started. Although they did not differ in their timing, they did differ along the dimensions of personal ability and task performance evaluation. The expectancy manipulation focused on the individual's relative skill at solving such puzzles over time. In contrast, the normative standard provided information directly relevant to current performance only. The feedback manipulation also focused on the level of current performance, but did so by supplying information for the retrospective evaluation of task performance.

We predicted that these cues would affect the importance of doing well (competence valuation), perceptions of competence, and task enjoyment. More specifically, our model suggests that these externally provided competence cues should affect interest through their effects on these intervening variables. We also hypothesized that these effects would be moderated by individual differences in achievement motivation. To examine the effects of independent and mediating variables on intrinsic interest, we conducted regression and path analyses according to guidelines for process analysis proposed by Judd and Kenny (1981a, 1981b). This approach allowed us to identify which variables mediated the effects of our experimentally manipulated competence cues on intrinsic interest. Although the details of this analysis are too complex to be reported here (see Harackiewicz, Sansone & Manderlink, 1985), the results may be summarized without reference to path diagrams.

The effects of the three competence cues were independent of each other, suggesting that different configurations of performance information could be understood in terms of the component cues. In a situation in which all subjects performed competently, these cues affected intrinsic motivation differently according to their impact on underlying mediational processes, and these effects differed dramatically according to the achievement orientation of subjects. High and low achievers performed equally well, but they appear to have appraised identical competence cues quite differently in terms of perceived competence and personal importance. Striking differences in task enjoyment resulted.

Across experimental conditions, subjects high in achievement orientation expected to do better on the puzzles before they began them, and believed that they had performed better after completing them, compared to low achievers. For high achievers, the critical mediating variable was importance: the more they cared about doing well at the outset of the performance period, the more they enjoyed the puzzles at its conclusion. The expectancy manipulation increased the level of importance for high achievers, and enhanced their interest through the competence valuation process. In other words, when given the personalized expectancy, doing well on the puzzles became more important to them, and their subsequent interest was higher. The effect of importance on task enjoyment was strongest when a normative standard had been provided, showing that competence valuation was most relevant to enjoyment when task performance could be evaluated during task engagement. High achievers, then, responded positively to both types of information provided before task engagement. Both cues enhanced their subsequent intrinsic interest, especially when they cared about performing well. Normative feedback supplied after task completion, however, did not influence their task enjoyment.

For low achievers, the critical mediating variable was anticipated performance, suggesting that perceived competence was the process most relevant to their intrinsic motivation. If their initial performance expectations were high, task enjoyment was higher following task completion. The normative standard was the only competence cue that enhanced interest through this process; it raised interest most for those with higher expectations for performance. If low achievers began the puzzles with relatively high expectations, their subsequent interest was enhanced by the availability of positive information during the performance period. Therefore, cues that facilitate the development of perceived competence during task engagement may be most effective in raising interest for low achievers.

Although perceptions of competence clearly are important to the task interest of low achievers, it seems difficult to give these individuals positive information that does not detract from their task enjoyment. The expectancy and feedback manipulations both lowered their intrinsic interest in the puzzles. These negative effects were not mediated by the process variables that we measured in this study (importance and perceived competence), but they are consistent with a third process outlined in our model: performance anxiety. Low achievers began the puzzles with low expectations for performance, and neither cue provided objective information about the task during the performance period. If low achievers are led to focus on performance evaluation, yet expect to perform poorly, anxiety and doubts about ability may occur (Geen, 1980). Objective information that counters self-doubts during the performance period (e.g., a performance standard) should be optimal in persuading them of their competence, and in maintaining task involvement. Cues that create an evaluative climate without supplying objective standards, or those that reduce uncertainty only after the task is completed, should be quite detrimental for low achievers.

The results of this study indicate that competence cues can influence intrinsic motivation through the processes described in our model. Furthermore, these processes varied according to achievement orientation: anticipated performance mediated interest for low achievers, whereas importance mediated interest for high achievers. These mediation effects were strongest in the presence of a competence cue that focused attention on task performance at the outset (i.e., the standard). When subjects were able to assess their performance while involved in the task, the perceived competence and competence valuation processes were particularly relevant to enjoyment. If low achievers expected to do well, and were able to confirm their expectations during the course of task engagement, their interest was enhanced. If high achievers cared about doing well, and were able to evaluate their performance during the performance period, their interest was enhanced. Thus, the availability of objective task information prior to performance appears to have been beneficial for subsequent interest.

The effects of the competence cues on interest varied as a function of their timing in a behavioral sequence, and as a function of whether they emphasized personal ability or task performance. The normative standard clearly was superior to the identical information presented as feedback, suggesting that the timing of such information is critical for intrinsic motivation processes. The standard raised perceptions of competence for all subjects, and its availability facilitated the enhancement of task interest through the perceived competence and competence valuation processes already discussed.

The expectancy manipulation also was presented prior to task engagement, but its effects on mediating processes and subsequent interest were quite different from those of the normative standard. The manipulation emphasized ability assessment, and initiated different motivational processes, depending on achievement orientation. High achievers, whose initial performance expectations were high, responded positively: they cared more about doing well, and they enjoyed the puzzles more as a consequence of their enhanced competence valuation. Low achievers, whose initial expectations were lower, responded to the emphasis on ability evaluation quite differently: their task enjoyment was undermined, possibly by performance anxiety. These results suggest that a focus on ability assessment, as opposed to task performance, may be most likely to initiate the competence valuation and performance anxiety processes (cf. Harackiewicz, Abrahams & Wageman, 1987; Harackiewicz & Sansone, 1991).

The fact that the feedback manipulation also affected intrinsic motivation differently according to achievement motivation suggests that low achievers may have been particularly sensitive to the evaluative implications of the positive feedback. Feedback that was relevant to a retrospective evaluation of task performance reduced interest for low achievers, but not for high achievers. Because this information could not be used to monitor ongoing task performance, subjects may have had little to concentrate on besides an evaluation of their recent performance. Thus, ability assessment may be relatively more salient in feedback manipulations than in normative standards. However, focusing on ability is not as extreme as in other competence cues (e.g., expectancy manipulations), since task performance is still central to the evaluation.

It is important to note that the negative effects of feedback observed in low achievers in this study were found in a situation in which competence evaluation had been salient before and during task performance. Subjects worked on the puzzles along with other students from their class (who also formed the peer group on which the performance norms were ostensibly based). Furthermore, 75 percent of the subjects who received feedback already had received some performance information (the expectancy and/or the standard) prior to beginning the activity. Thus, the informational impact of the feedback may have been reduced, and its evaluative features made particularly salient in this experimental context.

An analysis of the components of performance feedback

When competence is not emphasized prior to task engagement, and when feedback is the only performance information provided, this feedback may have a greater impact on perceived competence, and more positive implications for intrinsic motivation. Several studies have found that positive normative feedback has enhanced perceptions of competence and subsequent intrinsic motivation (Boggiano, Harackiewicz, Bessette & Main, 1985; Boggiano & Ruble, 1979; Deci, 1972; Harackiewicz, 1979). To fully understand feedback effects on subsequent intrinsic motivation, however, the nature of the stimulus information that conveys a sense of competence must be made explicit.

As noted in the previous study, normative feedback involved information only about an individual's performance relative to that of others. In naturalistic settings, however, social comparison feedback often conveys additional information. For example, when a student receives the results of an exam, he or she learns how many of the questions were answered correctly. Competence may be inferred from this raw information, but because it is ambiguous, grades are assigned. The grade tells a student how well he or she has done compared to some external standard of performance, which typically is based on the performance of others in the class (normative feedback). In addition, the student may learn the correct answers to the questions he or she answered incorrectly (task feedback). When we compare the effect of receiving this array of information with that of receiving no feedback at all, we do not know whether perceptions of competence are primarily or exclusively due to the social comparison component, as opposed to individual standards. All of the information conveyed may have relevance for intrinsic motivation, either through competence processes or through other processes.

When individuals do not have well-formed expectations about the task, or about their ability, the social comparison component of feedback should be the most important determinant of perceived competence. The normative information also may be the aspect of the feedback that directs attention to ability assessment. Task feedback, on the other hand, may redirect attention to the task itself, even though the individual has finished it. As such, it might be an important determinant of continuing task involvement and subsequent intrinsic motivation.

Thus, normative and task feedback appear to vary along the dimensions of ability assessment and task-performance evaluation, with task feedback providing the most performance-relevant information. However, normative feedback does not emphasize ability assessment to the exclusion of performance information. In contexts in which no other competence cues are provided, the availability of objective performance information may be more salient than the evaluative features of normative feedback. Thus both kinds of feedback may enhance intrinsic motivation. We would expect achievement motivation differences to moderate reactions to the social comparison component of feedback, and to make less difference for the other kinds of information.

To examine these issues, Sansone (1986) conducted a study in which she manipulated positive normative feedback and task feedback independently, in a setting in which no competence cues were provided prior to task performance. The experiment was conducted in individual sessions in which subjects performed a challenging and enjoyable activity (a trivia game) that involved identifying the names of specific parts of everyday objects. Subjects were asked to match an object part in a drawing (e.g., the triangle over the rotary dial of a telephone) with a name from a set of four alternatives (e.g., finger stop, dial block, rotary gate, or plate bar). Because the task was unfamiliar and involved arcane knowledge, subjects experienced considerable uncertainty about the correct names of the object parts, and about the number of correct identifications that would constitute good performance. Consequently, the operationalizations of task feedback reduced confusion about the correct answers, and normative feedback reduced uncertainty about performance level. Groups that received either normative or task feedback were compared with a control group that received no feedback about performance.

After completing a set of eleven identifications, subjects in the two feedback conditions were able to determine their number of correct identifications. Subjects' scores were experimentally constrained at an ambiguous absolute performance level (five out of eleven correct). Subjects in the task feedback conditions were ostensibly given the actual names of the object parts. In contrast, normative feedback subjects never learned the actual names of the parts. However, they did receive information concerning the ostensible eightieth percentile score (more than three correct), which they could use to evaluate their performance.

The results of this study indicated that subjects who played the trivia game were uncertain about both the correct solutions and their performance. In this context, both normative and task feedback appeared to provide meaningful information. Subjects who received normative feedback experienced the highest level of perceived competence, as expected. Task feedback also enhanced perceptions of competence, relative to the no-feedback control, but to a lesser extent. Both normative and task feedback enhanced enjoyment, relative to the no-feedback control, and to comparable degrees. The effect of normative feedback on enjoyment appeared to be due to its impact on perceived competence. However, perceived competence did not adequately explain the positive effect of task feedback on enjoyment, because task feedback enhanced interest to the same degree as normative feedback. Information about task solutions, which focused on the task itself, rather than personal outcomes, was beneficial for subsequent interest. This study suggests that social comparison information is not the only element of feedback that can affect intrinsic motivation (cf. Sansone, 1989; Sansone, Sachau & Weir, 1989).

It also was found that normative feedback enhanced task enjoyment most for achievement oriented individuals. This effect is consistent with the findings discussed earlier suggesting that high achievers are more responsive to competence cues with implications for ability assessment. Because task feedback provides minimal information about ability level, it may be less likely to evoke different responses as a function of individual differences in achievement motivation. These findings, together with those of Harackiewicz and colleagues (1985), suggest that intrinsic motivation processes are most likely to differ as a function of achievement orientation when competence cues focus on ability assessment rather than task performance.

Goal proximity

Harackiewicz and colleagues (1985) demonstrated that providing individuals with normative standards for performance before they begin an activity can enhance perceived competence and intrinsic motivation. The standard allowed individuals to monitor their performance during the course of task engagement, and to determine for themselves how well they were doing. Effects on perceived competence and intrinsic motivation were obtained even though subjects were not encouraged to adopt the standards as goals. In this section, we will present research in which subjects were explicitly instructed to consider the normative information as goals for performance.

Goal setting is one of the most commonly used tactics to motivate task performance. Laboratory and field research has demonstrated reliably that providing standards as performance goals is an effective technique for improving performance (Locke, Shaw, Sarri & Latham, 1981). Individuals who are assigned specific performance goals are more productive than those without goals. It appears, however, that other outcomes associated with goal setting are less desirable (cf. Harackiewicz & Sansone, 1991). For example, several studies suggest that assigned goals produce feelings of pressure and external constraint and interfere with task satisfaction (Umstot, Bell & Mitchell, 1976; White, Mitchell, & Bell, 1977).

The effects of performance standards on intrinsic motivation may differ according to the method of presentation. If they are provided simply as information about the task at hand, they may be viewed primarily as a source of competence information and should enhance intrinsic interest to the extent that they provide positive feedback. If they are assigned as performance goals by external agents, however, issues of control may also be raised (Manderlink & Harackiewicz, 1984; Mossholder, 1980). If they are interpreted as attempts to direct behavior, reductions in interest will occur. Within this line of inquiry, deadlines and assigned goals have been found to undermine interest, suggesting that they are seen as controlling (Amabile, DeJong & Lepper, 1976; Mossholder, 1980).

Certain attributes of goals may influence perceptions of competence and the extent to which individuals perceive their actions as externally constrained while goal directed. An important dimension in characterizing goals is temporal proximity (Bandura, 1982b). When involved in a task over a period of time, a person may focus on distal goals (e.g., finish writing the play by the end of the month), or on relatively proximal goals (e.g., complete the second act by the end of the week). With proximal goal setting, ongoing behavior easily may be assessed against performance standards, offering frequent instances of feedback during a performance episode. In contrast, distal goals may not provide as much feedback during the task because they are too far removed in time. They may be less effective than proximal goals in enhancing self-efficacy and perceptions of progress (Bandura & Schunk, 1981). Thus goal proximity moderates the timing of competence information during task engagement, and its effects may be interpreted within the framework of our model.

Externally mediated proximal and distal goal setting also may affect perceptions of external constraint differentially. Proximal goal setting continually demands that performance meet some criterion, and as a result may be perceived as controlling. Because distal goal setting imposes fewer requirements on ongoing performance, controlling properties should be less salient. Therefore, the inhibitory effect of goal setting on intrinsic motivation might be greater when proximal goals are assigned.

In an initial experiment, Manderlink and Harackiewicz (1984) compared the effects of proximal and distal goals on intrinsic interest in a word game (similar to the one used in the study discussed earlier). College students were given eleven puzzles in a timed trials procedure. One group received specific goals to be achieved on each of the trials (proximal goals condition). Another group was given an overall goal to be attained by the completion of the last trial (distal goal condition). Goals were set low enough to be attained by most subjects, and thus provided positive competence feedback. Moreover, the proximal and distal goals were equally attainable. A control group was not assigned specific performance standards.

It was found that relative to the other conditions, proximal goals subjects developed a greater sense of self-efficacy. More specifically, proximal goal setting fostered more positive goal attainment expectations while subjects worked on the task. However, the distal goal group had a higher level of intrinsic interest at the conclusion of the study. Furthermore, only the distal goal subjects grew more interested in the task over time.

That immediate goals undermined interest relative to more distant goals was consistent with the hypothesis that proximal goal setting would be experienced as more controlling. The performance feedback made available by proximal goal setting had a positive effect on perceived competence, but failed to enhance interest. This finding suggests that the controlling processes initiated by proximal goal setting outweighed its informational value. The distal goal, on the other hand, increased interest relative to a no-goals group, suggesting that goal setting can enhance intrinsic motivation through an informational process. Distal goals provide some positive feedback, but in a context that allows individuals to experience personal control over their performance. Distal goals, therefore, may be optimal for enhancing intrinsic motivation.

Recent studies by Kirschenbaum and his coworkers (Kirschenbaum, Humphrey, & Malett, 1981; Kirschenbaum, Malett, Humphrey, Tomarken, 1982; Kirschenbaum, Tomarken, & Ordman, 1982) also suggest that perceptions of control mediate the effects of goal proximity. In these experiments, students planning their study behavior on a daily basis (proximal planners) showed negative performance effects relative to those with more distal, monthly plans. In accounting for these deficits, Kirschenbaum proposed that proximal planning may interfere with perceptions of internal control by limiting subjects' freedom in the scheduling of goal-relevant behavior.

As our general model suggests, differences in achievement motivation may influence the optimal distance at which to set goals. High achievers perform better when assigned goals (Atkinson & Reitman, 1956; Steers, 1975) and become more involved in tasks that provide feedback. In contrast, low achievers generally approach goal-setting situations with more negative expectations and evaluation apprehension. For high achievers, goals provide valued competence information; for low achievers, goals often represent external performance pressure. If these response tendencies were exaggerated when goals were projected only a short distance in time, goal proximity might affect the intrinsic interest of low and high achievers differently. Proximal goals may enhance high achievers' interest by providing opportunities for frequent performance feedback. Low achievers should experience proximal goal setting as particularly controlling because evaluative cues are pervasive. Proximal goals, therefore, would interfere with low achievers' task interest.

Features of the activities themselves also may affect the relationship between goal proximity and interest motivation. Whether a task continues to provide new challenges seems particularly relevant to intrinsic interest in goal-setting contexts. An activity that becomes progressively more difficult seems more likely to sustain interest than one that is fixed at a single level of difficulty, or offers an irregular sequence of challenges. An important aspect of accelerating difficulty is that perceived competence can develop gradually. This perception may not be clarified unless proximal goals are pursued at each new level of difficulty. With distal goal setting, by contrast, it is more difficult for individuals to recognize gradual improvements in performance. Thus the undermining effects of proximal goals on intrinsic motivation may be attenuated when they are provided in a context of incremental challenge.

A second study (Manderlink, 1985) evaluated whether achievement orientation and pattern of task difficulty moderated the relationship between goal proximity and intrinsic motivation. High school students worked on sixteen word puzzles, a quarter of which were ostensibly drawn from each of four difficulty levels. In reality, the puzzles were of comparable difficulty. Half of the subjects began with the least difficult puzzles and concluded with the most difficult (progressive pattern); half were presented with the puzzles in an essentially random order that provided early experience at all levels of difficulty (variable pattern).

As in the first study, proximal goal setting was found to enhance self-efficacy (i.e., goal-attainment expectations) relative to distal goal setting. The most important result was an interaction of goal proximity by achievement by difficulty pattern on intrinsic motivation, indicating that the effects of goal proximity were moderated by both the task and personality variables. Low achievers' subsequent intrinsic interest was undermined by proximal goal setting in the variable condition. However, this negative effect was reduced when the task was structured to yield the impression of gradual competence development. For high achievers, proximal goals were more likely to enhance interest in the variable condition.

These results are consistent with the notion that proximal goal setting will enhance intrinsic motivation when the feedback provided is in harmony with initial performance expectations. For low achievers with characteristic low expectations, a gradual rate of improvement (as suggested by proximal goal attainments in the progressive condition) seems more beneficial than a faster but more erratic pace. Sudden evidence of a high level of mastery (as provided by proximal goal setting in the variable condition) may not be incongruous with the more positive expectations of high achievers. By contrast, the same information may seem unreliable or confusing to low achievers. This reasoning was supported further in that low achievers were found to have lower initial expectations than high achievers, and felt more satisfied with their performance outcomes in the progressive condition. It seems that both low and high achievers can benefit from the competence information made available through proximal goal setting, depending on the task environment.

The results of the two goal-setting studies indicate that the timing of competence cues can influence intrinsic motivation through the processes of perceived competence and perceived control. Proximal performance goals provided positive feedback throughout the performance period, and made subjects feel more competent, but subsequent interest was reduced, relative to the effect of distal goals. This negative effect appeared due to the controlling processes that were initiated by the assigned goals. In the second study, the timing of competence feedback was critical with respect to features of the task itself. When the activity was structured to support the gradual development of perceived competence, through a series of progressively more difficult puzzles, proximal goals had the effect of raising interest for low achievers. The frequent positive feedback allowed their perceptions of competence to develop gradually over the course of task involvement. These results are consistent with those of Harackiewicz and colleagues (1985), indicating that low achievers can benefit from positive performance information under some circumstances. Competence cues must focus on task performance and provide believable positive feedback during task involvement.

Conclusions

The studies discussed here are quite supportive of our model of competence processes, and more recent work has provided converging support (Epstein & Harackiewicz, 1992; Harackiewicz, 1989; Harackiewicz et al., 1987; Harackiewicz & Larson, 1986; Harackiewicz & Sansone, 1991; Sansone, 1989; Sansone et al., 1989). A variety of competence cues were shown to both enhance and undermine intrinsic motivation through the processes of perceived competence, competence valuation, performance anxiety, and perceived control. Furthermore, the effects of these cues could be interpreted with respect to two critical dimensions: their timing in the process of task engagement, and their focus on ability assessment versus task performance. The timing of competence cues seems most relevant to perceived competence and perceived control, whereas the ability assessment versus task performance dimension is most relevant to competence valuation and performance anxiety.

The effects of competence cues on motivational processes were moderated by individual differences in achievement motivation in a consistent pattern across studies. High and low achievers differed in their performance expectations before beginning the experimental activities (independent of any competence cues received), and the differences in their reactions to positive performance information were striking. Moreover, these differences were observed in experimental contexts where there were no achievement differences in actual performance level. Achievement orientation was particularly important in moderating the effects of competence cues that focused on ability assessment, and the competence valuation and performance anxiety processes were most affected.

Cues that stressed personal ability rather than task performance were most likely to arouse evaluative concerns, with very different implications for low and high achievers. When the situation provided an opportunity for self-assessment of personal skills and ability, high achievers became more interested in the pursuit of competence and cared more about doing well. Their subsequent interest was enhanced by this affective involvement in the activity. In contrast, low achievers may have worried about their performance level, or become anxious about their performance. The negative effects on their subsequent interest were consistent with the process by which performance anxiety interferes with task involvement and subsequent intrinsic motivation (Harackiewicz et al., 1984, 1987; Wine, 1971).

Our results indicate that communications that provide clear, positive feedback about an individual's competence at an enjoyable activity may not always have their intended effects on self-perceptions of competence, task involvement, and continuing motivation. Rather, these competence cues can affect interest differently as a function of their timing in the process of task engagement, their focus on ability assessment versus task performance, individual differences in achievement motivation, and characteristics of the task and of the social context. Cues that lead individuals to perceive themselves as competent, or to value competence, may have positive effects. However, competence cues also may undermine perceptions of personal control, and they can arouse performance anxiety, both of which have negative implications for subsequent interest. Fortunately, some of our results point to strategies that may optimize the development of perceived competence, competence valuation, and intrinsic motivation.

References

Amabile, T.M., DeJong, W., & Lepper, M.R. (1976). Effects of externally imposed deadlines on subsequent intrinsic motivation. *Journal of Personality and Social Psychology, 34,* 92–98.

Anastasi, A. (1982). *Psychological testing* (5th ed.). New York: Macmillan.

Atkinson, J.W. (1974). The mainspring of achievement oriented activity. In J.W. Atkinson and J.O. Raynor (Eds.), *Motivation and achievement.* Washington, D.C.: Winston.

Atkinson, J.W., & Reitman, W.R. (1956). Performance as a function of motive strength and expectancy of goal attainment. *Journal of Abnormal and Social Psychology, 53,* 361–366.

Bandura, A. (1977). *Social learning theory.* Englewood Cliffs, N.J.: Prentice-Hall.

Bandura, A. (1982a). The self and mechanisms of agency. In J. Suls (Ed.), *Psychological perspectives on the self* (Vol. 1). Hillsdale, N.J.: Lawrence Erlbaum Associates.

Bandura, A. (1982b). Self-efficacy mechanism in human agency. *American Psychologist, 37,* 122–147.

Bandura, A., & Schunk, D.H. (1981). Cultivating competence, self-efficacy, and intrinsic motivation. *Journal of Personality and Social Psychology, 41,* 586–598.

Boggiano, A.K., Harackiewicz, J.M., Bessette, J.M., & Main D.S. (1985). Increasing children's interest through performance-contingent reward. *Social Cognition, 3,* 400–411.

Boggiano, A.K. & Ruble, D.N. (1979). Competence and the overjustification effect: A developmental study. *Journal of Personality and Social Psychology, 37,* 1462–1468.

Boggiano, A.K. & Ruble, D.N. (1986). Children's responses to evaluative feedback. In R. Schwarzer (Ed.), *Self-related cognitions in anxiety and motivation.* Hillsdale, N.J.: Erlbaum.

Deci, E.L. (1972). Intrinsic motivation, extrinsic reinforcement, and inequity. *Journal of Personality and Social Psychology, 22,* 113–120.

Deci, E.L., & Ryan, R.M. (1980). The empirical exploration of intrinsic motivational processes. In Berkowitz (Ed.), *Advances in experimental social psychology* (Vol. 13). New York: Academic Press.

Deci, E.L. & Ryan, R.M. (1985). *Intrinsic motivation and self-determination in human behavior.* New York: Plenum.

Epstein, J.A. & Harackiewicz, J.M. (1992). Winning is not enough: The effects of competition and opponent information on intrinsic motivation. *Personality and Social Psychology Bulletin, 17,* in press.

Festinger, L. (1954). A theory of social comparison processes. *Human Relations, 7,* 117–140.

Fiske, D.W. (1973). Can a personality construct be validated empirically? *Psychological Bulletin, 80,* 89–92.

Geen, R.G. (1980). Test anxiety and cue utilization. In I.G. Sarason (Ed.), *Test anxiety: Theory, research, and applications.* Hillsdale, N.J.: Erlbaum.

Greenwald, A.G. (1982). Ego task analysis: An integration of research on ego-involvement and self-awareness. In A.H. Hastorf & A.M. Isen (Eds.), *Cognitive social psychology.* New York: Elsevier North Holland.

Hackman, J.R. & Oldham, G.R. (1980). *Work redesign.* Reading, Mass: Addison-Wesley.

Harackiewicz, J.M. (1979). The effects of reward contingency and performance feedback on intrinsic motivation. *Journal of Personality and Social Psychology, 37,* 1352–1361.

Harackiewicz, J.M. (1989). Performance evaluation and intrinsic motivation processes: The effects of achievement orientation and rewards. In D.M. Buss & N. Candor (Eds.), *Personality psychology: Recent trends and emerging directions.* New York: Springer-Verlag.

Harackiewicz, J.M., Abrahams, S., & Wageman, R. (1987). Performance evaluation and intrinsic motivation: The effects of evaluative focus, rewards and achievement orientation. *Journal of Personality and Social Psychology, 53,* 1015–1023.

Harackiewicz, J.M., & Larson, J.R., Jr. (1986). Managing motivation: The impact of supervisor feedback on subordinate task interest. *Journal of Personality and Social Psychology, 51,* 918–931.

Harackiewicz, J.M., & Manderlink, G. (1984). A process analysis of the effects of performance-contingent rewards on intrinsic motivation. *Journal of Personality and Social Psychology, 20,* 531–551.

Harackiewicz, J.M., Manderlink, G. & Sansone, C. (1984). Rewarding pinball wizardry: Effects of evaluation and cue value on intrinsic interest. *Journal of Personality and Social Psychology, 47,* 287–300.

Harackiewicz, J.M. & Sansone, C. (1991). Goals and intrinsic motivation: You *can* get there from here. In Maehr, M.L. & Pintrick, P.R. (Eds.), *Advances in motivation and achievement* (Vol. 7). Greenwich, CT: JAI Press.

Harackiewicz, J.M., Sansone, C., & Manderlink, G. (1985). Competence, achievement orientation, and intrinsic motivation: A process analysis. *Journal of Personality and Social Psychology, 48,* 493–508.

Harper, F.B.W. (1975). The validity of some alternative measurements of achievement motivation. *Educational and Psychological Measurement, 35,* 905–909.

Heckhausen, H. (1968) Achievement motivation research: Current problems and some contributions towards a general theory of motivation. In W.J. Arnold (Ed.), *Nebraska Symposium on Motivation.* Lincoln: University of Nebraska Press, 103–174.

Jackson, D.N. (1974). *Manual for the Personality Research Form.* Goshen, N.Y.: Research Psychologists Press.

Judd, C.M., & Kenny, D.A. (1981a). *Estimating the effects of social interventions.* Cambridge: Cambridge University Press.

Judd, C.M., & Kenny, D.A. (1981b). Process analysis: Estimating mediation in treatment evaluations. *Evaluation Review, 5,* 602–619.

Kanouse, D.E., Gumpert, P. & Canavan-Gumpert, D. (1981). The semantics of praise. In J. Harvey, W. Ickes & R. Kidd (Eds.), *New directions in attribution research* (Vol. 3). Hillsdale, N.J.: Erlbaum.

Kirschenbaum, D.S., Humphrey, L.L., & Malett, S.D. (1981). Specificity of planning in adult self-control: An applied investigation. *Journal of Personality and Social Psychology, 40,* 941–95.

Kirschenbaum, D.S., Malett, S.D., Humphrey, L.L., & Tomarken, A.J. (1982). Specificity of planning and the maintenance of self-control: 1 year follow-up of a study improvement program. *Behavior Therapy, 13,* 232–240.

Kirschenbaum, D.S., Tomarken, A.J., & Ordman, A.M. (1982). Specificity of planning and choice applied to adult self-control. *Journal of Personality and Social Psychology, 42,* 576–585.

Kukla, A. (1978). Foundations of an attributional theory of performance. *Psychological Review, 79,* 454–470.

Lepper, M. (1980). Intrinsic and extrinsic motivation in children: Detrimental effects of superfluous social controls. In W.A. Collins (Ed.), *Minnesota Symposium on Child Psychology* (Vol. 14). Morristown, N.J.: Erlbaum.

Locke, E.A., Shaw, K.N., Saari, L.M., & Latham, G.P. (1981). Goal setting and task performance: 1969–1980. *Psychological Bulletin, 90,* 125–152.

Manderlink, G. (1985). The effects of proximal vs. distal goal-setting on intrinsic motivation. Unpublished manuscript, Columbia University.

Manderlink, G. & Harackiewicz, J. (1984). Proximal vs. distal goal setting and intrinsic motivation. *Journal of Personality and Social Psychology, 47,* 918–928.

McClelland, D.C. (1961). *The achieving society.* Princeton, NJ: Van Nostrand.

Mossholder, K.W. (1980). Effects of externally mediated goal setting on intrinsic motivation: A laboratory experiment. *Journal of Applied Psychology, 65,* 202–210.

Murray, H.A. (1938). *Explorations in personality.* New York: Oxford University Press.

Nicholls, J.G. (1979). Quality and equality in intellectual development. *American Psychologist, 34,* 1071–1084.

Nicholls, J.G. (1984). Achievement motivation: Conceptions of ability, subjective experience, task choice, and performance. *Psychological Review, 91,* 328–346.

Pittman, T.S., Davey, M.E., Alafat, K.A., Wetherill, K.V., & Kramer, N.A. (1980). Informational versus controlling verbal rewards. *Personality and Social Psychology Bulletin, 6,* 228–233.

Rosenberg, M.J. (1969). The condition and consequences of evaluation apprehension. In R. Rosenthal & R.L. Rosnow (Eds.), *Artifact in behavioral research.* New York: Academic Press.

Ruble, D.N., Boggiano, A.K., Feldman, N.S., & Loebl, J.H. (1980). The concept of competence: A developmental analysis of self-evaluation through social comparison. *Developmental Psychology, 16,* 105–115.

Ryan, R. (1982). Control and information in the intrapersonal sphere: An extension of cognitive evaluation theory. *Journal of Personality and Social Psychology, 43,* 450–461.

Ryan, R.M., Mims, V., & Koestner, R. (1983). Relation of reward contingency and interpersonal context to intrinsic motivation: A review and test using cognitive evaluation theory. *Journal of Personality and Social Psychology, 45,* 736–750.

Sansone, C. (1986). A question of competence: The effects of competence and task feedback on intrinsic interest. *Journal of Personality and Social Psychology, 51,* 918–931.

Sansone, C. (1989). Competence feedback, task feedback, and intrinsic interest: An examination of process and context. *Journal of Experimental Social Psychology, 25,* 343–361.

Sansone, C., Sachau, D.A., & Weir, C. (1989). The effects of instruction on intrinsic interest: The importance of context. *Journal of Personality and Social Psychology, 57,* 819–829.

Sarason, I.G. (1980). Introduction to the study of test anxiety. In I.G. Sarason (Ed.), *Test anxiety: Theory, research, and applications.* Hillsdale, N.J.: Erlbaum.

Schlenker, B.R. & Leary, M. (1982). Social anxiety and self-presentation: a conceptualization model. *Psychological Bulletin, 92,* 641–669.

Spence, J.T. & Helmreich, R.L. (1983). Achievement-related motives and behaviors. In J.T. Spears (Ed.), *Achievement and achievement motives: Psychological and sociological approaches.* San Francisco: W.H. Freeman.

Steers, R.M. (1975). Task-goal attributes, achievement, and supervisory performance. *Organizational Behavior and Human Performance, 13,* 392–403.

Trope, Y. (1975). Seeking information about one's own ability as a determinant of choice among tasks. *Journal of Personality and Social Psychology, 32,* 1004–1013.

Umstot, D.D., Bell, C.H. & Mitchell, T.R. (1976). Effects of job enrichment and task goals on satisfaction and productivity: Implications for job design. *Journal of Applied Psychology, 61,* 379–394.

Wine, J. (1971). Test anxiety and direction of attention. *Psychological Bulletin, 76,* 92–104.

White, R.W. (1959). Motivation reconsidered: The concept of competence. *Psychological Review, 66,* 297–333.

White, S.E., Mitchell, T. & Bell, C. (1977). Goal setting, evaluation apprehension, and social cues as determinants of job performance and job satisfaction in a simulated organization. *Journal of Applied Psychology, 62,* 665–673.

7 Developmental changes in competence assessment

Diane N. Ruble, Ellen H. Grosovsky, Karin S. Frey, and Renae Cohen

It is well established that a sense of competence has a powerful impact on achievement-related behavior and motivation (Deci & Ryan, 1985; Fincham & Cain, 1986; Ruble & Boggiano, 1980). Several studies, for example, have suggested that children with a positive sense of competence were more likely to adopt an intrinsic orientation toward achievement, thereby demonstrating an interest in challenge, mastery, and curiosity, relative to children with a negative perception of competence (Boggiano, Main, & Katz, 1988; Harter, 1981; Chapter 9, this volume). Other research has shown that even among the most academically competent, some children were vulnerable to the negative effects of low perceived competence, showing lower expectancies of success, less persistence, and so on (Phillips, 1984). Such behavior has been termed by Langer (1979) "the illusion of incompetence."

What leads to such differences in self-perceptions even among comparably skilled children? Most speculation has focused on socialization processes, such as varying experiences with and feedback from parents and teachers (Eccles, Midgley, & Adler, 1984; Harter, 1981). An alternative approach, however, is to focus on the child's active, constructive processes involved in his or her assessment of competence – a "self-socialization" process (Ruble, 1987). This approach is characterized by the study of developmental changes in what children do, such as what information they seek and use, rather than on what is done to them by external socializing agents. Previous research has suggested that children's perceptions of competence changed during their first few years of school (Dweck & Elliott, 1983; Nicholls & Miller, 1984; Stipek, 1984), and that variations in achievement interest over time were related to these changing perceptions of competence (Boggiano & Ruble, 1979). We do not yet understand, how-

Preparation of this chapter was supported in part by two grants from the National Institute of Mental Health: Grant 37215, and a Research Scientist Development Award, Grant 00484, to the first author.

ever, how children form these different conclusions about their competence. That is, what information do children use to evaluate competence, and how does this process change with age? This chapter addresses these questions.

One significant source of information for an individual about his or her competence is social comparison. According to Festinger's (1954) social comparison theory, when unambiguous criteria for ability and performance are not available, people look to other individuals for subjective standards. The social-psychology literature has documented the pervasiveness and significance of these comparative standards for self-evaluation (e.g., Latane, 1966; Suls & Miller, 1977; Suls & Wills, 1991). Previous research also has suggested that both interest in and use of social comparison for self-evaluation of competence increased during the early school years (Ruble, 1983; Suls & Mullen, 1982). In the present chapter, we extend this line of research in two ways. The first contrasts self-evaluation with other-evaluation in children of different ages, in hopes of illuminating the processes underlying developmental changes in competence assessment. The second related issue concerns developmental changes in preference for and use of different standards in competence assessment. Veroff (1969), for example, has suggested that the basis of children's achievement motivation shifts as they grow older from autonomous evaluation (i.e., determining whether one meets one's own personal standards) to social comparison. In this chapter we will present studies that evaluate this hypothesis.

Self- versus other-evaluation

One way in which children's competence assessments change with age involves changes in how positive their judgments of themselves are. Numerous studies have indicated that children's self-assessments and expectations for performance become less optimistic with age (e.g., Frey & Ruble, 1987; Parsons & Ruble, 1977; Stipek & Hoffman, 1980). The reasons for young children's unrealistically optimistic self-evaluations have been puzzling for some time; they have recently been the subject of careful and provocative theoretical analyses (Eccles, Midgley & Adler, 1984; Stipek, 1984; Stipek & MacIver, 1989).

One productive way to approach this problem is to compare how children at different ages evaluate themselves with how they evaluate another child's performance at the same task. If the developmental differences observed were due to fundamental changes in ability to integrate and remember evaluation-relevant information, then similar patterns would be expected across self and other evaluation. Some previous research, however, suggested that young children were likely to evaluate themselves and others quite differently. Specifically, kindergartners appear to use social-comparison information when evaluating another child's ability (Ruble, Feldman, & Higgins, 1986, Study 1), even though a number of previous studies suggested that such young children demonstrated little or no use of social-comparison information when evaluating their own ability (e.g., Aboud, 1985; Chafel, 1986; Ruble, Boggiano, Feldman, & Loebl, 1980). In addition, related work by Stipek and her colleagues found similar self/other differences for evaluations based on feedback about one's previous performance (i.e., autonomous information). Specifically, preschool children's expectations and judgments of competence were affected by information about their previous success or failure only when they were evaluating another child; they did not use this information when evaluating themselves. Such self/other differences were not observed in older children (see Stipek, 1984).

Previous research suggested two major alternative explanations of self/other differences in evaluation. The first explanation points to the different perspectives of actors and observers towards a particular task: For actors, information about the task itself is likely to be salient, whereas observers tend to focus on the persons performing the task (Jones & Nisbett, 1971). Because actors' attention is focused on the task, various task factors, such as difficulty and novelty, may be most relevant to evaluations. Observers, however, are relatively more likely to attribute performance levels to person than to task factors. This actor/observer difference may be greater for younger children, because their judgments are more influenced than are those of older children by salience of information (e.g., Odom & Corbin, 1973). One recent study, for example, showed that the attributions of five- to seven-year-olds were more likely to be influenced by the salience of those being judged (i.e., which person's picture was available on a slide) than were the attributions of children eight years old and older (Pryor, Rholes, Ruble, & Kriss, 1984). Research reported by Stipek (1984), however, revealed no support for the hypothesis that differences in visual orientation accounted for differences in self/other evaluations at the preschool level.

The second possible explanation is derived from research suggesting that certain factors associated with evaluating oneself lead one to interpret and apply feedback information differently when evaluating the self versus another (Damon & Hart, 1982; Snyder, Stephan, & Rosenfield, 1978; Stevens & Jones, 1976; Wigfield, 1988). Damon and Hart (1982) highlighted two factors that distinguished a judgment about the self from a judgment about another: (a) the availability of direct knowledge about one's internal state, such as the amount of effort expended on a given task; and (b) emotional investment. Both of these factors might be expected to have the greatest impact on preschool and primary children. At these ages, children are likely to equate effort with ability (Nicholls & Miller, 1984). Thus, the perception that one has tried hard may lead to a positive evaluation about one's performances. In addition, young children are thought to be particularly likely to confuse wishes with reality (Piaget, 1930); indeed, previous research has suggested that preschoolers tend to evaluate themselves more positively than do older children, regardless of the nature of the feedback received (Stipek, 1984).

In a test of this "wishful thinking" hypothesis, Stipek, Roberts, and Sanborn (1984) found that preschool children had higher expectations for another child's performance when the preschoolers' rewards were made contingent on the other child's success. The tentative conclusion, based on these data, is that young children's unrealistic optimism regarding their performance probably is due not to an inability to use previous-performance feedback, but rather to an age-related cognitive-motivational factor: the tendency to make judgments consistent with desires. This conclusion must be drawn with caution, however, because it was based on an interaction of marginal statistical significance. Furthermore, developmental conclusions cannot be drawn, as only four-year-olds were included in this study. The research described in the next section extends this line of analysis to differences in self- versus other-evaluation in the use of social-comparison information and to a direct examination of predicted developmental differences.

Use of social comparison for self- versus other-evaluation

In one study (Grosovsky, 1985), differences between children's evaluations of themselves and others were examined in two ways: (a) as a between-subjects condition, in which some children focused on their performance and others focused on another child's performance and (b) as a within-subjects rating of the target (self or other) versus a hypothetical other. Subjects were thirty-six children at each of two age levels (five to six years and nine to ten years), randomly assigned to one of three conditions. The first (actor-self) condition replicated previous studies of self-evaluation in that the child performed a task, received feedback, and then was asked to evaluate his or her performance. The second (observer-other) condition was a standard observer-evaluation condition employed in actor-observer studies, in which the subject evaluated the performance of another child, shown on videotape. The basic prediction was that subjects in the observer-other condition would evidence greater use of social comparison information than children in the actor-self condition, and that this difference would be greater in the younger children.

A third (observer-self) condition was added to distinguish between the two alternative explanations for differences in accuracy in self- versus other-evaluation. In this condition, children evaluated themselves after watching videotapes of their performances, thereby experiencing simultaneously both the factors associated with evaluating the self and the visual orientation associated with evaluating another. If children were affected primarily by the differences in visual perspective, then social comparison information would be used more in both observer conditions than in the actor-self condition. In contrast, if children were affected primarily by the knowledge and emotional investment associated with evaluating oneself, then social comparison would be used less often in the two self conditions than in the observer-other condition. In either case, the differences were expected to be greater for the younger children.

The subjects in the two self conditions were asked to perform counting tasks utilizing different senses (e.g., seeing hidden faces and feeling different materials attached to cardboard). The correct answer was ambiguous, so success or failure could be conveyed to the subject by the experimenter in terms of comparative feedback. Specifically, after the subject responded, he or she was told, in the success condition, that four other children who had done the same task had not found nearly as many hidden faces as the subject, and, in the failure condition, that the other children had found many more. After receiving this feedback, subjects were asked to evaluate their performance and the performance of one of the hypothetical four children. The procedure for children in the observer-other condition was the same except that these subjects evaluated a target child shown on videotape, rather than themselves.

The tendency to use comparative information to evaluate self and others was assessed with three measures: (a) the child's prediction as to whether the self or the hypothetical other would perform better at the game if it were played again, (b) the child's rating of the self's and the other's absolute level of ability at the task ("How good do you think you are [he or she is] at this kind of puzzle?"), and (c) the child's ratings of the self's and the other's relative level of ability at the task ("Do you think you [he or she] did better, worse, or the same as most other kids your age?"). Responses that were compatible with the comparative feedback were scored as "correct." For example, a response would be scored as correct if a child in the success condition rated his or her relative ability higher than the hypothetical child's relative ability. In this way, an index of social comparison usage was created for each subject, ranging from 0 (no usage) to 3 (usage each time).

The results showed that older children tended to use comparison information marginally more than younger children (M = 1.83 vs. 1.57). As predicted, the greatest use of comparison information was by children in the observer-other condition (M = 1.94) and the least use was in the actor-self condition (M = 1.48). The mean score for the observer-self condition (M = 1.68) fell in the middle and thus was not informative about the two possible explanations of self- and other-evaluation differences proposed earlier. Moreover, contrary to predictions, this main effect of condition did not vary with age. Finally, judgments more closely mirrored social-comparison information after success feedback than after failure feedback. In summary, the younger children tended to use comparison information more when evaluating another than when evaluating themselves, as expected. Unexpectedly, however, the older children evidenced the same tendency.

The hypotheses also were examined in terms of the children's responses to open-ended questions. The children were asked why they had predicted that they would perform better or worse than the hypothetical other child and why they had achieved the score that they did. Their responses were scored in terms of whether or not they referred to social comparison (e.g., "She found more monkey faces than I did."). Mean references to social comparison as a function of age, outcome, and condition are shown in Table 7.1.

As expected, children in the observer-other condition made more references to social comparison than did children in the actor-self condition in response to both questions. Moreover, for the question concerning why they got the score that they did, the responses of children in the observer-self condition were similar to those in the actor-self condition, suggesting that factors associated with evaluating the self, such as emotional investment in protecting self-esteem, influenced children's use (or nonuse) of social comparison information. Indeed, for this question, social-comparison seemed to be irrelevant when children were evaluating themselves from either an actor or an observer perspective, but highly relevant when they were evaluating another. Perhaps a particular score is more easily viewed as affected by factors other than social comparison, such as effort, interest, or luck, than is a question about future relative performance.

In fact, deviation from the overall pattern did occur for the question concerning who would do better in the future. Specifically, children in the observer-self condition made more references to social comparison after

Table 7.1. *Proportion of subjects giving social comparison as a reason for their predictions and for their scores as a function of age, condition, and success/failure outcome*

Age and Outcome	Condition: Actor-Self	Observer-Self	Observer-Other
Prediction–6 years			
Success	0.22	0.18	0.80
Failure	0.22	0.73	0.70
Prediction–9 years			
Success	0.67	0.27	0.75
Failure	0.33	0.64	0.83
Score–6 years			
Success	0.11	0.00	0.55
Failure	0.11	0.00	0.64
Score–9 years			
Success	0.18	0.08	0.58
Failure	0.09	0.00	0.67

failure than after success. This result seemed to conflict with an emotional-investment explanation of self- and other-evaluation differences; and, in fact, the similarity of the children's responses in the two observer conditions suggested that visual orientation may have affected responses to this question. (Perhaps this phenomenon is what people refer to when they say they need some distance from a negative outcome to assess their situation objectively. People do not seem to require distance from a positive outcome.)

In brief, children's open-ended casual reasoning supported predictions about their tendency to use social comparison more for other- than for self-evaluation. These data also suggested that the basis for such differences may depend on other factors, such as the particular judgment being made (i.e., previous vs. future performance) and previous success versus failure experiences, although age was not a significant factor.

For the within-subjects analyses, subjects' ratings of absolute ability for the target and for the hypothetical other were compared (see Table 7.2). As expected, children's ratings of absolute ability at the task showed greater use of social comparison for other- than for self-evaluation. In addition, as shown in Table 7.2, subjects appeared to make higher ratings of their

Table 7.2. *Mean ratings of absolute task skill as a function of age, performance outcome, and target of evaluation*

	Age and Target of Evaluation			
	6 years		9 years	
Performance Outcome	Self	Other	Self	Other
Success	8.7	6.7	8.6	8.1
Failure	8.3	4.8	7.5	6.6

Note: Scale ranged from 1 (least positive evaluation) to 10 (most positive evaluation).

ability after failure, consistent with an emotion-based/self-protection interpretation of self/other differences. Finally, the results indicated, as expected, that, compared to older children, younger children showed a greater difference in the tendency to use social comparison when evaluating the self as opposed to when evaluating others.

In summary, this study provided reasonably clear support for the prediction that children would show greater use of relevant social-comparison information when evaluating another child than when evaluating themselves. This difference was found for the following: (a) between-subjects ratings of ability for self versus other in an actor versus observer role; (b) between-subjects analyses of open-ended casual explanations involving social comparison; and (c) within-subjects ratings of ability for the target versus a hypothetical other child. This study provided mixed support, however, for the prediction that younger children would show this difference more than older children because evidence for this effect occurred only in the within-subjects' analysis. Moreover, an attempt to examine the bases of this difference yielded mixed results. A second study examined the generality of differences in self- versus other-evaluation.

The second study (Ruble, Feldman, & Higgins, 1986) compared children's use of autonomous versus social-comparison information in evaluating others relative to the self. The subjects were forty children at each of three grade levels (kindergarten, second grade, and fourth grade). Half of the children at each grade evaluated themselves and half evaluated a hypothetical child. In the self-evaluation condition, pairs of subjects, matched on sex and grade, performed four trials of different prototype-matching tasks in which the outcomes were ambiguous. The four trials were (a) baseline control (no information); (b) social comparison (performing better or worse than the partner); (c) autonomous comparison (performing better or worse than one's previous performance); and (d) a conflict situation, in which both social and autonomous information were available. The order of the last three trials was counterbalanced. For the last three trials, subjects received information controlled by the experimenter regarding their performance and, when appropriate, about the performance of the other child. Subjects in the other-evaluation condition were taken through a procedure that paralleled the one for self-evaluation, except that they did not perform the tasks. Instead, they heard stories describing the performances of children who had completed the tasks. After each trial, subjects were asked to evaluate their performance on that trial, the affect they experienced, and their ability at that kind of task.

The results showed that children utilized the information more for other- than for self-evaluation, consistent with predictions and with the Grosovsky (1985) results reported earlier. The prediction that the differences between self- and other-evaluation would vary with age was supported only for children's rating of ability based on social comparison. Only fourth graders used this information for self-evaluation, whereas children at all three grade levels used the information appropriately when evaluating the hypothetical other child.

The results also indicated that for most comparisons differences between self and other ratings were greater after failure feedback, suggesting an influence of self-protective mechanisms on self-evaluation, as expected. This conclusion was supported by comparisons with the baseline ratings made by the control group, which received no performance information. Within-success analyses showed no significant effects of self-other evaluation, whereas within-failure analyses showed that decreases in performance evaluations relative to baseline were evident for other-evaluation only; for self-evaluation, most of the means were about equal to or even greater than the baseline means. That is, subjects apparently minimized the impact of the evaluative information when it indicated that they had performed poorly. These effects were highly significant for the measures based on social comparison but only marginally significant for the measures based on autonomous comparison. Thus it appeared that differences in self- versus other-evaluation were particularly pronounced when failure information was derived from social comparison.

Perhaps the most interesting information about differences in self- versus other-evaluation emerged from the analyses of the conflict trials. Unlike the results of previous studies, these data allowed us to examine the impact of social-comparison information on competence assessment when conflicting information was available.

Not surprisingly, the results showed that for all three measures – i.e., performance evaluation, affect, and perceived ability – self ratings were higher than other ratings. Moreover, for ratings of specific performance and ability, this difference between self- and other-evaluation decreased with age, as expected. Of greatest interest, however, was a three-way interaction for ratings of ability. As shown in Figure 7.1, the impact of comparative failure on self-evaluation increased with age, particularly between kindergarten and second grade, consistent with the results from previous research (Ruble, 1983). More importantly, the differences between self- versus other-evaluation in the use of social comparison decreased dramatically with age. Young children's ratings of another's competence showed a large effect of comparative success versus failure, whereas such information had virtually no effect on their assessment of their own competence. In contrast, by fourth grade, social comparison had a modest effect on the assessment of competence, with no difference between self and other ratings except for a slight self-enhancement bias. A similar pattern was found for ratings of affect, although the three-way interaction was only marginally significant. Thus, with multiple sources of evaluation-relevant information, children's ratings of competence showed strong support for our major predictions. Young children used social comparison when evaluating another child, but not when evaluating themselves, and the difference between self- and other-evaluation decreased with age.

Summary

Differences in evaluating oneself versus another were examined in these two studies, in part to address possible reasons for age differences in self-evaluation that were observed in previous research. Specifically, suggestions that preschool children used social comparison in evaluating others implied that their failure to utilize relative-feedback information in self-evaluation was not due to an inability to understand the information or to make relevant inferences. Instead, it would imply that something about the process of self-evaluation, at least as operationalized in these studies, created problems for younger children. The two studies described in this section represented the first direct comparison, as well as an examination of a predicted interaction, of such differences with age.

As expected, in both studies, evaluation-relevant information was used more for other- than for self-evaluation, supporting Stipek's (1984) findings based on autonomous performance feedback. It was difficult, however, to draw clear conclusions from these data. First, there was mixed evidence regarding predicted interactions with age. In both studies, the predicted decrease with age in self/other differences in use of social comparison

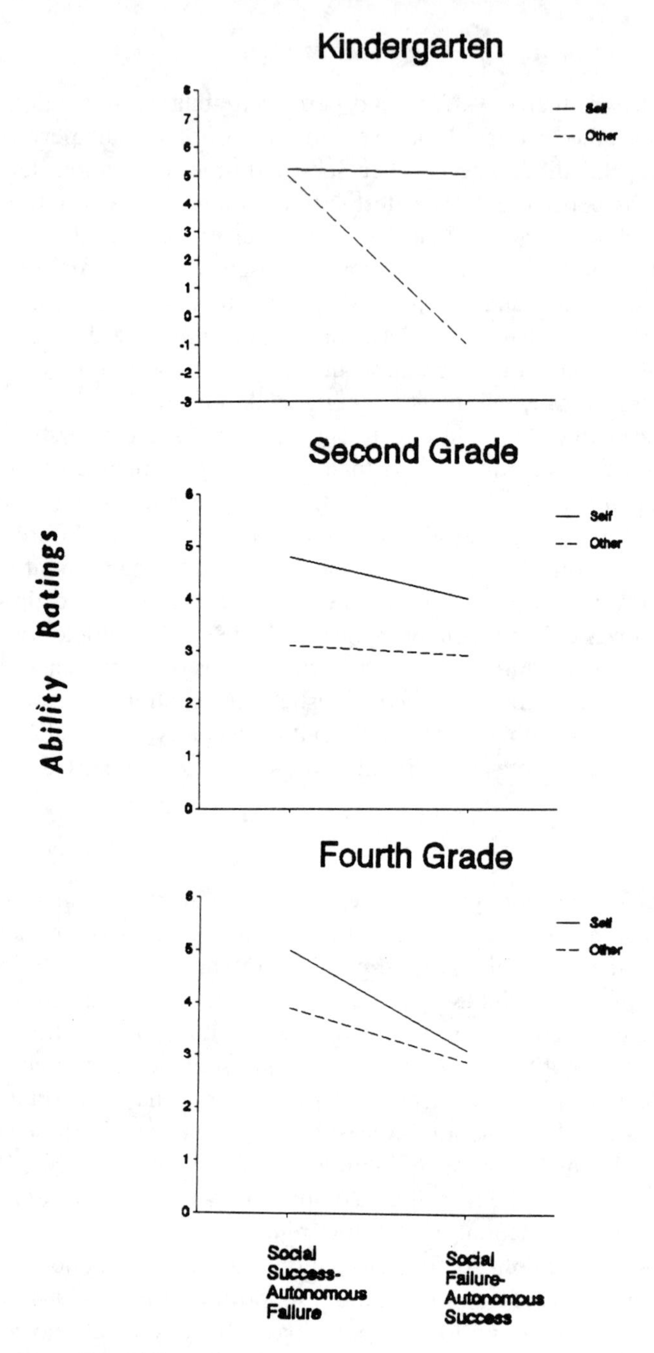

Figure 7.1. Ability ratings for self versus other as a function of grade and type of feedback.

information was reflected in some measures but not in others. Thus, although differences associated with a self- versus other-orientation during evaluation appeared to contribute to age-related differences in self-evaluation, other factors also appeared to be involved. Moreover, recent research suggested that in some circumstances older children showed greater self/other differences than younger ones (Ruble, Eisenberg, Feldman & Higgins, 1990). It may be that certain defenses or self-enhancement biases are elicited by different features of the task or context in children at different ages.

Second, younger children showed considerable use of evaluative information. This was particularly likely for measures focused on specific performance – i.e., open-ended responses concerning children's predictions of who would win another trial at the same game (Grosovsky, 1985) and children's feelings about their most recent performance (Ruble et al., 1986). In contrast, for self-evaluation of ability (i.e., "How good are you at this kind of game?"), only the oldest children showed any indication of using social comparison information, a finding that was consistent with previous studies. Perhaps with a specific, concrete referent, younger children could perceive more clearly the implications of the comparison information. Certainly, these differences were consistent with a number of studies suggesting that children younger than approximately seven years had difficulty making dispositional inferences implying a stable, general trait, such as ability or generosity (Rholes & Ruble, 1984; Rotenberg, 1982). It also is possible in both of these studies that the practice children had in evaluating both themselves and another child on multiple trials made the evaluative information more salient, when compared to other research involving self-evaluation only after performance of a single task.

Social versus autonomous comparison

The second issue to be addressed in this chapter concerns the standards children use in assessing competence. The kind of information children seek or use is likely to affect their conclusions about competence. For example, one may look to signs of improvement over time or to relative standing at the moment, drawing positive conclusions from one perspective and negative conclusions from the other. Moreover, the emotional consequences of self-evaluation vary depending on the standard for performance that is used (Higgins, Strauman, & Klein, 1986). Social comparison among children, for example, is likely to result in less complimentary conclusions than autonomous or temporal comparison (i.e., comparison with one's own performance over time).

Such distinctions also are important to recent theoretical analyses of achievement motivation. Dweck and Elliott (1983), for example, distinguish between *learning* and *performance* goals, in the sense that learning goals emphasize mastery and improvement over time, while performance goals emphasize judgments of competence in the immediate situation. Dweck and Elliott argue that the standards of evaluation for learning goals are likely to be personal (i.e., autonomous), whereas standards for performance goals are likely to be normative (i.e., social comparison). Similarly, Nicholls (1984) distinguishes between *task-involvement,* in which competence is judged with reference to mastery and effort, and *ego-involvement,* in which competence is judged with reference to social comparison.

In an early consideration of developmental changes in bases of competence assessment, Veroff (1969) suggested that young children's evaluations were based primarily on autonomous (self-oriented) standards rather than on comparative standards. Veroff's analysis further implied that after a few years in school, children would shift from using autonomous standards to using social comparison standards. According to Veroff (1969), even after children entered school, they did not automatically use social comparison information in ambiguous conditions, as Festinger's theory would suggest. Instead, a motive to compare oneself with others develops only after "considerable reinforcement" and the "larger socialization by the community through school" (p. 50).

This prediction seems reasonable if one assumes that younger children are more attentive to what they have done rather than to what others have done; perhaps the concept of egocentrism, loosely applied, would support this assumption. Moreover, there are developmental trends in children's conceptualizations of competence that are directly relevant to the distinctions made among types of achievement motivation (Dweck & Elliott, 1983; Nicholls, 1984). Specifically, during the first few years of school, children often equate competence with effort and mastery (Nicholls & Miller, 1984). Only later does the concept of competence as capacity (Nicholls & Miller, 1984) and as a stable, dispositional trait (Frey & Ruble, 1985; Rholes & Ruble, 1984) emerge. Thus, it would appear that learning goals (Dweck & Elliott, 1983) and task involvement (Nicholls, 1984) would more likely characterize the achievement behavior of younger children and that, therefore, their standards of competence assessment would emphasize autonomous comparison rather than social comparison.

The few relevant studies that have been conducted have tended to support this developmental hypothesis. Children younger than approximately seven years tend not to base self-evaluations of ability on social comparison

(Aboud, 1985; Harter & Pike, 1984; Ruble et al., 1980; Stipek & Tannatt, 1985). Instead, younger children's assessments seem to be more influenced by their meeting an absolute standard of success (Boggiano & Ruble, 1979; Butler, 1989b; Ruble, Parsons, & Ross, 1976), such as the number of items completed on a particular task.

To date, however, this developmental hypothesis has not been tested directly, that is, autonomous comparison has not been manipulated simultaneously with social comparison. Thus alternative hypotheses remain plausible. An information-processing analysis, for example, might predict no difference in use of social versus temporal (autonomous) comparison, since the use of both types of information requires an integration of other outcomes with the present performance. Instead, differences in use would be predicted by such factors as the magnitude of the discrepancy or the number of elements involved (Higgins, 1981).

Studies of social versus autonomous comparison

The study by Ruble and her coworkers (1986), described earlier, provided several ways of evaluating the impact of social versus autonomous comparison on competence assessment. First, the main effects of success or failure outcome were observed when autonomous and social comparison trials were examined separately. Thus, for the most part, both social comparison and autonomous comparison were used. The developmental hypothesis, however, would suggest that use of the two kinds of information would vary with age. Younger children were expected to base judgments of competence on autonomous standards, such as improved performance over time, whereas older children were thought to be more likely to base judgments on social comparison. Despite this prediction, the results showed little indication that children of any age based their evaluations on improvement. In fact, in most cases, the means showed no difference or were in the opposite direction (i.e., general ability was rated higher after temporal "failure" than after "success").

As a second test of the hypothesis, analyses were conducted to compare ratings for the tasks for which either social comparison or temporal comparison, but not both, were presented. In contrast to the developmental hypothesis, but consistent with information-processing predictions, the results of these analyses indicated no significant age differences in evaluation as a function of the type of information made available. There was, however, a marginally significant trend that was consistent with the developmental hypothesis. Younger children's ratings of affect were more positive when they experienced autonomous success than when they experienced social-comparison success; second graders showed the reverse trend; and fourth graders showed no difference, consistent with Veroff's (1969) suggestion that the two bases of competence assessment become integrated in older children.

The third test of the hypothesis involved the trial in which conflicting autonomous and social comparison cues were presented simultaneously (i.e., if social comparison indicated success, autonomous comparison indicated failure, and vice versa). Thus, for example, if children based their judgments on social comparison, then ratings would be more positive when they were told that they did better than other children, even though the autonomous information indicated they had done worse than they had previously. The results of this analysis showed no indication that children of any age based their evaluations of self or others on incremental improvement over trials. Indeed, analyses conducted separately for actors and for observers showed only one significant interaction with age. In direct contrast to the developmental hypothesis, kindergartners used social comparison information more than the two older age groups when evaluating the general ability of the hypothetical other child.

Finally, since the developmental hypotheses applied primarily to self-evaluation, analyses for actor subjects were conducted only for the trials in which either autonomous or social comparison information was presented. Children's ratings based on autonomous information were higher when performance improved across the two trials than when it declined, indicating that the autonomous-comparison information was used as expected. There also was partial support for the developmental hypothesis – the second graders used this type of information the least. In direct contrast to the hypothesis, however, for ratings of performance, fourth graders used the autonomous information *more* than the children at the two younger grade levels. For ratings based on social-comparison information, the results showed higher ratings after relative success than after relative failure, indicating that social comparison information also was used. The only interaction with age, however, was for the general ability ratings, with older children showing the greatest use of social comparison. Thus, in contrast to the developmental hypothesis, age-related results indicated that, if anything, the older children used autonomous information more for self-evaluation than did the younger children and, for performance and affect ratings, more than they used social comparison.

A similar conclusion emerged from another recent study examining age differences in the type of information children *sought* as opposed to the type of information they *used* when it was offered (Ruble & Flett, 1988). Children aged seven, nine, and eleven years performed a series of arithmetic tasks, for which they were given ambiguous outcome information. During "rest" periods, they could review two kinds of information relevant to evaluating their performance. The social-comparison information told them how other children their age had performed on the same tasks. The autonomous information included both a report of the subject's performance on previous tests at the same level of difficulty and answer keys for the tests the subjects had just taken. Thus, in this study, autonomous information involved self-standards of a more absolute nature as well as temporal comparison. As a way of examining possible self-protective motives affecting self-assessment strategies, individual differences in arithmetic achievement level (high, medium, and low) served as a factor in the design. It was expected that low-achieving children would show the least interest in self-evaluation overall, because they would anticipate receiving information that would violate self-protective goals. The results supported this prediction.

The results also revealed an intriguing interaction across age and achievement level in the type of information the children preferred. For high achievers, interest in social comparison decreased with age, whereas interest in autonomous evaluation increased dramatically. Medium achievers preferred social to autonomous-evaluation information at all age levels, with only nonsignificant increases in preference with age. Low achievers preferred social- to autonomous-evaluation information at the nine- and eleven-year-old levels. At seven years, they showed equal levels of interest (or disinterest?) in both.

Thus, once again, in contrast to the developmental hypothesis, the only age level showing a clear preference for autonomous evaluation was the oldest level. It is noteworthy that this finding was consistent across the two quite different measures used in the two studies: (a) use of information in performance ratings, and (b) interest in information during free choice. The results for the second measure are especially relevant to the self-socialization emphasis with which we began this chapter.

The Ruble and Flett (1988) study suggested further that this preference for autonomous information in the upper grades may be specific to high-achieving children. One interpretation of this result is that children who had concluded that they were very capable regarded further comparisons with peers as unnecessary. Thus, these children may focus on task mastery and autonomous evaluation (via information available in the answer keys and evidence of progress in relation to previous performance) more than on social comparison. Such a shift toward mastery orientation has important major implications for subsequent performance and self-esteem.

Within this context, it is interesting to ask why the low and middle-achievers maintained their preference for social comparison. One might have expected that once children in these groups defined their ability level as poor or average, they would be discouraged by continued comparison. It may be, however, that such children never quite accept the conclusion that they are not near the top, and this continued uncertainty maintains their interest in relative standing. Alternatively, social comparison may serve different functions at different ages and achievement levels. For low and average achievers, it may be a great relief to note that there are others doing worse than they are. Indeed, low and medium achievers engaged in more downward comparison by the second choice (39.6% and 22.9% respectively) than did high achieving children (19.4%). It would be informative in future research to examine the affective impact of downward comparison as a function of age and ability level.

Summary

Direct comparisons of the use of autonomous versus social comparison for self-assessment provided only minimal support for the predicted developmental changes in the relative impact of these two sources of information on performance and competence assessment. Consistent with Veroff's (1969) hypothesis, second graders were least attentive to autonomous standards; but, in contrast to developmental predictions, kindergartners did not utilize autonomous standards significantly more than they used social comparison standards. Instead, it appeared that even young children were able to use both kinds of information, at least when evaluating others, and that use of and interest in autonomous information, was, if anything, greatest for the oldest children. The association of autonomous evaluation with high achievement in older children seems quite important and suggests that the motivational implications of different bases of competence assessment may be considerable.

General discussion

A significant body of research indicates that a positive view of one's level of competence has various beneficial consequences for achievement, including positive affect, greater effort, and persistence (e.g., Phillips, 1984). More recent theoretical analyses have focused on the motivational impact of different definitions of competence. Dweck and Elliott (1983), for example, argue that a *learning* goal facilitates mastery strivings relative to a *performance* goal because the former emphasizes ability as something that can be learned, whereas the latter emphasizes ability as a fixed trait that is either present or absent. Similarly, Nicholls (1984) suggests that mastery is the goal of an achievement orientation based on *task-involvement,* whereas for *ego-involvement,* mastery is a means to an end rather than an end in itself.

Both aspects of competence assessment (i.e., positivity/negativity and learning/performance) appear to vary with age. Positive self-evaluations decline with age, at least during the first several grades of elementary school (Stipek, 1984), as does the prevalence of learning and mastery goals (Harter, 1981). The studies presented in this chapter examined developmental changes in how competence was assessed as a way to understand these age-related differences. An examination of differences in self- and other-evaluation was intended to shed light on processes that might lead to decreased positive self-assessment with age; change in the use of autonomous versus social comparison information was examined because of its relevance to learning versus performance goals.

Our approach to both issues was based in part on the question of why young children do not seem to base self-evaluations of competence on social comparison. It appears that this question is somewhat misleading in that the present results, as well as those from a number of previous studies (Butler, 1989b; Frey & Ruble, 1985; Levine, 1983; Mosatche & Bragonier, 1981) indicated quite clearly that children engaged in social comparison in kindergarten and that the shift was more one of focus and degree of engagement than of use versus non-use. The present results, taken together with previous findings, suggested that whether or not comparative standards were important in competence assessment seemed to depend, in part, on various qualities of the response measure. If the assessment required reasoning too far removed from the immediate task, particularly if it involved inferences about ability or predictions of performance on different tasks (Ruble et al., 1980), younger children might not be influenced by the performance of others. On the other hand, if the measure involved fairly concrete information integration, such as predicting a specific outcome on a task identical to one just completed (Grosovsky, 1985), young children might make quite sophisticated judgments. Interestingly, if the response measures were of potential threat to the self-esteem of older children, these children might fail to engage in social comparison (Frey & Ruble, 1985; Ruble, Eisenberg, Feldman, & Higgins, 1990). In this sense, then, failure to acknowledge social-comparison information actually may indicate that it has had a greater impact. Studies with college students also indicated this apparent failure to integrate information under some conditions (Stevens & Jones, 1976).

Although the present findings were not straightforward confirmations of empirically and theoretically derived predictions, some clear and consistent patterns did emerge and some developmental changes in competence assessment were observed. The results suggest the following conclusions:

1. Self-evaluations tend to be more positive and to be based less frequently on performance feedback than are other-evaluations, especially after failure. These differences emerged in all analyses.
2. Older children tend to use social comparison more than younger children for ratings of their general competence. This conclusion is based on findings from both the Grosovsky (1985) and the Ruble, Feldman, and Higgins (1986) studies. In the Grosovsky study, there was a marginally significant age difference in accuracy of use of social comparison across measures and a decrease in the self-other difference with age for ratings of ability (see Table 7.2). Ruble and colleagues found that younger children's self-ratings of ability showed no effect of social comparison, both when this information was presented in isolation and when it conflicted with autonomous information (see Figure 7.1).
3. Young children use social comparison information to rate others on all measures and to rate themselves on concrete measures. Indeed, age differences in self- versus other-evaluations of ability in both studies suggested that younger children might use social comparison for assessing the competence of others more than older children did.
4. In direct contrast to predictions, older children tend to base self-evaluations more on autonomous information, relative to social comparison, than do younger children. In the study by Ruble and colleagues (1986), older children used autonomous information more than both younger age groups for self-ratings of performance and more than second graders for self-ratings of affect. Moreover, the only group in the Ruble and Flett (1988) study that sought autonomous information more than social comparison was the one comprised of the oldest high achievers.

Possible explanations of the findings

We began with a discussion of why differences in self- versus other-evaluation might occur. One approach to this issue is to compare these findings to actor/observer differences in the attribution literature. Although the present measures were not directly comparable (the actor/observer literature examines individuals' attributions regarding why they performed well or poorly, rather than an evaluation of how they performed), the experimental conditions were comparable. The common finding that observers attributed behaviors more to dispositions and less to situations than did actors (Jones & Nisbett, 1971; Watson, 1982) was consistent with the present findings that observers utilized information relevant to evaluating a personal disposition (i.e., relative ability) more than did actors. Indeed, perhaps the former finding depended on the latter.

Similar explanations may underlie both sets of findings. One likely explanation concerns processes specific to evaluating oneself – in particular, emotional investment in protecting one's self-esteem, or knowledge about internal processes, such as effort and intention. Evidence in the present studies that self/other differences occurred more after relative failure than after relative success would seem to support a self-protection explanation. This trend is evident particularly in the comparisons to baseline in the Ruble, Feldman and Higgins (1986) study in which, for success, there were no significant differences across self/other evaluation. In contrast, for failure there were clear differences between self- and other-evaluation, and for most comparisons, there were significant decreases from baseline for other-evaluation only. These results were stronger for feedback based on social comparison, suggesting that social comparison may be more threatening than autonomous comparison. A similar trend was observed in the Stevens and Jones (1976) study for use of consensus versus consistency information in making ability attributions among college students.

Thus, success/failure comparisons supported the hypothesis that one aspect of self- and other-evaluation differences involved the desire to maintain a positive self-image. These findings supported Stipek's (1984) conclusions that "wishful thinking" accounted, in part, for differences in evaluative judgments for self versus other. The importance of processes specific to evaluating the self also is suggested by the condition effects for the open-ended analyses in the Grosovsky (1985) study, showing little reference to social comparison as a reason for one's performance when evaluating the self, from either an actor or an observer perspective. These data, together with the differences observed across success and failure, would seem to diminish the plausibility of an explanation based primarily on visual orientation per se.

This visual-orientation explanation also is inconsistent with findings that, for other kinds of social judgments, ratings about the self showed greater sophistication than ratings about hypothetical others (Ruble & Rholes, 1981). Piaget (1930), for example, observed that children's moral reasoning was more likely to incorporate information about intentions in judgments about the self than in judgments about others. These apparent inconsistencies between achievement-related and moral judgments in the relative sophistication of self- versus other-evaluation may be understood with reference to self-protective motives. That is, one's positive image about oneself is maintained by ignoring failure information when judging one's competence, but by incorporating information about lack of intent in judging, for example, the naughtiness of a misdeed.

The self-protective motive does not seem sufficient to explain some of the data, however, such as children's reliance on social-comparison information for predictions following failure in the observer-self condition of the Grosovsky (1985) study. These data suggested that visual orientation affected some judgments. In addition, it seemed likely that knowledge of one's internal states, such as effort, also affected self-evaluation differently from other-evaluation. Differences across age in ratings of ability for self versus others, for example, may be, in part, due to younger children's tendencies to equate ability with effort (Nicholls, 1984). If young children thought that they tried hard, they may have rated themselves as competent regardless of their relative outcome.

It is interesting to note that analyses of actor/observer differences in attributions made by adult subjects generally have not supported explanations based on differences in knowledge or information level (Watson, 1982). The type of information examined, however, has been general knowledge about oneself or others (e.g., the similarity to self-ratings of ratings of friends versus ratings of acquaintances) rather than knowledge of the internal processes specific to the situation. Thus it may be that other kinds of knowledge partially account for self/other differences observed in the present research and in previous actor/observer studies. Future research might, therefore, examine how judgments are affected when knowledge about internal processes, such as effort and involvement, is manipulated.

With respect to developmental differences, the present findings suggest that relevant to recent theoretical distinctions between incremental learning and improvement, temporal comparison with one's own previous performance is not more common in younger children. This conclusion is somewhat surprising, in part because it might be supposed that younger children are more optimistic and less realistic because they tend to base competence assessments more on autonomous comparison than on social comparison. In fact, however, there was only one marginally significant effect, for ratings of affect, in the predicted direction despite the many different ways the hypothesis was examined. Moreover, there was no indication at any grade that assessments of general ability were based on a learning or incremental view of competence. Perhaps this view represents a minority opinion relative to capacity views, or perhaps the context of the present studies fostered an evaluation rather than a learning set (Nicholls, 1984; Ruble & Frey, 1991).

If anything, autonomous evaluation was found to be more common in older children, especially in those who were high achievers. These data suggest that the relation between mastery-oriented (i.e., autonomous standards) and perceived competence reflects a causal association precisely opposite to that implied by analyses of different approaches to achievement (Dweck & Elliott, 1983; Nicholls, 1984). That is, the development of self-perceptions of competence may promote forms of competence assessment that are mastery-oriented rather than the other way around.

The present findings do not, however, rule out the hypotheses that younger children base assessments of competence more on other forms of autonomous standards than do older children. A number of studies, for example, suggest that younger children judge their performance according to absolute standards of competence, such as getting most of the answers correct (for reviews see Stipek & MacIver, 1989; Ruble & Frey, in press). Young children also may base their evaluations more frequently on their knowledge about their experience with the task, such as the amount of effort they exerted, though some recent findings fail to support this interpretation (Ruble et al., 1990).

Social and achievement consequences of the findings

Differences in forms of evaluations may be viewed as functional, with implications for achievement behavior. First, a tendency to view the self more positively (but less realistically) than one views another person may be adaptive in fostering a mastery orientation in achievement situations. The learned helplessness literature, for example, suggests that non-depressed individuals tend to have unrealistically high perceptions of personal control whereas depressed individuals tend to have more accurate perceptions, the so-called "sadder but wiser" effect (Alloy & Abramson, 1982). In this sense, then, the tendencies to evaluate oneself less optimistically with age may be viewed with some alarm, even though it does represent, in part, growth toward more realistic evaluations.

Second, there are similar implications in the findings that children's self-evaluations incorporated less of the available evaluative information than did their evaluations of others. Researchers generally agree that attention to evaluative components of performance may distract an individual from pursuing the goals of mastering a task – i.e., it may undermine intrinsic motivation. This effect seems especially likely when there is a focus on social comparison. Failure relative to others on a task is more likely to imply lack of ability than is failure relative to one's personal standards or previous performance. Social comparison standards also tend to emphasize outcomes that are relatively stable. Thus, children who base their self-evaluations on social comparison may give up trying to achieve, after failure, whereas the logical response of children who base their self-evaluations on temporal comparison is to try harder. Indeed, there is considerable evidence that competition tends to undermine intrinsic motivation (Amabile & Hennessey, Chapter 4, this volume; Butler, 1989a; Nicholls, 1984). Developmental findings concerning the use of social comparison for general ability assessment, therefore, suggest that younger children would exhibit more intrinsic motivation, whereas older children would be more prone to learned helplessness. There is some support for both predictions (Butler, 1989a; Harter, 1981; Rholes, Blackwell, Jordan & Walters, 1980).

The Ruble and Flett (1988) findings, however, suggest that likely exceptions to this general trend are children with above-average ability. By the time they have reached conclusions about their competence, after the first few years of school, these children have the luxury of ignoring social comparison, at least relatively speaking. Recent findings by Boggiano and her colleagues (Boggiano et al., 1988) suggest a similar conclusion. In this study, the only children whose intrinsic motivation was not affected negatively by controlling conditions (e.g., "You should do well") were those with self-perceptions of high levels of competence.

Such observations take on added significance in light of the fact that school is central to children's self-esteem, just as jobs are to adults'. On the job, people tend to resolve various forms of stress, such as threats to self-esteem, by devaluing the job (Pearlin & Schooler, 1978). Anecdotal evidence suggests that these coping responses also may be representative of older schoolchildren. A friend recently told one of us that her early adolescent daughter was resisting going to school because, she said, the material covered in her classes was "trivial" and "meaningless." Unfortunately, such responses may be inevitable in all but the brightest or most self-confident children, in a context in which grades and other forms of social comparison evaluation are commonplace. Furthermore, the self-segregation of friends that occurs on the basis of performance level and attitudes (Levine, 1983; Miller & Suls, 1977) can result in cliques that reinforce anti-academic values.

A final caveat from a life-span perspective is in order. These conclusions are limited to *children's* evaluative behavior, yet competence assessments will affect such decisions as collegiate and vocational ambitions. These decisions, in turn, are critically related to future economic status, self-esteem, and choice of affiliates. Even in old age, people may base their living arrangements on their assessment of their ability to care for themselves.

In old age, when people must adapt to declines in some of their abilities, the bases used for competence assessment may profoundly affect their self-esteem. Poor performance, relative to previous performance in some areas, may be indicative of an irreversible trend. Thus it might be predicted that a shift away from temporal evaluation would occur in the interest of protecting self-esteem (Frey & Ruble, 1990). For example, athletes who continue to compete past their prime may shift their reference from "personal best" to social comparison, perhaps with others in the seniors category or even with peers who do not compete at all. Such a shift might help explain why persons who have suffered serious physical impairments can report normal levels of well-being, yet indicate that their happiness has declined over time (Schultz & Decker, 1985).

In fact, the ability to shift reference points in the service of the ego may be, to some extent, a hallmark of healthy adaption during adulthood. Persons who view themselves with the cold eye of reality may lack the motivation necessary to continue their achievement efforts. This may be true particularly when efforts do not result in improvements over time. Thus, the basis used for competence assessment may have important implications for the maintenance of an active, involved life-style throughout the lifespan.

References

Aboud, F.E. (1985). Children's application of attribution principles to social comparisons. *Child Development, 56,* 682–688.

Alloy, L.B., & Abramson, L.Y. (1982). Learned helplessness, depression, and the illusion of control. *Journal of Personality and Social Psychology, 42,* 1114–1126.

Boggiano, A.K., Main, D.S., & Katz, P.A. (1988). Children's preference for challenge: The role of perceived competence and control. *Journal of Personality and Social Psychology, 54,* 134–141.

Boggiano, A.K., & Ruble, D.N. (1979). Perception of competence and the overjustification effect: A developmental study. *Journal of Personality and Social Psychology, 37,* 1462–1468.

Butler, R. (1989a). Interest in the task and interest in peer's work in competitive and non-competitive conditions: A developmental study. *Child Development, 53,* 1567–1577.

Butler, R. (1989b). Mastery vs. ability appraisal: A developmental study of children's observations of peer's work. *Child Development, 60,* 1350–1361.

Chafel, J. (1986). A naturalistic investigation of the use of social comparison by young children. *Journal of Research and Development in Education, 19,* 51–61.

Damon, W., & Hart, D. (1982). The development of self-understanding from infancy through adolescence. *Child Development, 53,* 841–864.

Deci, E.L., & Ryan, R.M. (1985). *Intrinsic motivation and self-determination in human behavior.* New York: Plenum.

Dweck, C.S. (1986). Motivational processes affecting learning. *American Psychologist, 41,* 1040–1048.

Dweck, C.S., & Elliott, E.S. (1983). Achievement motivation. In E.M. Hetherington (Ed.), *Handbook of child psychology: Vol. 4. Socialization, personality, and social development.* New York: Wiley.

Eccles, J., Midgley, C., & Adler, T.F. (1984). Age-related changes in the school environment: Effects on achievement motivation. In J.H. Nicholls (Ed.), *The development of achievement motivation.* Greenwich, CT: JAI press.

Festinger, L. (1954). A theory of social comparison processes. *Human Relations, 7,* 117–140.

Fincham, F.D., & Cain, K.M. (1986). Learned helplessness in humans: A developmental analysis. *Developmental Review, 6,* 301–333.

Frey, K.S., & Ruble, D.N. (1985). What children say when the teacher's not around: Conflicting goals in social comparison and performance assessment in the classroom. *Journal of Personality and Social Psychology, 48,* 18–30.

Frey, K.S. & Ruble, D.N. (1987). What children say about classroom performance: Sex and grade differences in perceived competence. *Child Development, 58,* 1066–1078.

Frey, K.S. & Ruble, D.N. (1990) Strategies for comparative evaluation: Maintaining a sense of competence across the lifespan. In R.J. Sternberg and J. Kolligian (Eds.), *Perceptions of competence and incompetence across the lifespan.* New Haven, CT: Yale University Press.

Grosovsky, E. (1985). Social comparison, self-evaluation, and peer-evaluation: A developmental analysis. Unpublished master's thesis, New York University.

Harter, D. (1981). A model of mastery motivation in children: Individual differences and developmental change. In A. Pick (Ed.), *Minnesota symposium on child psychology* (Vol. 14). Hillsdale, NJ: Erlbaum.

Harter, S., & Pike, R. (1984). The pictorial scale of perceived competence and social acceptance for young children. *Children Development, 55,* 1969–1982.

Higgins, E.T. (1981). Role taking and social judgment: Alternative developmental perspectives and processes. In J.H. Flavell and L. Ross (Eds.), *Social cognitive development.* New York: Cambridge.

Higgins, E.T., Strauman, T., & Klein, R. (1986). Standards and the process of self-evaluation. Multiple effects from multiple stages. In R.M. Sorrentino & E.T. Higgins (Eds.), *Handbook of motivation and cognition: Foundations of social behavior.* New York: Guilford Press.

Jones, E.E., & Nisbett, R.E. (1971). *The actor and the observer: Divergent perceptions of the causes of behavior.* Morristown, N.J.: General Learning Press.

Langer, E.J. (1979). The illusion of incompetence. In L.C. Perlmuter & R. A. Monty (Eds.), *Choice and perceived control.* Hillsdale, NJ: Erlbaum.

Latane, B. (Ed.) (1966). Studies in social comparison. *Journal of Experimental Social Psychology, Supplement* 1.

Levine, J.M. (1983). Social comparison and education. In N.M. Levine & M.C. Wang (Eds.), *Teacher and student perceptions: Implications for learning.* Hillsdale, NJ: Erlbaum.

Miller, R.L., and Suls, J.M. (1977). Affiliation preferences as a function of attitude and ability similarity. In J.M. Suls and R.L. Miller (Eds.), *Social comparison processes: Theoretical and empirical perspectives* (pp. 103–124). Washington, D.C.: Hemisphere.

Mosatche, H.S., & Bragonier, P. (1981). An observational study of social comparison in preschoolers. *Child Development, 52,* 376–378.

Nicholls, J.G. (1984). Conceptions of ability and achievement motivation. In R. Ames and C. Ames (Eds.), *Research on motivation in education* (Vol. 1, pp. 39–73). New York: Academic Press.

Nicholls, J.G., & Miller, A.T. (1984). Development and its discontents: The differentiation of the concept of ability. In J.G. Nicholls (Ed.), *The development of achievement motivation.* Greenwich, Ct.: JAI Press.

Odom, R.P., & Corbin, D.W. (1973). Perceptual salience and children's multidimensional problem solving. *Child Development, 44,* 425–432.

Parsons, J.E., & Ruble, D.N. (1977). The development of achievement-related expectancies. *Child Development, 48,* 1075–1079.

Pearlin, I., & Schooler, C. (1978). The structure of coping. *Journal of Health and Social Behavior, 19:* 2–21.

Phillips, D. (1984). The illusion of incompetence among academically competent children. *Child Development, 55,* 2000–2016.

Piaget, J. (1930). *The child's conception of physical causality.* London: Routledge & Kegan Paul, 1930.

Pryor, J.B., Rholes, W.S., Ruble, D.N., & Kriss, M. (1984). A developmental analysis of salience and discounting in social attribution. *Representative Research in Social Psychology, 14,* 30–48.

Rholes, W., Blackwell, J., Jordan, C., & Walters, C.A. (1980). A developmental study of learned helplessness. *Developmental Psychology, 16,* 616–624.

Rholes, W.S., & Ruble, D.N. (1984). Children's understanding of dispositional characteristics of others. *Child Development, 55,* 550–560.

Rotenberg, K.J. (1982). Development of character constancy of self and other. *Child Development, 53,* 505–515.

Ruble, D.N. (1983). The development of social comparison processes and their role in achievement-related self-socialization. In E.T. Higgins, D.N. Ruble, & W.W. Hartup (Eds.), *Social cognition and social development: A socio-cultural perspective.* New York: Cambridge University Press.

Ruble, D.N. (1987) The acquisition of self-knowledge: A self-socialization perspective. In N. Eisenberg (Ed.), *Contemporary topics in developmental psychology.* New York: Wiley.

Ruble, D.N., & Boggiano, A.K. (1980). Optimizing motivation in an achievement context. In B.K. Keogh (Ed.), *Advances in special education* (Vol. 1). Greenwich, CT: JAI Press.

Ruble, D.N., Boggiano, A.K., Feldman, N.S., & Loebl, J.H. (1980). A developmental analysis of the role of social comparison in self-evaluation. *Developmental Psychology, 16,* 105–115.

Ruble, D.N., Eisenberg, R., Feldman, N.S., & Higgins, E.T. (1992). Developmental changes in achievement evaluation: motivational implications of self-other differences. Manuscript submitted for publication.

Ruble, D.N., Feldman, N.S., & Higgins, E.T. (1986). Developmental changes in ability evaluation for self and others. Unpublished manuscript, New York University.

Ruble, D.N., & Flett, G.L. (1988). Conflicting goals in self-evaluative information seeking: Developmental and ability level analyses. *Child Development, 59,* 97–106.

Ruble, D.N. & Frey, K.S. (1991). Changing patterns of comparative behavior as skills are acquired: A functional model of self-evaluation. In J. Suls & T.A. Wills (Eds.), *Social comparison: Contemporary theory and research.* Hillsdale, N.J.: Lawrence Erlbaum Associates.

Ruble, D.N., Parsons, J.E., & Ross, J. (1976). Self-evaluative responses of children in an achievement setting. *Child Development, 47,* 990–997.

Ruble, D.N. & Rholes, W.S. (1981). The development of children's perceptions and attributions about their social world. In J.H. Harvey, W. Ickes, & R. Kidd (Eds.), *New directions in attribution research* (Vol. 3). Hillsdale, NJ: Erlbaum.

Schultz, R., & Decker, S. (1985). Long-term adjustment to physical disability: The role of social support, perceived control, and self-blame. *Journal of Personality & Social Psychology, 48:* 1162–1172.

Snyder, M.L., Stephan, W.G., & Rosenfield, D. (1978). Attributional egotism. In J.H. Harvey, W.J. Ickes, & R.F. Kidd (Eds.), *New directions in attribution research* (Vol. 2). Hillsdale, NJ: Erlbaum.

Stevens, L., & Jones, E.E. (1976). Defensive attribution and the Kelley cube. *Journal of Personality and Social Psychology, 34,* 809–820.

Stipek, D.J. (1984). Young children's performance expectations: Logical analysis or wishful thinking? In J. Nicholls (Ed.), *The development of achievement motivation* (pp. 33–56). Greenwich, CT: JAI Press.

Stipek, D., & Hoffman, J. (1980). Development of children's performance-related judgments. *Child Development, 51,* 912–914.

Stipek, D. & MacIver, D. (1989). Developmental change in children's assessment of intellectual competence. *Child Development, 60,* 521–538.

Stipek, D., Roberts, T., & Sanborn, M. (1984). Preschool-age children's performance expectations for themselves and another child as a function of the incentive value of success and the salience of past performance. *Child Development, 59,* 1983–1989.

Stipek, D., & Tannat, L. (1985). Children's judgments of their own and their peers' academic competence. *Journal of Educational Psychology, 76,* 75–85.

Suls, J.M. & Miller, R.L. (1977). *Social comparison processes: theoretical and empirical perspectives.* Washington, D.C.: Hemisphere.

Suls, J.M., & Mullen, B. (1982). From the cradle to the grave: Comparison and self-evaluation across the life-span. In J.M. Suls (Ed.), *Social psychological perspectives on the self* (Vol. 1, pp. 97–125). Hillsdale, N.J.: Erlbaum.

Suls, J.M., & Wills, T. (Eds.) (1991). *Social comparison: contemporary theory and research.* Hillsdale, NJ: Erlbaum.

Veroff, J. (1969). Social comparison and the development of achievement motivation. In C.P. Smith (Ed.), *Achievement-related motives in children.* New York: Russell Sage Foundation.

Watson, D. (1982). The actor and the observer: How are their perceptions of causality divergent? *Psychological Bulletin, 92,* 682–700.

Wigfield, A. (1988). Children's attributions for success and failure: Effects of age and attentional focus. *Journal of Educational Psychology, 80,* 76–81.

Part III

Motivation and achievement

The final group of chapters share achievement motivation as a primary theme. In addition, these chapters explicitly address the influences of extrinsic pressures on an individual's reaction to achievement-relevant settings.

In Chapter 8, Richard Ryan, James Connell, and Wendy Grolnick present a compelling theoretical analysis of achievement behavior that may *not* be intrinsically motivated. They propose three points on a continuum of extrinsically motivated self-regulation, which vary according to the degree of internalization of external standards. External regulation, in which extrinsic contingencies in the form of rewards and punishments control the child's behavior, involves the least amount of internalization. Introjected regulation, involving a greater degree of internalization, links performance to self-esteem and the approval of others. Identification occurs with higher levels of internalization; the formerly external value becomes part of the individual and is experienced as part of the self. Using this fruitful theoretical analysis, the development of these styles of self-regulation in elementary school students is examined. The authors describe an index of self-determination, and report their findings on teacher and parent influences on regulatory style, as well as findings on self-regulation in high school students.

In Chapter 9, Cheryl Flink, Ann Boggiano, Deborah Main, Marty Barrett, and Phyllis Katz investigate extrinsic and intrinsic motivation in achievement settings. The authors discuss factors that influence achievement in elementary school children, starting with an analysis of teachers' motivational strategies. Students of teachers who employ controlling strategies have been found to be more likely to adopt an extrinsic motivational set than students whose teachers employ strategies that encourage autonomy. The authors also found that as pressure on teachers increased, teachers were more likely to employ such controlling strategies, which in turn negatively impacted students' performance. The authors then explain how controlling strategies increase susceptibility to learned helplessness, as shown in several studies using different tasks. In addition, the nature of adults' and students' beliefs about the efficacy of controlling interventions is examined. The results of these latter studies clearly suggest the need for intervention programs focused on the erroneous beliefs held by adults and students about the effectiveness of teaching strategies that are controlling.

Achievement motivation takes center stage in Philip Costanzo's, Erik Woody's, and Pamela Slater's optimal-pressure model of achievement motivation (Chapter 10). The authors first review prior work on undermotivation (motivation that is too low for optimum performance), focusing on the roles of motives to achieve success and avoid failure, expectations of and values placed upon potential success, and expectations of and constructs associated with possible failure. They review in detail the controversial literature on undermotivation and achievement behavior in women. They then report on studies that have examined the effects of overmotivation (motivation too high for optimal performance), and discuss theoretical positions based on arousal, cognitive deficits, and distraction. The authors then integrate the findings on under- and overmotivation into a model of optimal pressure, and report the results of an experimental test of the model with high school students.

In the final paper (Chapter 11), Janet Riggs focuses on achievement motivation and undermotivation in a unique way. The chapter begins with a review of attributional models of achievement motivation. Making the point that individuals often may arrange to avoid self-threatening inferences from performance failures, she introduces the concept of self-handicapping (creating real or apparent external handicaps so that they, rather than personal shortcomings, may be blamed for poor performance). The experimental literature on self-handicapping is reviewed, and the author then analyzes the development of self-handicapping styles in adolescence and reports the results of two studies involving high school students. Given the concern over drug and alcohol abuse by young people, their potential as self-handicapping devices must be understood. The chapter concludes with a discussion of the central role played by concerns about one's competence image, as held by self and by others, and some thoughts on how the use of self-handicapping strategies might be minimized.

8 When achievement is *not* intrinsically motivated: A theory of internalization and self-regulation in school

Richard M. Ryan, James P. Connell, and Wendy S. Grolnick

Perhaps the central problem of all education is that of fostering students' motivation to learn. The question of motivation, however, can be viewed from two perspectives. From an "outer perspective" – that of the educator – it is a question of how to create conditions that facilitate learning, how to support, guide, inspire, and promote the learning process. But these issues can also be seen as derivative, insofar as they are attainable only through an understanding and appreciation of the "inner perspective" – what it is inside the learner that leads her to focus on something, take interest, and assimilate it. Learning is purposive activity, and motivational principles need to be guided by knowledge of what *regulates* the process, what governs or directs it.

"Back-to-basics" advocates and other educational conservatives have recently voiced their own answers to the question of how to motivate students to learn. In their "search for excellence" they are calling for more discipline, longer hours, fixed curricula, and higher external standards. They represent an age-old view that education is something produced from without, by firm contingencies or reinforcements and "no nonsense" approaches. The policies and practices that describe their outer perspective are well articulated – more authority and structure, more external direction, more salient rewards and constraints.

While this viewpoint is vocal and explicit with regard to what parents and teachers should do, it is usually silent with regard to the "inner perspective," or the students' experience of learning. Indeed, the "more discipline" advocates eschew discussion of experience and motivation. Nonetheless, their views of these matters are implicitly evident. They suggest that what regulates learning is the desire for rewards and the fear of punishment. From this view a child learns only if externally reinforced, or in order to stay out of trouble. The affective life and experience, by implication, alternates between satisfaction with reward attainment and fear of punishment or failure. It is hard to imagine a vision of children's inner life in school more opposed to our ordinary conception of ourselves and our motives, except under adverse conditions.

Nonetheless there is something compelling about the back-to-basics viewpoint. In an atmosphere with tight controls and strong, salient rewards, human experience does indeed become what we have just described. All of us probably had some experience in classrooms where our motivation consisted of just these factors – pressure to perform, balanced by fear of failure or of shame. The point is that given particular outer conditions and approaches to education, an inner world will eventually emerge which conforms to and matches it. That children *can* be regulated by external constraints and controls is without dispute. The question is whether this describes the atmosphere and goals of education to which we as educators, and as a culture, aspire.

An alternative perspective, more complex and subtle than the one just described, considers the motivation to learn to be a developmental issue. While learning can be wholly controlled and prompted from the outside (i.e., externally regulated), the goal of education is, from the alternative view, the development of *self-regulation* for learning. This is conceptualized as a movement away from heteronomy and toward autonomy in the acquisition of knowledge, away from reliance on others for the incentives to learn and toward internal satisfaction with accomplishment and the learning process itself. It is also seen as a movement away from external pressure and control, and toward an inner sense of the value of learning, its importance and centrality. Finally, it involves a movement away from tentativeness, insecurity, and dependence upon the environment for direction, and toward confidence and responsibility.

These terms, autonomy, value, responsibility, self-confidence, are *psychological* in nature; they have their referents in internal, experiential aspects of the person. A set of persistent, historical questions has involved whether such concepts can ever be adequately described and empirically studied, and whether effective principles for fostering them can be clearly articulated and applied. It is the purpose of the current chapter to describe an initial attempt to do just that: to explicate a theory of motivational regulation in schools; to describe attempts to empirically verify it; to offer evidence concerning what factors influence it; and to ground the discussion in more general theories of motivation and development.

Achievement and its motivations

The initial study of motivation in schools was concerned with the description and measurement of *achievement motivation.* The pioneers of this research defined achievement in quite general terms as all those activities in which an individual compares his or her performance with some standard of excellence (e.g., McClelland, Atkinson, Clark, & Lowell, 1953; Atkinson, 1964). Because comparisons of one's behavior with standards or goals is a ubiquitous aspect of human activity, the domain of achievement could encompass nearly all goal-related or purposive activity. However, most of the research on achievement has focused rather narrowly on school (for children) and work (for adults). McClelland (1961), for instance, focused nearly his entire volume entitled *The Achieving Society* on entrepreneurial and business activities. More recently, Dweck and Elliott (1983) in their review of the literature on the development of achievement motivation considered schools and education to the exclusion of all other domains. The choice of these content areas undoubtedly reflects the centrality of school and work in the cultural value system. However, that which is called "achievement" will vary considerably by culture, by gender, and by developmental level (Spence, 1985). In short, the content of achievement must be considered relativistically: it is relative vis-à-vis one's values, one's social comparison group, and one's capacities.

Equally varied are the motives subsumed under the all-too-singular term achievement motivation. Even cursory reflection upon achievement-related activities suggests that they can be incited or energized by quite different motives (Ryan, Connell, & Deci, 1985; Spence & Helmreich, 1983). For example, some individuals are motivated to achieve primarily by financial rewards or fame, others by needs for approval and self-esteem, and still others by intrinsic satisfactions such as inherent interest in the activity or opportunities for self-expression. Thus it appears important to distinguish between persons not only in the *level* or strength of their achievement motivation, but also in terms of the *orientation* of that energy (Ryan & Connell, 1989). Put differently, it is of great significance to understand not only how strongly people are motivated to achieve something, but also *why* they strive to succeed. Both the level and orientation of motivation are important determinants of performance, persistence, and experience vis-à-vis achievement-related action. However, the history of this literature reveals that a great deal of attention has been paid to the former issue, whereas the latter has only recently become a central focus.

In contrast, our own conceptualization of the motives to achieve and their development focuses primarily on the orientation of achievement-related motives rather than on the general level of achievement motivation per se (Ryan, Connell & Deci, 1985; Ryan & Connell, 1989). First we differentiate two broad classes of motives that energize achievement, each with its own identifiable subtypes, characteristics, and dynamics – namely, intrinsic and extrinsic motives.

We define *intrinsic motivation* as an innate, rather than derivative, propensity to explore and master one's internal and external worlds. It is manifest as curiosity and interest, which motivate task engagement even in the absence of outside reinforcement or support. Intrinsic motivation represents an organismic tendency that plays an important role in development by energizing the exercise and elaboration of one's capacities (Elkind, 1971; Ryan, 1991). It also plays a significant role in achievement, although not all achievements are intrinsically motivated.

Intrinsically motivated behavior is "autotelic" (Csikszentmihalyi, 1975), meaning that it is "done for its own sake," or for the satisfaction inherent in the process of activity. Nonetheless, at a more fundamental level one can relate intrinsic motivation to two basic or primary psychological needs, those for *autonomy* and for *competence* (Deci & Ryan, 1987; see also Chapter 1, this volume). Indeed, intrinsic motivation occurs primarily under conditions which afford autonomy and optimal challenge, and is itself an expression of the characteristic of organisms to actively pursue more independent and effective interactions with the world around them. While the needs for autonomy and competence in this sense underlie intrinsically motivated action, they can also play a role in energizing other classes of behavior, as we shall see.

Extrinsic motivation, on the other hand, pertains to activity that is more directly instrumental and adaptational, based upon people's needs to respond to socially prescribed demands, limits, and patterns of behavior. When extrinsically motivated, individuals behave *in order to* attain some external reward, avoid some threat, gain some recognition by another, or conform to some extant value. Thus while intrinsic motivation concerns activities energized by their inherent interest or challenge, extrinsic motives are oriented towards separable goals, rewards, or values that lie beyond the inherent satisfaction of the task or activity per se. A great deal of achievement-related activity is, accordingly, extrinsically motivated. It is non-intrinsically motivated achievement that is the primary focus of this chapter.

Even within the category of extrinsically motivated achievement, however, very distinct types of goals and motives can be observed. For example, a person can be extrinsically motivated to work at or learn something simply in order to gain an external reward or avoid punishment (Ryan & Stiller, 1991). Thus the extrinsic incentive or goal is something completely external to or removed from the person, and the initiation of and persistence at the activity is dependent upon the presence or absence of external contingencies; the activity is *externally regulated.*

But extrinsic motives can also be in evidence even when no external rewards are apparent. Take the case of a child who achieves in order to maintain a fragile sense of self-esteem, or to gain real or projected approval from parents or teachers. Here learning is not done wholly "for its own sake" as in intrinsic motivation, but neither is it done for tangible external rewards or contingencies. Instead the extrinsic incentives are internal to the child, that is, they involve intrapsychic dynamics which, although they may have been derived from external conditions, have some functional independence. We sometimes refer to such processes as *introjected regulation.* Finally there are many instances in which one accomplishes something or achieves a result because of its centrality to future goals or because it is personally valued. Many children and adults work hard not simply for intrinsic satisfaction, or even necessarily because of rewards or introjected contingencies. Rather they value work, and part of their identity involves engaging work fully and energetically. Such self-determined or choiceful behavior we refer to as *regulation by identification;* it has a less conflicted, more flexible character than the previous extrinsic styles we have described.

These three types of regulation – external, introjected, and identification – are all extrinsic by definition, in the sense that they represent the performance of an activity for reasons separable from its inherent satisfactions. But both the nature of the goals involved *and* the quality and dynamics of the regulation vary from type to type.

Reconceptualizing extrinsic motives: the continuum of internalization

One way in which the variation among the different types of extrinsic motivation can be described is through the concept of *internalization.* The concept is not a new one; indeed, it has enjoyed currency in psychological theory for over fifty years (Ryan, Chandler, Connell, & Deci, 1983). It is also a concept with important developmental and individual difference implications.

Internalization, as we view it, refers to the process by which an individual initially acquires beliefs, attitudes or behavioral regulations from external sources and progressively transforms these external regulations into personal attributes, values, or regulatory styles. Numerous authors have defined and described this process within various theoretical frameworks (e.g., English & English, 1958; Hartmann & Loewenstein, 1962; Schafer, 1968; Collins, 1977; Meissner, 1981). Most definitions emphasize a very active component to this process; internalization takes place only when individuals are motivated to take in, transform, and fully assimilate values or ways of behaving that were initially not their own. Internalization thus represents the active, internal pole of the dialectic between the organism and its social context, while the term *socialization* describes the external pole, that is, the activities through which the culture trains, teaches, and acculturates its members (Connell & Ryan, 1987; Ryan & Deci, 1985).

The domain of internalization concerns all those activities and regulations that are not spontaneously driven or intrinsically motivated. Thus there are many kinds of motivated actions to which internalization processes do not apply. One example is primitive drive-based behavior. Children will eat or excrete without any outside prompt or prod. Thus, the motives to eat or excrete need not be "taken in." The internalization process would be more pertinent to the acquisition of regulations modifying such natural functions. Neither does internalization concern most intrinsically motivated actions. Children rarely have to be taught or trained to explore novel objects, play, or engage optimal challenges with interesting tasks. They value such activity naturally (White, 1959; Deci & Ryan, 1985). Indeed, internalization more usually comes into play when caretakers attempt to curtail spontaneous or intrinsically motivated activities (Koestner, Ryan, Bernieri, & Holt, 1984).

Internalization, then, pertains to the development of internal regulations both for limiting or rechanneling "what comes naturally" and for doing new things that are not themselves either natural or intrinsically motivated. Thus, children may love to scream and shout, or get dirty, or avoid all sorts of onerous tasks, and it is only initially through external regulation that they may learn to do differently. *Internalization processes are thus relevant to all behavior and regulations whose occurrence initially depended upon extrinsic incentives.* The beginnings of internalization emerge from social contingencies, controls, and values.

Compliance with such social demands and regulations can be motivated by a number of needs and drives. One may initially comply in order to obtain drive-relevant gratifications or to avoid harm or pain. More usually compliance is based upon one's need to sustain love, esteem, and connectedness with others. All humans have a basic psychological need for *relatedness,* the social motive which has us concerned with and caring about what others look for in and from us (Ryan, 1991).

To know what motivates compliance does not, however, tell us what motivates the *process* of internalization, the taking in and making one's own of regulations and values that were originally merely externally imposed. We maintain that the process of internalization has its roots in three basic psychological needs, namely those for *autonomy, competence,* and *relatedness.* Autonomy is implicated in the fact that internalization represents a movement away from heteronomy or control by external forces, and toward self-determination in one's behavior. Competence needs are reflected in internalization because, generally speaking, more internalized forms of behavioral regulation are also more transferable, flexible, and effective than less internalized forms. Finally, our view suggests that relatedness needs are also involved in the process of internalization. To a great extent those behaviors which tend to be internalized are those that are important to significant others; those that when accepted tend to increase the integration of the individual into the social matrix; and those that involve the assimilation of values and functions that transcend individual gains or instrumentalities. In addition, relatedness with others is a vehicle for emulation, through which the behavior change of internalization can occur (Ryan, Stiller & Lynch, 1992). In sum, we believe that at the most basic level *the psychological process of internalization has its origins in the primary psychological needs of persons to be autonomous and competent in the context of relatedness to others.* This is, of course, merely a metapsychological assumption, one that primarily serves to organize hypotheses and which itself awaits empirical confirmation. Nonetheless it provides a framework for the study of the motives supporting internalization across the life span, and within various domains.

Internalization and achievement in schools

Given that internalization processes are relevant to the regulation of all those behaviors that are not natural or intrinsically motivated, it is clear that such processes will play an important role in school adjustment and achievement. First of all, while learning in children is often intrinsically motivated in the natural context (White, 1959; Danner & Lonky, 1981), much of what children are asked to do and learn in school is not intrinsically motivating. Evidence for this has been provided in several studies which suggest that there may be a progressive *decrease* in intrinsic motivation for classwork in the average child as he or she advances through school (Harter, 1981; Resnick & Robinson, 1975).

Two major factors can be hypothesized to account for this trend. First it may be that schools are increasingly "controlling" and therefore undermine intrinsic motivation in students, or fail to provide optimal challenges. A number of studies have shown that controlling classroom climates and/or non-optimal challenges can be deleterious to intrinsic motivation (Deci, Schwartz, Sheinman, & Ryan, 1981; Ryan & Grolnick, 1986; Deci & Ryan, Chapter 2 of this volume). A second hypothesis is that as children advance through school the agenda of education, both with regard to its cognitive tasks and its behavioral requirements, is inherently less interesting than other activities in the child's life. Schools are, after all, the primary agency of socialization outside the nuclear family, and much of the socialization process involves the conveying of information and ways of acting that are initially neither natural nor interesting. Put more simply, schools often serve the function of teaching not only *what interests the child* but also that which is felt to be *in the child's interest.* Some of that which is deemed to be in the interest of the child to learn will require extrinsic support if it is to be attended to and acquired. Motivational theories must address the question of how children adapt to and cope with these social demands, and more importantly how they can develop the capacity to be *self-regulated* with respect to them and eventually to assimilate such regulations into their own values and goals.

Self-regulation in elementary school children

Ryan and Connell (1989) distinguished between several styles of self-regulation that were evident in elementary school children, and they conceptualized these as lying along a continuum of internalization. At the lowest end of the internalization continuum was *external regulation,* in which a child is motivated to perform a prescribed behavior or inhibit a forbidden one primarily on the basis of extrinsic contingencies such as reward or punishment. A somewhat greater degree of internalization was described as *introjected regulation,* in which children perceive self-esteem and the approval of others to be linked to their performance and behavior. Thus they might, for example, do homework or try hard in school not solely for rewards, or because it is seen as inherently valuable, but because they might feel "bad," anxious, or guilty if they did not. In introjected regulation the external regulation has been "taken in" in the form of intrapsychic, self-approval based contingencies. A third internalized form of regulation was defined as regulation through *identification,* which represented a further progression along the internalization continuum. Identification with a behavioral regulation is evidenced whenever the child experiences action as initiated out of his or her own values or choice. Thus a child who has identified with achievement-related values works, in school and out, because of a personal sense of the importance of learning. Here the regulation of behavior is characterized by greater autonomy and self-valuing. The child has internalized what were formerly external regulations and values, and now experiences them as his or her own. Finally, Ryan and Connell argued that internalization can proceed further, through the increasing *integration* of separate identifications into a flexible, coherent hierarchical system of motives and values. However, because of the developmentally advanced nature of integration, it was not a focus of inquiry at the elementary school level.

To empirically investigate the process of internalization Ryan and Connell developed a technique which assesses students' *reasons* for engaging in various school-related behaviors. Children rate various answers to the question of "why do you do X," where X is a behavior that is central to the achievement domain. Although the endorsement of reasons for behaving reflects only those forces and motives which are conscious and salient to the child for engaging in a behavior, it was felt that such responses might capture important phenomenal components of the self-regulatory process. For example, a child who rates highly the response that he does his homework "because I'll get in trouble if I don't" or "because that's what I'm supposed to do" can be assumed to experience external others (parents and teachers) as prime movers of homework behavior. An external regulatory orientation is thus evidenced. Introjected regulation would be indexed by reasons such as "I'd feel bad about myself if I didn't" or "so the teacher will think I'm a good student." Identified regulation is represented by reasons such as "I want to understand the subject" or "it's important to me to do well." Intrinsic reasons, such as doing schoolwork for enjoyment or "because it's fun," are also included. These reason categories were designed to tap *orientations* toward (rather than *levels* of) academic motivation, and such orientations are referred to as *self-regulatory styles*.

Correlates of self-regulatory style in elementary school

We have examined motivational orientations in both elementary and high school children in urban, suburban, and rural school systems, along with a number of other relevant measures of school achievement and adjustment, including teacher ratings, standardized test scores, and student self-evaluations. The network of findings that has emerged suggests that each of the assessed self-regulatory styles is associated with theoretically coherent attitudes, beliefs, coping styles, and self-related processes. We will briefly describe this construct network, which attests to the significance of motivational styles for children's school experiences and performance.

External regulatory style

Children whose school-related activity is primarily externally regulated depend upon teachers and parents for their motivation. They do their schoolwork in order to stay out of trouble, avoid punishment, or because of salient externally imposed constraints. Not surprisingly, children who are highly externally regulated, as assessed by the SRQ, are rated by parents and teachers as less independent and motivated, and are described as requiring more outside attention, pressure, and prodding to do their work. Reciprocally these same children perceive the classroom environment to be more pawnlike (deCharms, 1976) or controlling, and they see their mothers as less involved and autonomy-supportive (Grolnick, Ryan, & Deci, 1990). They are more likely to see the control over outcomes in school to be in the hands of "powerful others" or to be "unknown" (Connell, 1985). Similarly they tend to see themselves as less autonomous, less mastery-motivated (Harter, 1982), and as having less internal control over outcomes.

Evidence thus far suggests that external regulatory styles are associated with more defensive styles of coping with setbacks in school (Skinner, in press). In particular, external regulation is associated with projection, in which blame for failure is externalized, and denial, in which the significance of failure is minimized or avoided (Tero & Connell, 1983). Despite the fact that external regulators have not internalized the values of achievement, they do worry about outcomes in school, as reflected by measures of cognitive anxiety (Buhrmester, 1980). They have also evidenced, in most of our samples, a significantly lower sense of academic or cognitive competence. Even more noteworthy is the negative association between external regulation and self-report measures of general self-confidence and self-worth (e.g., Harter, 1982). Children who tend to be externally regulated are correspondingly seen by teachers as having lower confidence and self-esteem. We would argue that, because these children do not see their behavior in school as choiceful or do not experience internal responsibility for their actions, they can derive no true sense of worth or esteem from their experiences in school.

Of the four styles of self-regulation assessed by the SRQ, external is most frequently associated with poor achievement and learning difficulties, although typically not with intelligence. It appears that, independent of intellectual factors, external regulation results in poorer performance in school (Grolnick & Ryan, 1987; Grolnick, Ryan & Deci, 1991). It is also likely that children with learning problems experience more pressure from others, which in turn promotes an external regulatory style. Teachers report an excess of learning difficulties and acting-out behaviors among high external regulators relative to the other assessed styles. In sum, it appears that an external regulatory style is a central feature in children who are alienated and discouraged in school, those "at risk" for a variety of adjustment and academic difficulties.

Introjected regulatory styles

The concept of introjection has been used in various theoretical contexts, often with varied meanings (Meissner, 1981). Nonetheless it invariably connotes (a) a relatively non-integrated but "internal" form of a previously external regulation, and (b) a dynamic pattern wherein self-esteem or sense of worth is hinged upon particular outcomes. The concept of non-integration implies that the regulatory principle or value has not been fully assimilated or strongly competes with other (often unrecognized) needs of the person. However, the regulation is dynamically supported by the contingent self-worth and perceived approval of others.

Introjection is an "internalized" regulatory style. In behavioral terms it represents one form of *self-control.* The person regulates him or herself, but the motivators or goals are the avoidance of negative self-evaluative experiences, or the attainment of self- and other-approval and feelings of worth. Introjection can vary in its valence (positive to negative) and its strength, but it involves some degree of pressure and conflict. It can also be related to the concept of "ego involvement" (Nicholls, 1984; Ryan, 1982; Plant & Ryan, 1985; Koestner, Zuckerman, & Koestner, 1987) in which one is motivated to demonstrate ability in order to attain self-enhancing feedback, or to avoid self-disparagement.

Introjection is thus characterized by a focus upon doing one's schoolwork for approval or to avoid negative self-related feelings. Our empirical evidence has indicated that it is associated with a coping style referred to as anxiety amplification (Tero & Connell, 1983), in which failure may be responded to with further self-disparagement and worry. Self-esteem generally has been uncorrelated with the degree of introjected regulation, but is rather expected to strongly fluctuate on the basis of social comparisons and visible outcomes.

Introjected regulatory style is also uncorrelated with teacher and parent ratings of independence or motivation. Similarly, in elementary school children's self-reports, introjection is unrelated to perceived autonomy or mastery motivation. It thus appears to be midway between external regulation, which is negatively associated with these variables, and identification, in which autonomy is more in evidence. Introjected regulation is, however, related to perceived internal control over outcomes in school. This reflects the fact that children who regulate themselves through introjection have internalized the responsibility for performance. They also, however, tend to be anxious with respect to that performance, as indexed by cognitive anxiety measures.

In sum, our evidence suggests that introjection represents one form of internalized regulation of behavior, in which the child is not solely dependent on the environment for the impetus to behave, but also is not autonomous or independent. Self-worth is variable and dependent on whether specific standards have been met, and there is strong evidence of anxiety as a primary "enforcer" of the behavioral regulation that occurs.

Identification and regulation

An important goal of development in school is coming to accept and to value the process of learning and to accept personal responsibility for it. Children who have identified with the goals of achievement evidence this by doing homework or schoolwork "because they want to understand better" or because it feels personally important. Children who endorse such reasons for working also perceive themselves to be highly mastery motivated (Harter, 1982) and autonomous (deCharms, 1976) in school. Teacher and parent ratings corroborate this. These children are rated as more motivated, independent, and in need of less outside pressure to work. In turn, these children perceive their teachers and parents as more autonomy oriented and supportive, rather than controlling.

Highly "identified" forms of self-regulation are associated with positive self-evaluation as well. These children report higher perceived cognitive competence and generally higher self-esteem. They report more confidence (Lorion, Cowen, & Caldwell, 1975) and less anxiety (Buhrmester, 1980) than those who rely more on external or introjected regulation. Furthermore, identified regulators are more likely to "positively cope" after failure (Tero & Connell, 1983). That is, they rebound after failure by seeking ways to "do better next time."

There is also a strong positive correlation between identification as a style of regulation in school and intrinsic motivation in school. Both of these motivational orientations are relatively highly self-determined or autonomous. It is plausible that a child who values school, and is in turn not reciprocally overcontrolled or pressured by parents and teachers, will experience less salient external constraints and accordingly be more intrinsically motivated when conditions allow.

Relative autonomy index

Having conceptualized self-regulatory styles as lying along a continuum from less to more internalization of originally externally regulated behaviors, Ryan and Connell (1989) proposed a structural pattern, called a "simplex model" (Guttman, 1954), that should fit the data. In a simplex model, adjacent levels should be more highly correlated with one another than those that are non-adjacent. Because we conceive of external regulation as "adjacent" to introjection, these orientations should evidence a greater intercorrelation than, for example, external regulation and identification. Surveys assessing motivational orientations have been shown to have a simplex-like structure in multiple independent samples drawn from urban, suburban, and rural schools representing a wide range of socioeconomic backgrounds.

A simplex model suggests that the constructs within it can be meaningfully organized along a single dimension or parameter. In our theory, the underlying dimension is one of relative autonomy or perceived locus of causality (deCharms, 1968). As something becomes internalized, it is characterized by greater autonomy, and it is perceived as being "caused" or endorsed by the self (Ryan, in press). Intrinsic motivation, which is paradigmatically self-determined, can therefore be related to the simplex model of internalization. It will be "adjacent" to identification, lying at the outer extreme of the matrix, although this does not suggest that internalized regulation can eventually become intrinsic motivation. Rather, it indicates that all types of motivated behavior, whether intrinsically motivated or extrinsically motivated, can be evaluated for their degree of autonomy.

The continuum of autonomy underlying this assessment framework has many implications. It "fits" with a developmental conceptualization – that is, that there is a developmental tendency toward greater internalization – but it does not in any way confirm it. More importantly, it represents a significant individual difference dimension of the degree of self-determination in behavioral regulation in school.

In some studies, we have obtained a "relative autonomy" index by weighting the various reason categories previously described. This index has shown important relationships with a wide range of constructs (see also Vallerand & Bissonnette, in press, for a similar model). For example, in elementary school samples, more autonomously oriented students have higher self-esteem, higher perceived cognitive competence, and are less projective in coping with perceived failure. Such children are seen by parents and teachers as more motivated and independent in school, and they themselves experience more autonomy and freedom. They also experience more internal control and less anxiety with respect to academic pursuits.

Connell and Wellborn (1990) reported several studies relating relative autonomy to student engagement and achievement outcomes. Across several diverse samples, they identified a path model in which students higher in relative autonomy were more engaged in school, and in turn obtained better grades and achievement test scores. Furthermore, they showed significant differences in relative autonomy between urban students labeled "at risk" for becoming school dropouts and a non-labeled comparison group.

Grolnick and Ryan (1987) explored the significance of individual differences in students' relative autonomy in an experimental study of children's learning. They asked children to read passages containing grade-level social studies material under various conditions, including doing it for a grade (extrinsic), doing it for challenge (intrinsic), or doing it without any specific direction to learn (nondirected). Children were then tested for their learning, and were followed up later to assess their long-term retention of the material. Across conditions, long-term retention of material was predicted by the degree to which children were more versus less autonomous. Children who were stylistically more autonomous in school were more likely to integrate material into long-term memory. Especially striking was the relationship between autonomy and learning within the nondirected condition. Here, in the absence of external supports or regulations for learning, individual differences in relative autonomy strongly predicted retention of material. Such results suggest that the less salient the external controls, the more crucial are internalized ones.

Teacher and parent influences on self-regulation

Thus far we have suggested that motivational orientations or regulatory styles with respect to school behavior can be meaningfully conceptualized along a continuum of self-determination. The more internalized and integrated the regulation of behavior, the more the student will experience autonomy, confidence, and flexibility, and the more others will experience the student as independent and self-motivated. There is also evidence which suggests that the quality of learning and adjustment is enhanced when the behavioral regulation is more self-determined. Together these results suggest that an appropriate goal of education would be the promotion of more internalized and self-determined regulatory styles (Ryan & Connell, 1989; Krathwohl, Bloom, & Masia, 1974).

Elsewhere (e.g., Deci & Ryan, 1985; Ryan & Deci, 1985; Ryan, Connell, & Deci, 1985) we have argued that the internalization and integration of regulations is a natural developmental process. This means that under appropriate conditions persons will move toward greater autonomy and competence in their regulation of action, as well as toward more socially integrated and responsible forms of action. Indeed, we see the process of internalization (though not its content) as intrinsically motivated, "for its own sake," without outside prod or prompt. This metapsychological assumption is heuristically valuable because it allows us to detail aspects of the environment which should either optimize or forestall the integrative process underlying progressive internalization.

We hypothesize that there are three dimensions of interpersonal environments which can directly influence internalization processes. First and foremost is the degree of *autonomy* afforded to the child. A regulation that is originally externally imposed will come to be one's own only under conditions of minimal control. Surplus pressures or controls create conflict with the psychological need for self-determination, making it less likely that the person will be motivated to actively assimilate the regulation. Put differently, external regulators must gradually give over control and responsibility to the child if self-regulation is to occur. Support for growing autonomy is thus the primary agar of self-regulation.

However, while stressing the importance of providing autonomy, we do not wish to imply that children will automatically internalize regulations if left on their own. Rather, the environment must support the child's autonomy by providing a context which includes both *structure* and positive *involvement.* For internalization to occur, the meaning and value of regulations must be conveyed. We refer to this aspect of environments as the provision of structure. Structure thus includes providing information regarding social expectations, why they are important, and delineating the consequences of meeting or not meeting these expectations. Both autonomy and structure will be most conducive to internalization, however, if provided in the context of warm, responsive, and involved significant others. When a child feels a sense of relatedness to and regard for significant others he or she will be most likely to identify with values or rules imposed by them and thus to internalize the regulations they communicate. Furthermore, it is through relations with others that common cultural elements are *shared,* and accordingly affectively integrated into personality (Parsons, 1952; Ryan, 1991).

We suggest that these three aspects of interpersonal environments – support of autonomy, involvement, and structure – influence internalization processes primarily because they are tied to the three psychological needs discussed earlier, namely the needs for autonomy, competence, and relatedness. It follows then that conditions which support these needs by affording autonomy, providing adequate structure, and maintaining a high level of positive involvement are those that are conducive to taking in external regulations and assimilating them as one's own. When, on the other hand, the environment affords little of these nutriments, or potentiates conflict between the various needs, identification and integration will be forestalled.

The correlational findings that have emerged from studies of self-regulatory style offer support for, but not confirmation of, the "autonomy hypothesis," namely that autonomy-supportive contexts facilitate the internalization and integration of regulation in the academic domain. We noted, for example, that elementary school children who experience their teachers and parents as more autonomy-oriented with respect to school-related behaviors were also more likely to evidence more self-determined regulatory styles. Nonetheless these correlations could reflect that those children who are more independent and self-determined in their regulation are actually given more freedom (Ryan & Grolnick, 1986) and/or that the experience of the environment as supportive of autonomy *is an aspect of* more self-determined regulation.

Grolnick and Ryan, in a recent series of studies in a rural school system, more directly assessed teacher and parent attitudes and behavior and related them to children's self-regulatory styles. As one aspect of their research they performed a short-term longitudinal analysis of changes in children's regulatory styles between the first days of the school year (September) and approximately five months later (February). These changes were related to teacher attitudes toward autonomy versus control as assessed by a measure developed by Deci, Schwartz, Sheinman, and Ryan (1981). Autonomy-oriented teachers, as measured by this questionnaire, are those who provide support for children's solving their own problems in the context of a warm, structured atmosphere. It was found that children who were in classrooms of more autonomy-oriented teachers increased in their identification with the value and importance of achievement-related behaviors between the two assessments, relative to children in classrooms of more controlling teachers. Furthermore, within-classroom analyses suggested that those students who, by teacher report, were allowed to take more responsibility and who were less externally pressured, were likely to report more self-determined forms of regulation at the second assessment.

In another part of this project (Grolnick & Ryan, 1989) mothers and fathers of fifty children in grades three through six were separately interviewed by trained raters. The focus of this structured interview was the assessment of the aforementioned three dimensions of parenting behavior: autonomy versus control, involvement, and provision of structure. For both mothers and fathers the autonomy dimension was strongly related to the students' self-reported relative autonomy on the self-regulation questionnaire. Parents who valued autonomy, used less controlling techniques for motivating their children, and encouraged more independence in their children had children with more self-determined styles of regulation in school. Furthermore, more autonomy-oriented parents had children who by elementary school teacher report were less likely to act out in school, and less likely to have learning difficulties. In addition, there were interactive effects of the three dimensions for both mothers and fathers. For example, mothers who were rated as low on autonomy and structure had children with the least autonomous styles of regulation. Similarly, children of fathers high on autonomy and structure were the most self-determined.

Grolnick, Ryan, and Deci (1990) recently extended this model by examining children's perceptions of their parents' autonomy support and involvement. They developed a survey which separately assesses perceived autonomy support and involvement in mothers and fathers and related it to measures of motivation and achievement. It was found that autonomy support and involvement dimensions of parent style were directly related to increases in perceived competence, control understanding, and relative autonomy. In turn, these three "inner resources" were predictive of both standardized and teacher-rated achievement indices.

It thus appears from our preliminary evidence that both teachers and parents have a significant impact upon the development of self-regulatory capacities and adjustment in school primarily through the process of support of autonomy. This returns us to the idea that self-regulation is a developmental achievement that can be either facilitated or forestalled by the interpersonal environment. We suggest that conditions which are conducive to self-regulation – i.e., the child's acquisition of volition with respect to learning and performance – represent an important area for further study.

Internalization, development, and social context

We have suggested that there is a natural developmental process through which children will tend to assimilate extant cultural conventions and values and eventually make them their own. Further, it appears that internalization is most likely to proceed when (a) the environment affords the maximal possible autonomy and adequate involvement and structure, and (b) there exists social support for the process and involvement from significant others, so that relatedness needs can simultaneously be met.

Having specified some of the environmental conditions which can facilitate or undermine the processes of internalization, several points need to be clarified. The first concerns the significance for internalization of the child's developmental level. We assume that a regulation cannot be assimilated until the actions and meaning it entails are within the structural capacities of the child. Thus, we suggest that there is an optimally challenging developmental period for any given regulation, such that there is a match between the regulatory demand and the child's capability to understand and carry out the actions it entails. Efforts to socialize a child too early, for example, will generate excessive conflict and anxiety.

Second, we do not maintain that all behavioral regulations are capable of being fully internalized. Those regulations that conflict with basic needs, drives, or tendencies will necessarily create conflict and add resistance to the processes of internalization and integration. For example, one could not expect a child to fully internalize such regulations as: to be uniformly emotionally controlled; to always sit still and "pay attention"; or to forgo exploratory tendencies and curiosity when in school. Such rules or conventions, and others that are organismically incongruous or which inevitably conflict with significant psychological needs of the individual, will never become fully self-determined. At best they can be "introjected," and conflictually or inflexibly effected by the person. This further suggests that people are not infinitely malleable, as for example social learning theorists might hold. Indeed, the limits to human malleability might be studied by looking precisely at those regulations which do not (i.e., *can*not) become fully assimilated even under optimal conditions. We might even learn something about human "nature" by systematically examining these limits.

Finally, even where regulations are potentially integratable or fitting, they will be actively assimilated only under conditions which provide autonomy. One cannot force responsibility and self-regulation; it, by definition, must be volitional. Thus one will not promote the self-regulation of achievement merely by "more discipline" or control, but rather by making the learning process challenging and personally relevant to the student. The latter is of course more difficult to design and effect than the former. But it does suggest that school environments must be capable of shifting the ratio of freedom and control in response to the capacity for self-regulation of the student. By gradually being allowed more responsibility, the student may over time grow to take more responsibility. On the other hand, if students are not allowed more responsibility and freedom to exercise their capacities, the growth of self-regulation predictably will stagnate.

Most recently we have been examining the model of internalization described herein in nonacademic domains. Our preliminary evidence suggests that within areas as distinct as prosocial behavior, religious motivation, and health care, our general model has application (e.g., Avery & Ryan, 1988; Ryan & Connell, 1989; Ryan, Rigby & King, 1992). That is, contextual support of autonomy, positive relatedness, optimal challenge, and structure facilitate internalization processes, and at the same time engage the person's own inherent tendencies toward autonomy, relatedness, and competence. It is of course a general model of internalization toward which motivation theory must increasingly direct itself.

Summary

Motivation in school is a central problem of all education. Students can be motivated in many ways, and it is important to distinguish not only *how* motivated someone is (level) but also *why* one is motivated (orientation). One major distinction is between intrinsic and extrinsic motives. Moreover, even within the category of extrinsic motivation one can distinguish between externally regulated motives and more autonomous ones.

We have accordingly distinguished among four different orientations in children's school-related motives – namely, external regulation, introjected regulation, identified regulation, and intrinsic regulation. Each of these is associated with different incentives and experiences in the process of learning. Ryan and Connell (1989) assessed motivational orientations through children's *reasons* for performing achievement-type activities. Results supported the view that the orientation of motivation in school can markedly affect the quality of experience, learning, and adjustment of children and young adults within the academic domain.

Underlying the various motivational orientations is a dimension of autonomy. That is, the regulation of school-related behavior can be conceptualized as lying along a continuum from externally controlled to fully self-regulated. The dimension of autonomy also reflects a continuum of valuing, such that the more autonomous the regulation the more personal and integrated it is. Valuing is both an individual difference and a developmental process.

We have argued that motivational development proceeds away from heteronomy in regulation and toward autonomy under appropriate conditions. Those conditions include the provision of (a) autonomy, or the minimizing of external control, (b) adequate structure and information, (c) a context of warm, positive involvement on the part of socializers. Our research has specifically shown how both parents' and teachers' support for children's autonomy can enhance their self-regulatory capacities. This means that children can grow toward self-regulation if the environment gives over responsibility in accord with developmental capacity and makes non-arbitrary, potentially meaningful demands. In school this means the affordance of reasonable autonomy in learning by both parents and teachers, optimally challenging tasks and behavioral demands, and information regarding the relevance and meaningfulness of that which is required.

Research on the development of individual differences in self-regulation is still in its infancy, and its importance undoubtedly extends well beyond the academic domain. Nonetheless, schools are perhaps the most important socializing agency outside the family, and thus are fertile ground for the psychological exploration of the dialectic between the organismic, psychological needs for autonomy, competence, and relatedness on the one hand, and various cultural structures and demands on the other. Indeed, it is this dialectic more generally that defines the emerging field of social-developmental psychology.

References

Atkinson, J.W. (1964). *An introduction to motivation.* Princeton, NJ: Van Nostrand.

Avery, R.R., & Ryan, R.M. (1988). Object relations and ego development: Comparison and correlates in middle childhood. *Journal of Personality, 56,* 547–569.

Buhrmester, D. (1980). *The children's concern inventory.* Unpublished manuscript, University of Denver.

Collins, B.E. (1977). *Internalization: Towards a micro-social psychology of socialization or enduring behavior control.* Unpublished manuscript, University of California, Los Angeles.

Connell, J.P. (1985). A new multidimensional measure of children's perceptions of control. *Child Development, 56,* 1018–1041.

Connell, J.P., & Ryan, R.M. (1987). Development within the context of schools. *International Society for the Study of Behavioral Development Newsletter,* no. 2, serial, no. 12, 1–3.

Connell, J.P., & Wellborn, J.G. (1990). Competence, autonomy, and relatedness: A motivational analysis of self-system processes. In M. Gunnar & A. Sroufe (Eds.), *Minnesota symposium on child psychology: Vol. 22. Self processes in development* (pp. 43–77). Minneapolis: University of Minnesota.

Csikszentmihalyi, M. (1975). *Beyond boredom and anxiety.* San Francisco: Jossey-Bass.

Danner, F.W., & Lonky, E. (1981). A cognitive-developmental approach to the effects of rewards on intrinsic motivation. *Child Development, 52,* 1043–1052.

deCharms, R. (1968). *Personal causation: The internal affective determinants of behavior.* New York: Academic Press.

deCharms, R. (1976). *Enhancing motivation: Change in the classroom.* New York: Irvington.

Deci, E.L., & Ryan, R.M. (1985). *Intrinsic motivation and self-determination in human behavior.* New York: Plenum.

Deci, E.L., & Ryan, R.M. (1987). The support of autonomy and the control of behavior. *Journal of Personality and Social Psychology, 53,* 1024–1037.

Deci, E.L., Schwartz, A.J., Sheinman, L., & Ryan, R.M. (1981). An instrument to assess adults' orientations toward control versus autonomy with children: Reflections on intrinsic motivation and perceived competence. *Journal of Educational Psychology, 73,* 642–650.

Dweck, C.S., & Elliott, E.S. (1983). Achievement motivation. In P.H. Mussen (Ed.), *Handbook of child psychology* (Vol. 4, pp. 643–691). New York: Wiley.

Elkind, D. (1971). Cognitive growth cycles in mental development. In J.K. Cole (Ed.), *Nebraska symposium on motivation* (Vol. 19, pp. 1–31). Lincoln, NE: University of Nebraska Press.

English, H., & English, A.C. (1958). *A comprehensive dictionary of psychological and psychoanalytic terms.* New York: David McKay.

Grolnick, W.S., & Ryan, R.M. (1987). Autonomy in children's learning: An experimental and individual differences investigation. *Journal of Personality and Social Psychology, 52,* 890–898.

Grolnick, W.S., & Ryan, R.M. (1989). Parent styles associated with children's self-regulation and competence in school. *Journal of Educational Psychology, 81,* 143–154.

Grolnick, W.S., Ryan, R.M., & Deci, E.L. (1991). The inner resources for school achievement: Motivational mediators of children's perceptions of their parents. *Journal of Educational Psychology, 83,* 508–517.

Guttman, L. (1954). A new approach to factor analysis: The radex. In P. Lazarfeld (Ed.), *Mathematical thinking in the social sciences* (pp. 258–348). Glencoe, IL: Free Press.

Harter, S. (1981). A new self-report scale of intrinsic versus extrinsic orientation in the classroom: Motivational and informational components. *Developmental Psychology, 17,* 300–312.

Harter, S. (1982). The perceived competence scale for children. *Child Development, 53,* 87–97.

Hartmann, H., & Loewenstein, R.M. (1962). Notes on the superego. *The Psychoanalytic Study of the Child, 17,* 42–81.

Koestner, R., Ryan, R.M., Bernieri, F., & Holt, K. (1984). Setting limits in children's behavior: The differential effects of controlling versus informational styles on intrinsic motivation and creativity. *Journal of Personality, 52,* 233–248.

Koestner, R., Zuckerman, M., & Koestner, J. (1987). Praise, involvement and intrinsic motivation. *Journal of Personality and Social Psychology, 53,* 383–390.

Krathwohl, D.R., Bloom, B.S., & Masia, B.B. (1974). *Taxonomy of educational objectives, handbook II: Affective domain.* New York: David McKay.

Lorion, R.P., Cowen, E.L., & Caldwell, R.A. (1975). Normative and parametric analyses of school maladjustment. *American Journal of Community Psychology, 3,* 291–301.

McClelland, D.C. (1961). *The achieving society.* Princeton, NJ: Van Nostrand.

McClelland, D.C., Atkinson, J.W., Clark, R.A., & Lowell, E.L. (1953). *The achievement motive.* New York: Appleton-Century-Crofts.

Meissner, W.W. (1981). *Internalization in psychoanalysis.* New York: International Universities Press.

Nicholls, J.G. (1984). Achievement motivation: Conceptions of ability, subjective experience, task choice, and performance. *Psychological Review, 91,* 328–346.

Parsons, T. (1952). The superego and the theory of social systems. *Psychiatry, 15,* 15–25.

Plant, R. & Ryan, R.M. (1985). Intrinsic motivation and the effects of self-consciousness, self-awareness, and ego-involvement: An investigation of internally controlling styles. *Journal of Personality, 53,* 435–449.

Resnick, L.B., & Robinson, B.M. (1975). Motivational aspects of the literacy problem. In J.B. Carroll & J.S. Chall (Eds.), *Toward a literate society.* New York: McGraw-Hill.

Ryan, R.M. (1982). Control and information in the intrapersonal sphere: An extension of cognitive evaluation theory. *Journal of Personality and Social Psychology, 43,* 450–461.

Ryan, R.M. (1991). The nature of the self in autonomy and relatedness. In J. Strauss & G.R. Goethals (Eds.), *The self: Interdisciplinary approaches.* New York: Springer-Verlag, pp. 208–238.

Ryan, R.M., Chandler, C., Connell, J.P., & Deci, E.L. (1983). Internalization and motivation: Some preliminary research and theoretical speculation. Paper presented at the Society for Research in Child Development, Detroit, MI.

Ryan, R.M., & Connell, J.P. (1989). Perceived locus of causality and internalization: Examining reasons for acting in two domains. *Journal of Personality and Social Psychology, 57,* 749–761.

Ryan, R.M., Connell, J.P., & Deci, E.L. (1985). A motivational analysis of self-determination and self-regulation in education. In C. Ames & R.E. Ames (Eds.), *Research on motivation in education: The classroom milieu* (pp. 13–51). New York: Academic Press.

Ryan, R.M., & Deci, E.L. (1985). The "third selective paradigm" and the role of human motivation in cultural and biological selection: A response to Csikzentmihalyi and Massimini. *New Ideas, 3,* 259–264.

Ryan, R.M., & Grolnick, W.S. (1986). Origins and pawns in the classroom: Self-report and projective assessments of individual differences in children's perceptions. *Journal of Personality and Social Psychology, 50,* 550–558.

Ryan, R.M., Rigby, S., & King, K. (1992). *Two types of religious internalization and their relations to religious orientations and mental health.* Unpublished manuscript, University of Rochester.

Ryan, R.M., & Stiller, J. (1991). The social contexts of internalization: Parent and teacher influences on autonomy, motivation and learning. In P.R. Pintrich & M.L. Maehr (Eds.), *Advances in motivation and achievement: Vol. 7. Goals and self-regulatory processes.* Greenwich, CT: JAI Press, pp. 115–149.

Ryan, R.M., Stiller, J., & Lynch, J.H. (1992). *Representations of relationships to teachers, parents, and friends as predictors of academic motivation and self-esteem.* Unpublished manuscript, University of Rochester.

Schafer, R. (1968). *Aspects of internalization.* New York: International Universities Press.

Skinner, E.A. (in press). Perceived control: Motivation, coping, and development. In R. Schwarzer (Ed.), *Self-efficacy and psychological functioning.* Hillsdale, NJ: Erlbaum.

Spence, J.T. (1985). Achievement American style: The rewards and costs of individualism. *American Psychologist, 40,* 1288–1295.

Spence, J.T., & Helmreich, R.L. (1983). Achievement-related motives and behavior. In J.T. Spence (Ed.), *Achievement and achievement motives: Psychological and sociological approaches.* New York: Freeman.

Tero, P.F., & Connell, J.P. (1983, April). Children's academic coping inventory: A new self-report measure. Paper presented at the meeting of the American Educational Research Association, Montreal.

Vallerand, R.J., & Bissonnette, R. (in press). Intrinsic, extrinsic, and amotivational styles as predictors of behavior: A prospective study. *Journal of Personality.*

White, R.W. (1959). Motivation reconsidered: The concept of competence. *Psychological Review, 66,* 297–333.

9 Children's achievement-related behaviors: The role of extrinsic and intrinsic motivational orientations

Cheryl Flink, Ann K. Boggiano, Deborah S. Main, Marty Barrett, and Phyllis A. Katz

Central to most theories of achievement-motivated activity is the assumption that, independent of actual ability level, motivation has a profound influence on students' achievement (Dweck & Elliott, 1983). There are, however, markedly divergent assumptions about the kind of motivation that produces optimal learning or achievement in children. One approach has emphasized factors that maximize strength of motivation, with the implicit assumption being that achievement varies with motivational level. For example, according to this theory of achievement motivation, extrinsic incentives, such as social approval or tangible rewards, would have a positive effect on motivation by increasing students' willingness to pursue an academic activity (Atkinson & Raynor, 1974). Advocates of this perspective assume not only that reinforcements (such as praise and tangible rewards) discourage disruptive behavior and foster positive classroom behaviors such as attention, but also that use of such techniques enhances academically relevant behaviors including reading, arithmetic, and even creative problem solving (Kazdin & Wilson, 1980).

Although this assumption has been accepted widely in educational settings and demonstrated empirically when an extrinsic incentive is operative (Kazdin & Wilson, 1980), research presented in several chapters of this volume indicates that use of controlling techniques (e.g., evaluation, tangible reward, or even use of the term "should") leads to reduction in children's interest in pursuing the same activity after the extrinsic incentive or coercive technique is withdrawn. Theoretically, children come to see the reinforcement, rather than an interest in the task or desire to achieve mastery in a particular domain, as their primary reason for engaging in a school activity. Because the controlling strategy shifts a child's motivation for performing the activity from an intrinsic one (e.g., enjoyment, mastery over challenge) to an extrinsic one (e.g., obtaining the reinforcement, avoiding punishment), motivation decreases markedly when the extrinsic reason is no longer available, as more than fifty studies have demonstrated

(Deci & Ryan, 1985; Lepper & Greene, 1978). Curiosity, mastery strivings, a sense of effectance and perceptions of control over the environment – the core components of an intrinsic motivational orientation – are less prevalent after a child is exposed to controlling techniques (Deci, Nezlek, & Sheinman, 1981; Boggiano, Barrett, Shields, Flink, & Seelbach, 1991). The implication is that the ploy, "If you do your reading, then you can have extra recess," has a boomerang effect: The child shows a decrement in interest in the subject, and, ironically, more positive feelings toward and interest in the reward activity (Boggiano & Main, 1986; Lepper, Sagotsky, Dafoe, & Greene, 1982). Given the pervasive use of controlling strategies by educators, it may not be surprising that children show a dramatic developmental shift from a predominantly intrinsic motivational orientation toward learning to an extrinsic one as they progress through elementary school (Harter, 1981a).

This body of research raises an issue considered paramount to the primary goal of educators: the long-term effect of motivational techniques used by teachers on students' overall achievement. Intrinsic motivation to pursue a given school subject has been markedly attenuated for as long as six weeks after one exposure to a controlling technique (e.g., tangible reward) in a laboratory setting. What, then, is the long-range effect of continuous exposure to these controlling strategies on children's achievement – if these techniques indeed, leave children with little intrinsic motivation to pursue school subjects both inside and outside the classroom?

Based on a model of factors assumed to influence achievement in children (see Figure 9.1), this chapter addresses two interrelated issues. In our first section, we discuss the consequences of students' adopting an intrinsic versus extrinsic motivational orientation on a number of important indices of achievement: (1) students' approaches to performing achievement related activities; (2) students' achievement outcome (e.g., national test scores); and (3) students' performance following evaluation feedback. In our second section, we examine why adults may use controlling strategies, by discussing research addressing socializing agents' beliefs about the effectiveness of extrinsic incentives in enhancing children's achievement. We also present evidence regarding adults' beliefs about the advantages and disadvantages of extrinsic versus intrinsic motivational orientations in students.

Achievement-related behaviors: the role of motivational orientations

Extrinsic and intrinsic children theoretically would approach their schoolwork and respond to informational feedback about their performance in

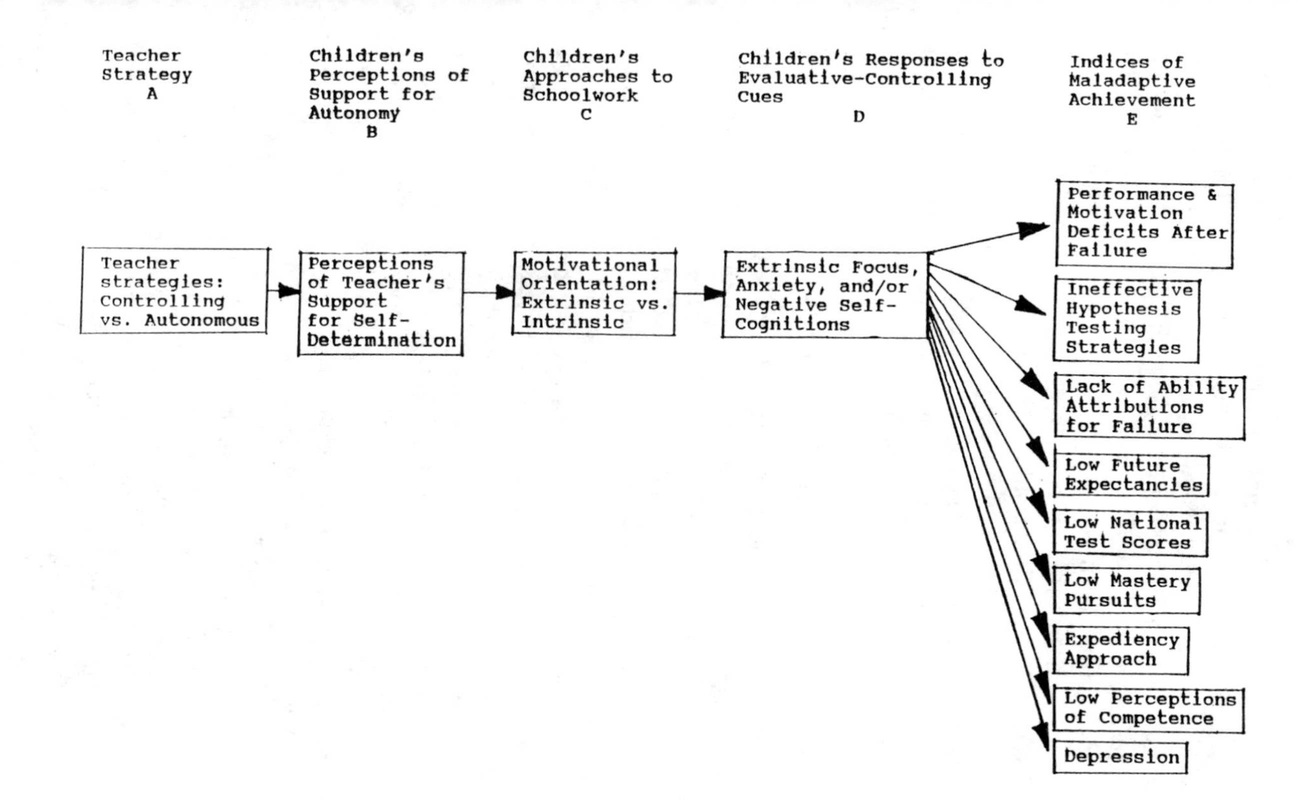

Figure 9.1. A model of factors influencing achievement in elementary school children. (Based on Bogganio, Main, Flink, Barrett, Silvern, & Katz, 1989; Boggiano, Barrett, Main, & Katz, 1985)

dramatically different ways. Extrinsic children are characterized by their preference for easy rather than challenging activities; their working to please the teacher and obtain good grades rather than to satisfy their interest and curiosity; and their dependence on the teacher rather than on their own judgment about how to solve problems (Harter, 1978). From this perspective, it has been proposed that extrinsic children would take an expediency approach to their schoolwork (see Pittman, Boggiano, & Ruble, 1983), attempting to expend the least amount of effort necessary to obtain the maximum gain. This orientation toward academic work has been termed the "mini-max" principle (Kruglanski, 1975). The adoption of a particular motivational set in students, then, would appear to have a number of important effects on achievement-related behaviors.

Students' approaches to performing schoolwork

One major consequence of adopting an extrinsic versus an intrinsic motivational orientation is divergent approaches to academic tasks. A hallmark of an intrinsically motivated child is his or her desire to seek and meet challenge (White, 1959). A child who adopts an intrinsic motivational set toward an activity will find that features such as enjoyment of task complexity, stimulation from the novelty of the task, and the desire for mastery are salient. In contrast, when an extrinsic orientation toward a task is engendered a child will prefer the opposite: easy tasks. In the latter case, a child performs the task primarily as a means to an end – to obtain a tangible reward, for example, or to avoid evaluation. This instrumental set toward an activity, with the concomitant disinterest in the "means" (Boggiano & Main, 1986), produces the desire to complete the task as quickly as possible to achieve the "end" or goal in question – for example, to avoid feelings of pressure from evaluation. Even more interestingly, it is assumed here that this set toward the activity would generalize over to any subsequent interactions with activities performed for extrinsic as opposed to intrinsic reasons, so that children would retain their initial set toward the task even after the goal was achieved.

Research has supported this theory by demonstrating that grades and tangible rewards lead to a preference for less challenging versions of a target activity (Harter, 1974; 1978; Harter & Guzman, 1986; Maehr & Stalling, 1972; Shapira, 1976) while the controlling technique is in effect. Moreover, children's preference for challenge has been found to "carry over" to subsequent sessions when extrinsic inducements were no longer present. After being offered a reward for working moderately difficult puzzles, children preferred the easiest puzzles even during a subsequent free choice session when the reward was no longer available. Children who had not been offered a reward chose the more difficult version of the puzzle during the subsequent free choice session (Boggiano, Pittman & Ruble, 1982; Pittman, Emery, & Boggiano, 1982).

The data suggest that, depending on motivational orientation, children categorize an activity as either a means to an end (i.e., as a way of obtaining a reward) or as an end in itself (e.g., an enjoyable task). This categorization and resulting reactions to activities (i.e., striving for mastery vs. an expediency approach) operate in subsequent approaches to and engagement in the activity (Boggiano, Pittman, & Ruble, 1982). Indeed, children's level of intrinsic interest in schoolwork predicts their preferences for challenge, even when perceptions of competence are taken into account (Boggiano, Main, & Katz, 1988). Thus, under conditions in which an extrinsic motivational set develops, children avoid the pursuit of challenge even when they are no longer being rewarded or evaluated. This provides evidence for the links between C and D in our model (Figure 9.1) and has clear implications for students' long-range achievement.

This research indicates that achievement-related behaviors, including mastery pursuits, are attenuated by the use of incentives even when the incentive value is trivial, for example, a sticker or a marshmallow. The implication of this analysis is that children who are continually exposed to controlling strategies used by educators to "motivate" children (e.g., incentives or surveillance) would develop a general and pervasive extrinsic orientation toward learning. More specifically, as described by Harter (1981b), children with an extrinsic orientation would be characterized by (1) a preference for easy assignments over more challenging ones, (2) a desire to work to please the teacher or to get good grades, rather than to satisfy curiosity or interest, (3) a reliance on the teacher for help, as opposed to an effort to master difficult problems on their own, (4) a dependence on the teacher's opinion or judgment, and (5) a reliance on external sources of evaluation (e.g., grades or teacher feedback) rather than on internal criteria.

We propose that these behaviors have negative consequences for achievement that are dramatic and far-reaching. First, students of teachers who reported using controlling, rather than autonomous, strategies as motivational tools were significantly more likely to adopt an extrinsic motivational set and were characterized by lower perceptions of control than were their intrinsic counterparts, even after only a few weeks of exposure to these different teachers (Boggiano, Barrett, Main, & Katz, 1985; Deci, Nezlek, & Sheinman, 1981). We hypothesized that these extrinsic children, because of exposure to controlling techniques, would exhibit decreased interest in and motivation for pursuing schoolwork, as well as an avoidance of difficult school material (Boggiano, Main, & Katz, 1988; Harter, 1981b). Because of converging evidence regarding the number and strength of effects that controlling techniques have on students, both in terms of children's self-concept and indirect indices of achievement (as noted in Figure 9.1), we proposed that use of controlling techniques by teachers would negatively impact their students' achievement. If our theoretical analysis were correct, the potentially deleterious impact of control on students after months of exposure to these strategies would be reflected in the students' national test scores.

To address the issue of the effects of teacher strategy on student achievement, Boggiano and colleagues (1991) conducted a longitudinal study with 297 children from grades four through six (13 classrooms), in which we collected the students' achievement scores from two consecutive years. We also assessed, by means of self-report measures, (1) teachers' preferences for using controlling techniques to motivate students in their classrooms; (2) children's perceptions of control over their classroom environment, that is, whether they felt more like "pawns" or "origins"; and (3) children's motivational orientation, as indexed by Harter's Motivational Orientation Questionnaire.

The data indicated strong support for our model of achievement (see Figure 9.2). Students of teachers who reported preferences for controlling rather than autonomous techniques were more likely to feel like pawns (rather than origins) and were more prone to adopt extrinsic orientations, in comparison to students whose teachers used autonomous techniques, such as providing choice options to students. Of particular interest was the finding that children who adopted an extrinsic, rather than an intrinsic, orientation toward schoolwork were more likely to do poorly on overall achievement, as indexed by national test scores, even when we controlled for achievement scores from the previous year.

This strong evidence that controlling strategies negatively impacted children's achievement led to a related question: What factors influenced teachers' adoption of more autonomous or controlling strategies? One likely factor is the amount of pressure exerted by administrators or parents to ensure that their students perform well. In other words, teachers may experience evaluative pressure and react by utilizing more controlling strategies because they assume that such strategies maximize students' achievement (Boggiano, Barrett, Weiher, McClelland, & Lusk, 1987).

Deci and his colleagues addressed the impact of external pressure on teaching strategies by pressuring college subjects who were assigned the

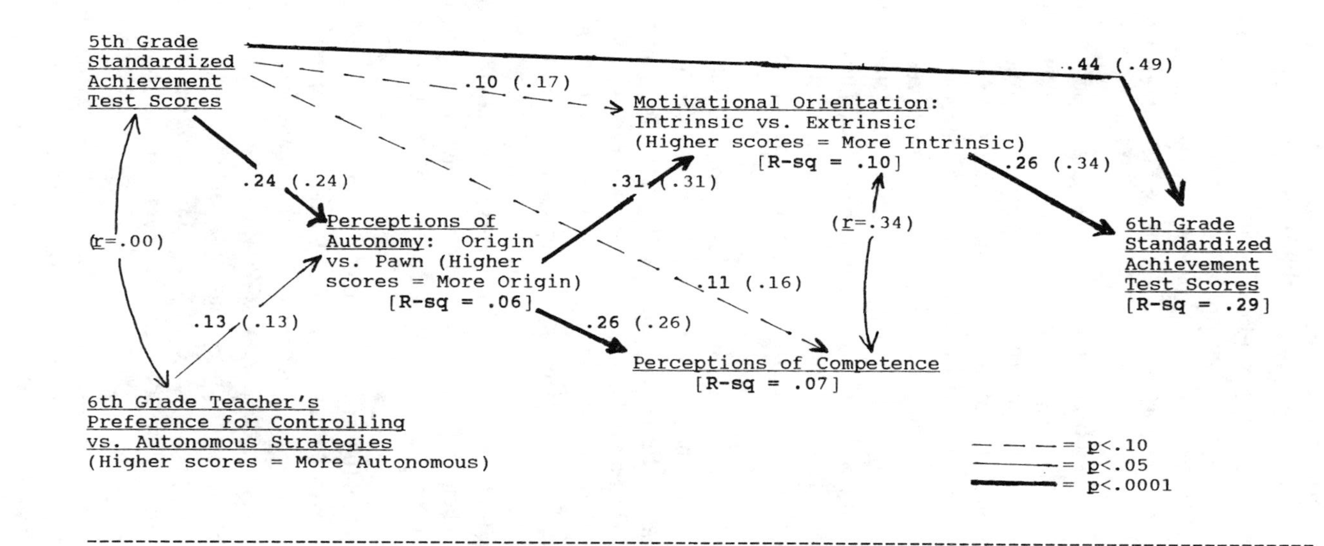

Standardized beta weights are shown on the path. Nonsignificant paths ($p>.05$) were deleted and path coefficients recomputed for remaining analysis (although marginal paths are included in the figure). Zero-order correlations are in the parentheses following the beta weights. R-squares are the adjusted R-square giving the percentage of variance accounted for for each criterion variable by all preceding predictor variables. Correlation between motivational orientation and competence is the partial correlation controlling for all preceding variables.

Figure 9.2

role of teacher in an experimental setting to ensure that their students performed well. The data indicated that when these "teachers" were told that their role was to ensure that their students performed up to standards (controlling manipulation) – rather than to facilitate students' learning (autonomous manipulation) – "teachers" in the controlling condition evidenced more controlling behaviors (Deci, Spiegel, Ryan, Koestner, Kauffman, 1982).

Although the results obtained by Deci and his colleagues supported the hypothesis that administrative pressure increased the use of controlling strategies by teachers, the study did not address the critical issue of the effects of such strategies on children's achievement. Deci's study was conducted in a laboratory, using introductory psychology students who role-played the part of teachers. To address the impact of external pressure on actual teachers and on their students' achievement, Flink, Boggiano, and Barrett (1990) conducted a field experiment in the classroom. They investigated both the strategies teachers adopted in response to induced pressure and the effects those strategies had on children's performance on academic tasks.

The authors hypothesized that pressured teachers would exhibit more controlling behaviors toward their students, which in turn would impair their students' performance. Fifteen teachers and 267 children in their classrooms participated in the study. The teachers received instructions about their roles before they taught two target activities: anagrams and a picture sequencing task. Teachers randomly assigned to the controlling manipulation were told their role was to ensure that their students performed well when tested. By contrast, teachers in the autonomous condition were told simply to help the children learn how to solve the problems. Teachers then worked with groups of students on the two tasks; each interaction was videotaped.

Once children completed the group-learning session, they completed three performance measures administered by an experimenter blind to condition. These tasks included a new set of anagrams and sequences, as well as a spatial-relations puzzle task. The data indicated that children whose teachers received the controlling manipulation did not perform nearly as well on the composite score of anagrams, puzzles, and sequences as did children whose teachers received the autonomous manipulation.

These findings were consistent with the results of one study in which elementary school students of peer teachers exhibited diminished performance when their tutors were pressured to ensure that their students performed well, in this case by offering the tutors rewards contingent on their students' performance. Garbarino (1975) found that tutors in the reward condition exhibited more negative affect towards their students than did tutors in the no-reward condition. Also, students whose tutors expected reward based on their tutees' performance level performed worse than their counterparts whose tutors were not offered a reward. Thus, effects of "pressure" led not only to tutors' negative feelings toward students, but to the use of more intrusive and controlling behaviors by tutors and, subsequently, to poorer performance by their students.

What factors might mediate the negative effects of controlling strategies on students' performance? One hypothesis is that teachers who felt pressured not only might be more directive, but also might phrase directives in a more demanding manner, be less responsive to students' questions, and place less emphasis on conceptual learning. To address this question, we analyzed videotapes of the teaching sessions to assess the degree to which teachers exhibited controlling strategies as a function of the manipulation they received. Indeed, teachers responded to the manipulation of pressure by using both verbal and nonverbal controlling techniques (Mehrabian, 1968), these techniques moderated students' inferior performance level. As Deci has demonstrated, even a very subtle induction of pressure increased the use of controlling strategies. It seems very likely, then, that teachers working within a school system that continually emphasized the importance of children's performance on evaluative tests would respond to that pressure by using controlling strategies. Evidence from the above three studies suggested that such strategies produced an effect opposite to the one intended by teachers and administrators: decreased, rather than enhanced, performance.

Studies described in several other chapters of this volume are consistent with our results: Children who performed schoolwork for extrinsic reasons (e.g., grades), as opposed to intrinsic ones, showed marked deficits in learning. For instance, children who performed activities for extrinsic reasons have been found to be less creative than intrinsics (see Amabile & Hennessey, this volume; and Kruglanski, Friedman, & Zeevi, 1971). Moreover, extrinsic children were found to be more likely than intrinsics to "guess" at the correct answer (Condry & Chambers, 1978), and were less likely than intrinsics to solve difficult problems (McGraw & McCullers, 1979) or to retain information (Grolnick & Ryan, 1987). Overall, then, contrary to the beliefs of educators that extrinsic incentives and other controlling techniques enhance learning in students (see Condry & Chambers, 1978), these techniques impair children's cognitive functioning and are detrimental to their long-range achievement.

Mediators of the relation between controlling techniques and achievement

We propose that children's responses to evaluative feedback determine their achievement in school. Although a number of situational and psychological factors mediate achievement in intrinsic and extrinsic children (and, undoubtedly, there are potential mediating variables that have not been considered theoretically or explored empirically), feedback given to children about their school performance is an inevitable part of the learning process and is routinely offered in educational settings. It also appears that although feedback may not occur more frequently with increasing grade level, the climate clearly becomes more evaluative as children progress through school. That is, competitive grading practices are more common in higher grades, and there are more sources of evaluation. For instance, in higher grades children are more likely to have several teachers who evaluate them in different subject areas. Social comparison with peers also grows increasingly normative and important (Eccles, Midgely, & Adler, 1984). The consequences of the evaluation process, then, become increasingly important to students as they advance through the education system, especially when they reach the upper elementary and lower junior high school years.

We have assumed that the increasing importance of evaluation, in conjunction with a more competitive grading process, would increase the likelihood that children would develop an extrinsic orientation as they progressed through school (see Chapter 5, this volume) and also would increase extrinsic children's negative affective reactions to evaluative feedback. The expectation of evaluative cues, then, would increase extrinsics' concerns about performance outcome, negative feedback, and the adequacy of their ability. Based on this line of reasoning, we have proposed that although extrinsics and intrinsics might exhibit comparable responses when evaluative and other controlling cues were *not* salient, the presence of such cues would produce dramatic differences in the ways children with different motivational orientations approached and performed schoolwork. We turn now to two important negative consequences of the use of controlling evaluative cues: children's susceptibility to helplessness after failure feedback, and preferences for easy rather than challenging activities.

Susceptibility to helplessness. One critical determinant of achievement in extrinsic children may be divergent susceptibility to helplessness deficits. Children who develop a pervasive and general extrinsic motivational orientation have lower self-esteem and less positive perceptions of their ability level than do their intrinsic counterparts (Deci et al., 1981; Chapter 5, this volume) – traits that typically characterize helpless children (Nolen-Hoeksema, 1987). Also, as noted previously, extrinsic children display less persistence when confronted with complex tasks and prefer easy rather than difficult tasks.

An additional factor – one central to learned helplessness theory – that differentiates extrinsic from intrinsic children is their perceptions of control over outcome: Extrinsic children tend to think that powerful others, rather than internal factors, control their performance outcomes, whereas intrinsics tend to think the opposite (Boggiano et al., 1985). Differences in perceptions of control have clear implications for how children with different motivational orientations respond to negative evaluative feedback, which theoretically would in turn render children differentially susceptible to helplessness deficits.

Would we characterize extrinsic children as having perceptions of less control over performance outcome than intrinsics? According to Boggiano and Barrett (1985), children who consistently performed schoolwork for extrinsic reasons (e.g., to gain approval or to avoid criticism from their teacher) were likely to regard achieving goals as less determined by their responses than were intrinsically motivated children. Attaining extrinsic goals, such as teacher approval, often is contingent on factors that lie outside of one's control – such as the teacher's mood or one's performance relative to others. Furthermore, the teacher's praise or criticism may at times seem unrelated to schoolwork and may seem based more on extraneous variables, such as neatness or time taken to complete the assignment. Because the primary goals held by extrinsic children depend heavily on factors outside their control, they may perceive the role of extraneous factors to be more important than their own effort in attaining their goals. A perception of effort-outcome independence thus develops, as demonstrated by extrinsic children's tendency to regard powerful others or unknown factors as the primary reasons for their success or failure (Boggiano et al., 1985).

In contrast, because intrinsically motivated children work for the pleasure inherent in an activity, their desired outcome – satisfaction won from task mastery – is largely dependent on their own effort. Moreover, intrinsically motivated children rely only partly on external evaluation of their performance and have internal criteria for success and failure (Harter, 1981a; 1981b). Consequently, the role of effort in effecting a given outcome is salient. Children who adopt an intrinsic orientation generally have perceptions of more control over desired outcomes and a sense of contingency between effort and outcome (Boggiano et al., 1985).

Based on findings demonstrating marked differences in perceptions of both control and competence in extrinsic versus intrinsic children, we formulated the following hypotheses. First, we assumed that use of pressure or evaluative techniques would produce helpless behavior in extrinsic, but not intrinsic, children. For extrinsic children, controlling conditions, such as the use of evaluative feedback or performance pressure, would serve as cues that heightened their attention to whether they could control the outcome or perform up to standard. The negative affect experienced by extrinsic children – feelings of pressure and tension, for instance (Ryan, 1982) – theoretically would interfere with a mastery orientation, resulting in performance decrement and less persistence. In contrast, intrinsic children who perceived themselves as in control would be impervious to evaluative pressure and, when faced with a challenging task, might show even enhanced performance and motivation.

To test these hypotheses about the effects of evaluative feedback on subsequent performance and motivation, Boggiano and Barrett (1985) gave fourth through sixth grade children who had developed either an extrinsic or an intrinsic motivational orientation (Harter, 1981a) success information, failure information, or no evaluative information about their performance on an incomplete picture task. The authors predicted that after failure feedback, only extrinsically motivated children would exhibit performance decrements on an additional task involving different skills (i.e., anagrams). Assuming that helplessness would generalize across situations, the authors additionally predicted that failure would negatively affect extrinsic children's subsequent motivation to perform activities similar to the failure task. Finally, because of the divergent mastery strivings of children with different motivational orientations, we expected information about success to have a positive effect on subsequent motivation for both the generalization and target task in intrinsics, and a negative effect in extrinsics.

The data revealed that children with different motivational orientations differed markedly on the anagram task as a function of initial success or failure feedback (see Figure 9.3). Specifically, children with an extrinsic motivational orientation showed performance impairment and less motivation on the generalization task following failure, whereas children with an intrinsic orientation showed facilitation following the same negative information. In addition, intrinsic children's performance increased after success, whereas extrinsic children's performance did not.

As can be seen in Figure 9.3, the performance of extrinsic and intrinsic children did not differ under conditions in which evaluative cues were *not* present. Our findings, then, did not imply that being extrinsic was either

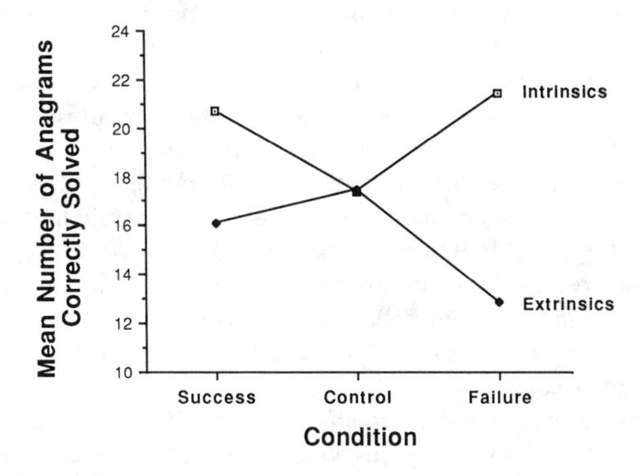

Figure 9.3.

necessary or sufficient to produce helplessness deficits. We proposed, therefore, that performance decrement in extrinsic children would be apparent primarily when cues were present that signified pressure or feelings of being controlled by a powerful other. This proposition concerning the importance of controlling or evaluative cues parallels the assumption in the learned-helplessness literature that children who were prone to helplessness would show achievement and emotional deficits when confronted with stress or negative life events (Nolen-Hoeksema, Girgus, & Seligman, 1986; Peterson & Seligman, 1984). An extrinsic motivational orientation, then, appears to be a risk factor for performance impairment and other helplessness deficits (Boggiano & Barrett, 1985), just as having a maladaptive attributional style to account for difficult life events is a risk factor for depression (Peterson & Seligman, 1984).

Response to evaluative pressure and ability concerns. The results of several recent studies have supported the assumption that differences between intrinsic and extrinsic children's achievement behaviors or strivings appeared primarily when cues were present that signified pressure about performance outcome or ability level. In one study, for instance, Boggiano, Main, and Katz (1988) gave either more or less controlling feedback to nine- to eleven-year-old extrinsically and intrinsically motivated children when the children played a moderately difficult shape-matching activity. We found that given a highly controlling directive ("I'll bet you'll want to do well on this next activity, as you *should,* as you *ought* to."), extrinsic children, who scored low on perceptions of competence and control, chose the easiest versions of the shape-matching activity during a subsequent free-choice session observed unobtrusively by a blind experimenter. In contrast, when provided with the same controlling directive, intrinsics, who scored high on competence and control, preferred the most challenging version of the shape-matching activity. No differences between these groups were observed when children received a less controlling directive ("I'll bet you'll want to do well on this activity.").

An additional recent study also examined the proposition that extrinsic children's achievement-related behavior differed markedly from that of intrinsics when cues were presented that either provided evaluative pressure or promoted concern about their ability (Main, 1987). That is, if information were available for assessing competence, extrinsics would avoid or ignore it. Conversely, this kind of pressure relevant to self-evaluative concerns theoretically would have little negative impact on intrinsics, whose goals center on learning and mastery over challenge. Based on this line of reasoning, we assumed that if children were given information about their ability that, although positive, was definitive about competence, extrinsic children would not seek further ability information in subsequent interactions with the target activity and would display behaviors consistent with a self-handicapping approach to positive feedback (see Chapter 11, this volume). Thus when given the choice of performing an easy or a difficult version of an activity, extrinsics theoretically would prefer the less challenging form, but only under conditions in which they could not clearly ascertain their ability level. This minimal effort strategy for extrinsics would appear primarily when situational variables made the issue of their ability salient. The strategy of avoiding information about competence would not be apparent, we reasoned, if ability were not an issue – that is, if adequacy of ability were not made salient or if feedback inherent in the task itself confirmed a high level of ability. Intrinsics, on the other hand, theoretically would evidence enhanced mastery strivings even if competence at a task were uncertain.

Main (1987) examined this relationship between children's motivational orientation and their reactions to feedback. Intrinsically and extrinsically oriented subjects solved logical sequence problems about which they were given information that provided either highly definitive (i.e., six of eight problems were solvable) or less definitive (i.e., six of eight were impossible) information about task competence. These students then received positive or no feedback regarding their performance. (It should be noted that although all the problems were impossible, manipulation checks indicated that students did not perceive the tasks as being insolvable.) Based on our theoretical analysis, we predicted that when intrinsic children were unsure about their ability, they would work to assess their mastery level by pursuing more challenging tasks than they would when their competence was easily ascertained. In contrast, we predicted that when extrinsics received identical information that made their ability level unclear, these children would avoid more difficult activities and thus prefer the easiest version. Finally, we expected no difference between extrinsics and intrinsics when the information indicated that they were very competent (i.e., clear positive feedback was available from task participation itself) or when competence assessment was not made salient (i.e., the control condition).

The data confirmed our hypotheses by showing that under conditions in which children were uncertain about their ability, extrinsically oriented subjects avoided the difficult activity, and intrinsically oriented individuals showed significantly greater preferences for challenge relative to extrinsics. In addition, as predicted, no differences existed between extrinsic and intrinsic students in the no-feedback control condition or in the condition in which positive competence information could be obtained from task participation.

Maximizing children's achievement: adults' beliefs

The findings reviewed in several chapters of this volume consistently have pointed to the negative impact of controlling techniques on important achievement-related behaviors, particularly conceptual learning, achievement scores, and creativity. Of course, when performing activities that require passive rather than active involvement in learning, rewards and other controlling techniques may not be detrimental to performance and may even facilitate performance. Indeed, the few studies that demonstrated a facilitation effect of rewards used tasks that were well learned and that generally required algorithmic solutions (McGraw, 1978). Given that a large body of research indicates that extrinsic incentives produce performance deficits in the type of academic activities deemed of critical importance by educators, it becomes increasingly important to examine the strategies adults think are useful for enhancing children's learning. Ryan, Connell, and Grolnick (Chapter 8, this volume) point out that educators are moving increasingly toward a "back-to-basics" philosophy. This includes an emphasis on longer school hours, more basic science, math, and English courses, and fewer electives. Such a philosophy reflects the belief that children must achieve some targeted level of proficiency in a given area in order to function in society. To balance one's checkbook, one must be able to add and subtract; to vote, one must be able to read the ballot.

If, however, controlling techniques preclude a deeper, conceptual understanding of certain subjects and interfere with problem solving, adults must face the difficult task of employing other motivating strategies that do not impair conceptual learning. Adults' beliefs about useful motivational strategies, then, are of serious concern.

Beliefs about controlling techniques

What techniques do adults prefer for maximizing children's motivation and achievement? This question is of applied as well as theoretical interest because of the impact that adults, and particularly parents, have on children's achievement-related behaviors. Despite the well-documented finding that the strategy of offering a child a reward to perform an activity adversely affects motivation and achievement (and, as a corollary, that the larger the reward, the more negative the effects), we proposed that adults would positively evaluate extrinsic incentives. Programs involving rewards and other salient controlling techniques are widespread in educational settings and are deemed valuable for maximizing achievement-related behaviors in children (Deci & Ryan, 1985; Kazdin & Wilson, 1980; O'Leary & Drabman, 1971). In fact, the use of stars, prizes, and the like by educators predates Skinnerian techniques and is widely assumed to be an effective tool in the classroom (O'Leary & Drabman, 1971). The fact that such extrinsic inducements, including grades, time deadlines, and surveillance, are frequently used in academic settings (Deci & Ryan, 1985) may have a number of predictable effects on adults' beliefs.

One important implication of pairing tangible rewards and prizes with academic work is that adults may be less likely to consider schoolwork per se, as opposed to nonacademic behavior (e.g., prosocial behavior), as an end in itself (Kruglanski, 1975). Instead, adults may perceive school activities as involving "work" typically performed for exogenous reasons – in other words, as a means to some ulterior end, whether that be good grades or fulfillment of some academic requirement. The normative acceptance of inducements or payment for academic tasks may lead adults to apprehend extrinsic inducements as an integral or endogenous feature of schoolwork. If adults do perceive reward as endogenous to an activity, then adults theoretically would expect rewards to increase, rather than decrease, subsequent motivation (Kruglanski, 1975). Reward does, in fact, increase subsequent motivation for tedious or rote activities of low interest that undoubtedly are composed of work-like features (Boggiano & Hertel, 1983; Calder & Staw, 1975). If adults saw both high- and low-interest activities as school "work," rather than differentiating them according to their unique features, they might infer that reward and other inducements augmented achievement for virtually all types of school activities. Thus "overly sufficient" incentives, such as tangible reward, might be preferred by adults over "minimally sufficient" strategies to motivate children to perform not only low-interest but also high-interest activities.

A second major implication of frequently pairing rewards with academic tasks is that the potential benefits, rather than the costs, of rewards may be more salient to the rewarder. In the short run rewards often have positive effect, not unlike compliance effects, on both high- and low-interest tasks. Productivity increases (Lepper, Greene, & Nisbett, 1973), performance on simple tasks improves (McGraw, 1978), and interest in boring tasks increases (Boggiano & Hertel, 1983; Calder & Staw, 1975; Kruglanski, 1975). Rewards for performing academic activities also produce positive effects, at least while the reward program continues (Boggiano & Hertel, 1983). If adults observed the immediate positive effects of reward on performance, they indeed would see this motivational tool as valuable for academic tasks in general. Adults may not differentiate between tasks of varying interest levels, so they may think that children's increased interest following reward for low-interest activities would generalize to high-interest activities. Consequently, any negative long-term effects of reward on activities that children initially found intrinsically interesting might be overlooked or ascribed to factors other than reward (e.g., fatigue).

To investigate adults' beliefs concerning effective techniques for maximizing children's interest in academic activities, we designed a series of six studies (Boggiano et al., 1987). Our major hypothesis was that adults prefer rewards for maintaining or increasing children's interest in *both* high- and low-interest academic tasks over other, less controlling strategies, such as inductive reasoning or a noninterference policy. In addition, adults were not expected to differentiate between the short- and long-term effects of extrinsic constraints on intrinsic interest – that is, compliance versus negative effects that persist after the incentive no longer is present.

In the first study, we examined adults' (parents and introductory psychology students) preference for rewards versus less controlling strategies (i.e., reasoning, punishment, and preference for noninterference) for increasing or maintaining children's intrinsic motivation for academic activities. Subjects were assigned randomly to read one of several scenarios of approximately equal length that described either ten-year-old boys or girls showing either high or low intrinsic interest in different academic activities. After reading the scenarios, subjects rated how effective they thought each of the four social control techniques (rewards, reasoning, punishment, noninterference) would be "in maximizing the child's enjoyment or interest in computers/reading," while the strategy was in effect (short term), and several months after the technique was used (long term).

Results indicated that both samples preferred rewards over the other three strategies (i.e., more than reasoning, punishment, and noninterference, respectively) to maximize children's interest in working with computers and reading. Moreover, subjects did *not* differentiate between tasks of high versus low interest. It appeared that subjects viewed both high- and low-interest academic tasks as requiring controlling techniques to increase children's enjoyment, and saw no differences in the short- and long-term effects of those strategies. This suggested that subjects may not discriminate carefully between tasks of varying interest levels, presumably because they see all school-related activities as work. Indeed, in a separate study examining this hypothesis, we found that adults perceived performing academic activities for money to be more like "work" than a number of other behaviors, for example, prosocial behaviors.

Our second study expanded on the previous experiment by comparing parents' preferences for reward to promote interest in academic and non-academic activities. Minimally sufficient, rather than controlling, techniques have been demonstrated to increase the likelihood of long-term maintenance of altruistic and interpersonal behavior (Lepper & Greene, 1978). However, we proposed that adults would prefer overly sufficient rewards more for academic tasks, as opposed to other techniques, because they would perceive academic tasks as "work." In this study, parents read scenarios describing children behaving in four domains: academic activity, aggression, altruism, and friendship. Parents rated how effective they thought the four social-control techniques used in the first experiment would be for maximizing children's interest in an activity or promoting a given behavior. As in the first study, parents preferred reward over reasoning, punishment, and noninterference, respectively, to motivate children academically. (Interestingly, for prosocial behavior, the preferences for reward and reasoning were reversed.) In addition, the prediction that reward would be more highly valued in the academic domains than in other domains received support. Overall, then, the results of the second study replicated and extended the findings from the first study.

An additional study examined the extent to which adults preferred large versus small rewards for increasing interest in academic tasks. If adults thought that reward was very beneficial for high-interest activities, they then theoretically would assume that interest covaried with the size of the reward: Increasing the size of a reward would enhance interest. Subjects read the scenarios used in the earlier studies and rated how effective five techniques would be in increasing children's willingness to engage in certain behaviors in three different domains (academic, prosocial, and aggressive). The five techniques were large reward, small reward, large punishment, small punishment, and noninterference. Analyses revealed that subjects preferred large reward over all other techniques in the academic domain. Adults' assumptions about the value of reward for academic versus other behaviors were again demonstrated: Subjects preferred both large and small rewards more for academic tasks in comparison to prosocial and aggressive behaviors.

The results of these studies suggested that adults may follow a strong implicit theory about the positive co-occurrence of rewards and increases in intrinsic interest in academic activities. If subjects thought rewards and subsequent interest in academic tasks were related positively, they might well perceive a positive relationship even when there was evidence to the contrary. To test this hypothesis, introductory college subjects viewed overhead transparencies reflecting either no relation ($r = .00$) or a negative relation ($r = -.55$) between two variables, academic interest and reward, or miles run and appliances used (control condition). Subjects were told that the purpose of the study was to assess the relation between two variables, and were given several examples depicting various relationships between different variables (e.g., cloud seeding and rain). Subjects then rated on a -100 to $+100$ scale (-100 = complete and total negative relation; 0 = no relation at all; $+100$ = complete and total positive relation) what number best represented the relationship they had been shown between certain variables. The data indicated that subjects saw a positive relation between reward and academic tasks, but not between the two variables in the control condition, although both pairs had identical values. Even when given disconfirming evidence, then, subjects judge reward and academic interest as being highly positively related because of their strong beliefs about the value of incentives to motivate academic achievement.

The above series of studies addressed adults' beliefs concerning the utility of controlling techniques for increasing children's willingness to engage in schoolwork, as opposed to other desired behaviors. Both parents and college students preferred reward over other techniques. Indeed, this belief persisted even when subjects viewed evidence to the contrary. Moreover, subjects preferred large rewards over small ones, a phenomenon termed the maximal operant principle, which obviously is discordant with the minimal sufficiency principle.

The persistence and strength of adults' beliefs that rewards increased interest in academic tasks pointed to a clear and consistent misuse of the minimal sufficiency principle when attempting to enhance children's interest in academic tasks. Adults perceived academic tasks as "work" and evidently assumed that interest in schoolwork, which they deemed to be uninteresting, boring, and repetitive, may be increased by reward. Ironically, in their attempts to maximize intrinsic motivation in academic tasks, adults unwittingly may encourage extrinsic orientation toward schoolwork, which is characterized by low interest in learning and poor achievement.

Mediators of achievement beliefs: perceived characteristics of extrinsic vs. intrinsic children

Although the research described above indicated that adults preferred use of controlling techniques, such as positive incentives, to maximize students' academic achievement, adults' beliefs about achievement-related characteristics typical of children who have adopted an intrinsic versus an extrinsic orientation seemed of great interest as well. We assumed that adults would see extrinsic children as more dedicated and responsive to teachers' evaluative feedback, relative to intrinsics – primarily because extrinsic children would express more concern with approval and grades (Barrett & Boggiano, 1988). To examine this issue, we asked a parents sample, as well as a college student sample, to read scenarios describing two elementary schoolchildren who exhibited either an extrinsic or an intrinsic orientation.

A and B are both fourth graders who enjoy and do well in school, although they approach school and relate to their teachers in different ways. For example, B did all this week's reading on the solar system knowing that completing assignments pleases the teacher. B made a couple of points during class discussion so the teacher would know B had done the reading. A also finished all the reading because A got really interested in knowing all about the solar system. A continued to ask questions during the discussion, even after some of the other kids seemed tired of the topic. Since A knows grades don't always reflect work quality, A isn't that interested in grades and doesn't pay much attention to them, but B pays close attention to grades and uses them as a gauge by which to judge how B has been doing on recent work . . .

Subjects indicated which character in the scenario (A or B) they thought would exert greater effort after failure and would show enhanced performance following success. Subjects also rated each child on several other dimensions, including overall effort in schoolwork, basic ability, degree of responsibility, and so on.

The data indicated that, as predicted, both the parent and college samples perceived extrinsics as more responsive to evaluative feedback: Extrinsic children were assumed to exert more effort after failure and to show enhanced performance following success. In a similar vein, adults perceived extrinsics as willing to exert more effort overall in schoolwork and to take more responsibility for completing their work. However, extrinsic children were thought to have lower self-esteem than intrinsic children, despite the fact that there was no perceived difference in basic ability.

Interestingly, several beliefs held by adults paralleled research findings. For example, our findings indicated that adults "correctly" thought that intrinsics had higher self-esteem, as previous research has suggested (Deci et al., 1981). Beliefs about differences between extrinsics and intrinsics which did *not* coincide with empirical findings, however, included parents' and collegians' beliefs that extrinsics put forth more effort in school and derived more benefit from evaluative feedback than did intrinsics (Barrett & Boggiano, 1988).

The above research examined adults' beliefs about children who displayed different orientations toward learning. This line of research bears a strong similarity to what commonly has been referred to as "teacher expectancy" effects. Jussim (1986) asserted that teachers developed expectations about their students, perhaps based on conversations with other teachers or on knowledge of the previous year's grades. As a consequence, teachers treated students differently. Numerous studies reviewed by Jussim indicated that when teachers expected a student to succeed academically, they offered that student more emotional support, favorable feedback, attention, and opportunities to learn difficult material. This introduces an interesting question about the teachers' potentially different treatment of extrinsic vs. intrinsic students. Findings from the Barrett and Boggiano (1988) study indicated that adults preferred the behavioral characteristics of extrinsically motivated children to those of intrinsically motivated children. Adults thought that extrinsics were more responsive to evaluative feedback and more likely to work hard in school. However, although teachers may "appreciate" the responses of their extrinsic (as compared to intrinsic) students, they also may offer greater learning opportunities to students whose achievement is higher, that is, to intrinsics. Cooper (1979) contended that teachers' tendencies to treat students differently, depending on their achievement levels, stemmed from teachers' belief that more able students could more easily understand a broad range of topics; thus, teachers feel more "satisfaction" from educating these children. Because intrinsics exhibit a higher quality of performance, as indexed both by their scores on national tests and their responses under stressful evaluative situations, it may well be that teachers' expectancies perpetuate intrinsics' high achievement and perceptions of competence (see Chapter 5, this volume). Moreover, the opposite set of expectancies for extrinsics may produce a spiraling negative set of interactions such that a myriad of academic and self-esteem problems emerge. Thus, adults' beliefs and expectations concerning children's abilities may have a powerful influence on the educational strategies chosen by parents and teachers, which in turn impacts children's achievements and, ultimately, their self-esteem and career goals.

Summary

We began this chapter by asking what the long-range effect on achievement would be if children had little intrinsic motivation to pursue school subjects. Clearly, the evidence presented here converges on one conclusion: Extrinsic motivation results in achievement deficits. Children who adopt an extrinsic orientation prefer easy tasks, work to please the teacher and to obtain good grades, and depend on others to evaluate their work. Such children are more likely to exhibit helplessness deficits, to respond negatively to evaluative feedback, and, consequently, to perform poorly in comparison to intrinsically motivated cohorts.

Motivational orientation also has an immediate and measurable effect on children's abilities to cope with pressure. Almost daily in school, children encounter pressure to perform: They receive grades, complete national standardized achievement tests, and compete with their classmates (see Chapter 7, this volume). Teachers may augment this pressure by using controlling strategies – emphasizing grades, using directives, allowing little independent work, or creating a less supportive environment in general. Extrinsic children respond poorly to such stressors, as evidenced by declines in performance and in interest in subsequent tasks. These children are much more detrimentally affected by controlling strategies and evaluative pressure than are intrinsic children, and are more at risk for helplessness or exhibiting behavioral and affective deficits.

The development of an intrinsic or extrinsic set may very well hinge on the techniques used by parents and teachers for facilitating learning. One of our most distressing findings is that adults consistently thought that reward (a subset of controlling strategies) enhanced learning. Most adults operate in a world in which extrinsic incentives are commonly offered: If you sell enough items, then you will receive a commission; if you succeed on the GRE, then you will be admitted to graduate school; if you publish enough research, then you will receive tenure. It is no wonder, then, that adults' heuristics for improving achievement depend heavily on rewards. Indeed, in accord with normative if-then contingencies in our society, adults' belief that "the larger the reward the greater the learning" comes as no great surprise. Even when presented with disconfirming evidence, this commonly held belief persisted, indicating a resistance to disconfirming instances of the "if-then" halo effects. Additionally, adults thought that students who displayed concern over grades (an extrinsic orientation) exerted more effort and took greater responsibility for schoolwork. However, when teachers use controlling techniques to increase achievement (techniques also used on them by administrators), the process backfires. Rote learning may improve, but conceptual learning and motivation to *continue* learning decrease. Yet these effects seem to go unnoticed by adults (Maehr & Stalling, 1972).

With regard to our proposed model, although not all of the links have been tested empirically, the research discussed in this chapter supports the causal relationship. Adults' strategies, whether they be autonomous or controlling, affect children's perceptions of competence and control (link A to B). To the extent that children adopt an intrinsic or extrinsic orientation, they exhibit diverging reactions to various stressors. Extrinsics display more helplessness, greater anxiety, increased vulnerability to pressure and fewer mastery pursuits; they also make more attributions to control by powerful others. Intrinsics, however, display the opposite set of responses (link B to C). These orientations differentially affect performance, as assessed through creativity measures, national test scores, and pursuit of challenging tasks (link C to D).

The studies discussed in this chapter have underscored the need for additional research relevant to these issues. First, more longitudinal work is needed to assess the antecedents of extrinsic, as well as intrinsic, orientations. Given that intrinsics seem less vulnerable to a competitive school environment and to other pressures, the question emerges of how children develop intrinsic sets and, moreover, how we may direct extrinsic children toward the development of more intrinsic sets (see Chapter 4, this volume). The evidence consistently suggests that performing a task for intrinsic reasons is qualitatively and quantitatively superior to performing the same task for extrinsic reasons. Realistically, of course, we cannot hope that every task will be inherently interesting. Children certainly will encounter situations in which they perform tasks for extrinsic reasons, and, as mentioned earlier, this will become more frequent as they grow older. However, if we want to encourage children's creativity, interest in challenging tasks, and persistence – behaviors critical for achievement – we would consider their adoption of an intrinsic set to be imperative. Second, and perhaps most importantly, intervention programs are needed to begin changing adults' beliefs. Parents and teachers have an enormously important influence on children's lives. If they continue to think that rewards and controlling strategies improved children's academic performance and motivation for learning, then our families and schools will continue to produce extrinsically motivated children, characterized by low perceptions of competence, a preference for easy tasks, anxiety over evaluative information, and little or no interest in learning.

References

Atkinson, J. W., & Raynor, J. O. (1974). *Motivation and achievement.* Washington, D.C.: Winston.

Barrett, M., & Boggiano, A. K. (1988). Fostering extrinsic orientations: Use of reward strategies to motivate children. *Journal of Social and Clinical Psychology, 6,* 293–309.

Boggiano, A. K., & Barrett, M. (1985). Performance and motivational deficits of helplessness: The role of motivational orientations. *Journal of Personality and Social Psychology, 49,* 1753–1761.

Boggiano, A. K., Barrett, M., Main, D. S., & Katz, P. (1985). Mastery-motivation in children: The role of an extrinsic vs. intrinsic orientation. Paper presented at the American Education Research Association (AERA), Chicago.

Boggiano, A. K., Barrett, M., Shields, A., Flink, C., & Seelbach, A. (1991). Use of controlling techniques: Effects on students' performance and standardized test scores. Unpublished manuscript, University of Colorado, Boulder.

Boggiano, A. K., Barrett, M., Weiher, A. W., McClelland, G. H., & Lusk, C. M. (1987). Use of the maximal operant procedure to motivate children's intrinsic interest. *Journal of Personality and Social Psychology, 53,* 866–879.

Boggiano, A. K., & Hertel, P. T. (1983). Bonuses and bribes: Mood effects in memory. *Social Cognition, 2,* 49–62.

Boggiano, A. K., & Main, D. S. (1986). Enhancing children's interest in activities used as rewards: The bonus effect. *Journal of Personality and Social Psychology, 51,* 1116–1126.

Boggiano, A. K., Main, D. S., & Katz, P. A. (1988). Children's preference for challenge: The role of perceived competence and control. *Journal of Personality and Social Psychology, 54,* 134–141.

Boggiano, A. K., Pittman, T. S., & Ruble, D. N. (1982). The mastery hypothesis and the overjustification effect. *Social Cognition, 1,* 38–49.

Boggiano, A. K., Ruble, D. N., & Pittman, T. S. (1981). Mastery and overjustification. Paper presented at meeting of the Society for Research in Child Development (SRCD).

Calder, B. J., & Staw, B. M. (1975). The interaction of intrinsic and extrinsic motivational orientation: Some methodological notes. *Journal of Personality and Social Psychology, 31,* 76–80.

Condry, J., & Chambers, J. (1978). Intrinsic motivation and the process of learning. In M. R. Lepper & D. Greene (Eds.), *The hidden costs of reward* (pp. 33–60). Hillsdale, NJ: Erlbaum.

Cooper, H. (1979). Pygmalion grows up: A model for teacher expectation communication and performance influence. *Review of Educational Research, 49,* 389–410.

Deci, E. L., Nezlek, J., & Sheinman, L. (1981). Characteristics of rewarder and intrinsic motivation of rewardee. *Journal of Personality and Social Psychology, 40,* 1–10.

Deci, E. L., & Ryan, R. M. (1985). *Intrinsic motivation and self-determination in human behavior.* New York: Plenum.

Deci, E. L., Spiegel, N. H., Ryan, R. M., Koestner, R., & Kauffman, M. (1982). Effects of performance standards on teaching styles: Behavior of controlling teachers. *Journal of Educational Psychology, 74,* 852–859.

Dweck, C. S., & Elliott, E. S. (1983). Achievement motivation. In Paul H. Mussen (Ed.), *Handbook of Child Psychology* (Vol. 4, pp. 643–691). New York: John Wiley.

Eccles, J., Midgely, C., & Adler, T.F. (1984). Age-related changes in the school environment: Effects on achievement motivation. In J. G. Nicholls (Ed.), *The development of achievement motivation.* Greenwich, Conn: JAI Press.

Flink, C., Boggiano, A. K., & Barrett, M. (1990). Controlling teaching strategies: Undermining children's self-determination and performance. *Journal of Personality and Social Psychology, 59,* 916–924.

Garbarino, J. (1975). The impact of anticipated reward upon cross-age tutoring. *Journal of Personality and Social Psychology, 32,* 421–428.

Grolnick, W. S., & Ryan, R. M. (1987). Autonomy in children's learning: An experimental and individual difference investigation. *Journal of Personality and Social Psychology, 52,* 890–898.

Harter, S. (1974). Pleasure derived from cognitive challenge and mastery. *Child Development, 21,* 34–64.

Harter, S. (1978). Effectance motivation reconsidered: Toward a developmental model. *Human Development, 21,* 34–64.

Harter, S. (1981a). A model of mastery motivation in children: Individual differences and developmental change. In W. A. Collins (Ed.), *The Minnesota symposia on child psychology: Vol. 14. Aspects of the development of competence.* Hillsdale, NJ: Erlbaum.

Harter, S. (1981b). A new self-report scale of intrinsic versus extrinsic orientation in the classroom: Motivational and informational components. *Developmental Psychology, 17,* 300–312.

Harter, S., & Guzman, M. E. (1986). The effects of perceived cognitive competence and anxiety on children's problem-solving performance, difficulty level choices, and preference for challenge. Unpublished manuscript, University of Denver.

Jussim, L. (1986). Self-fulfilling prophecies: A theoretical and integrative review. *Psychological Review, 93,* 429–445.

Kazdin, A. E., & Wilson, G. T. (1980). *Evaluation of behavior therapy.* Lincoln: University of Nebraska Press.

Kruglanski, A. W. (1975). The endogenous-exogenous partition in attribution theory. *Psychological Review, 82,* 387–406.

Kruglanski, A. W., Friedman, I., & Zeevi, G. (1971). The effects of extrinsic incentive on some qualitative aspects of task performance. *Journal of Personality, 39,* 606–617.

Lepper, M.R., & Greene, D. (1978). *The hidden costs of reward.* Hillsdale, NJ: Erlbaum.

Lepper, M. R., Greene, D., & Nisbett, R. E. (1973). Undermining children's intrinsic interest with extrinsic rewards: A test of the overjustification hypothesis. *Journal of Personality and Social Psychology, 28,* 129–137.

Lepper, M. R., Sagotsky, G., Dafoe, J. L., & Greene, D. (1982). Consequences of superfluous social constraints: Effects on young children's social inferences and subsequent intrinsic interest. *Journal of Personality and Social Psychology, 42,* 51–65.

Maehr, M. L., & Stalling, W. M. (1972). Freedom from external evaluation. *Child Development, 42,* 177–185.

Main, D. S. (1987). Effect of controlling strategies on mastery pursuits. Unpublished doctoral dissertation, University of Colorado.

McGraw, K. O. (1978). The detrimental effects of reward on performance: A literature review and a prediction model. In M. R. Lepper & D. Greene (Eds.), *The hidden costs of reward* (pp. 33–60). Hillsdale, NJ: Erlbaum.

McGraw, K. O., & McCullers, J. C. (1979). Evidence of a detrimental effect of extrinsic incentives on breaking a mental set. *Journal of Experimental Social Psychology, 15,* 285–294.

Mehrabian, A. (1968). Relationship of attitude to seated posture, orientation, and distance. *Journal of Personality and Social Psychology, 10,* 26–30.

Nolen-Hoeksema, S. (1987). Sex differences in unipolar depression: Evidence and theory. *Psychological Bulletin, 101,* 259–282.

Nolen-Hoeksema, S., Girgus, J. S., & Seligman, M. E. P. (1986). Learned helplessness in children: A longitudinal study of depression, achievement, and explanatory style. *Journal of Personality and Social Psychology, 51,* 435–442.

O'Leary, K. D., & Drabman, R. S. (1971). Token reinforcement programs in the classroom: A review. *Psychological Bulletin, 75,* 379–398.

Peterson, C., & Seligman, M. E. P. (1984). Causal explanations as a risk factor for depression: Theory and evidence. *Psychological Review, 91,* 347–374.

Pittman, T. S., Boggiano, A. K., & Ruble, D. R. (1983). Rewards and intrinsic motivation in children: Implications for educational settings. In J. M. Levine and M. Wang (Eds.), *Perceptions of success and failure: New directions in research* (pp. 319–341). Hillsdale, NJ: Erlbaum.

Pittman, T. S., Emery, J., & Boggiano, A. K. (1982). Intrinsic and extrinsic motivational orientations: Reward-induced change in preference for complexity. *Journal of Personality and Social Psychology, 42,* 789–797.

Ryan, R. M. (1982). Control and information in the intrapersonal sphere: An extension of cognitive evaluative theory. *Journal of Personality and Social Psychology, 43,* 450–461.

Shapira, Z. (1976). Expectancy determinants of intrinsically motivated behavior. *Journal of Personality and Social Psychology, 34,* 1235–1244.

Weisz, J. R., & Stipek, D. J. (1982). Competence, contingency, and the development of perceived control. *Human Development, 25,* 250–281.

White, R. W. (1959). Motivation reconsidered: The concept of competence. *Psychological Review, 66,* 297–333.

10 On being psyched up but not psyched out: An optimal pressure model of achievement motivation

Philip R. Costanzo, Erik Woody, and Pamela Slater

Simply stated, one central issue in the study of achievement motivation is to understand the psychological conditions under which people perform to the best of their capacities. Theorizing about such conditions is relatively complex due to two factors. First, there are many situational variables that might affect the intervening variable of motivation; and the question arises of how these multiple situational influences combine to raise or lower motivation. Second, the relation of motivation, in turn, to performance may not be a straightforward linear one; rather, motivation may be a mediating influence of which there is sometimes too little and sometimes too much. When the individual's level of motivation is too low to facilitate optimal performance, we may refer to a state of *undermotivation,* whereas when the individual's level of motivation is too high to lead to optimal performance, the problem is one of *overmotivation.*

The present conceptual framework and empirical research focuses on situational factors of a principally cognitive nature and their impact on motivation and performance. It advances a very simple but workable idea about how situational variables are integrated to affect motivation, and it also examines the nonlinear relation of motivation to performance. To set the stage for our own work, it will be useful to review some of the previous research on achievement motivation under the two rubrics already mentioned – the phenomenon of undermotivation and the phenomenon of overmotivation. This will allow us not only to trace the variety in how motivation affects performance, but also to flesh out the situational variables used in our work with a bit of their history.

Portions of this paper have been distilled from Pamela Slater's Ph.D. dissertation, *The relationship between pressure and performance: exploring and optimal achievement pressure model and its implications for gender-based theories,* completed at Duke University.

Perspectives on undermotivation

As is widely acknowledged, the origin of much work in achievement motivation is the Atkinson-McClelland expectancy-value theory (Atkinson & Feather, 1966). Atkinson and his colleagues argued that the behavior of people in competitive achievement situations reflects two acquired traits – the motive to achieve success and the motive to avoid failure. Although some people may be high or low in both traits, principal theoretical interest inhered in predicting the behavior of individuals characterized by the predominance of one motive or the other (Atkinson & Litwin, 1960). In a free-choice situation, people dominated by the motive to achieve success should tend to engage in achievement tasks, whereas ones dominated by the motive to avoid failure should prefer to avoid all achievement tasks. When people are constrained to perform, predictions become more complex, and it is necessary to consider the interaction of the achievement motives with two situation-specific variables – expectancy for success and the value of the incentive. Atkinson proposed that the strength of the motivation to perform an act is a multiplicative function of these variables. Thus, the tendency to approach a task is reflected by the product of the motive to achieve, the perceived likelihood of success, and the attractiveness of success. Likewise, the tendency to avoid a task is reflected by the product of the motive to avoid failure, the perceived likelihood of failure, and the unattractiveness of failure. Finally, the theory posits that behavior in an achievement situation is determined by the sum of these approach and avoidance tendencies.

In practice, the theory is simplified considerably by Atkinson's assumption that the incentive value of an outcome is entirely determined by its subjective likelihood. Other researchers have pointed out that this assumption is too simplistic, since factors accruing from success, such as social or material gains, may affect the value of an outcome in addition to expectancy (Canavan-Gumpert, Garner, & Gumpert, 1978). Nonetheless, it is likely that the more difficult the task, the greater the attractiveness of success; and the easier the task, the more anxiety is aroused by the prospect of failure. It follows that both the tendencies to approach and to avoid a task are maximized when the difficulty of the task is intermediate – that is, when the likelihood of success and failure are equal. Thus, moderately difficult tasks are the most attractive to individuals dominated by the motive to achieve success, and the most anxiety-arousing to individuals dominated by the motive to avoid failure.

Variations on a theme: the issue of achievement behavior in women

Although the Atkinson-McClelland model has garnered some empirical support (e.g., Weiner, Frieze, Kukla, Reed, Rest, & Rosenbaum, 1972), there have been many proposals to modify and extend it. One of the most interesting lines of proposed modification has come out of work on gender differences in achievement motivation. Some studies have suggested that females tend to perform less successfully than males on real-world indicators of educational and occupational achievement (Frieze, Parsons, Johnson, Ruble, & Zellman, 1978); and although there are obviously many possible causes for this, motivational underpinnings are one interesting possibility. In addition, by the early seventies, the few experimental studies on achievement motivation that had been conducted with females seemed to produce results inconsistent with the theoretical predictions of the Atkinson-McClelland model and with male achievement behavior (Horner, 1973). Consequently, a number of theories were advanced to explain the relatively greater difficulty shown by women in performing optimally in competitive achievement circumstances. These theories constitute a set of variations on the basic Atkinson-McClelland model, in the sense that they propose that gender differences in trait motives, values, or expectancies produce gender differences in achievement behavior.

Horner (1973) argued that the fundamental difference between the sexes in the determinants of achievement behavior is a difference in motives, such that males value success whereas females are ambivalent about it. She hypothesized that in addition to the motives to achieve success and to avoid failure, there is a third trait – the motive to avoid success – which is unique to women. In essence, it is an unconscious tendency to anticipate negative consequences as a result of success, including loss of femininity, low self-esteem, and social rejection.

Horner proposed that this female-specific disposition is acquired in conjunction with female sex role standards. That is, women learn early in life that femininity is incompatible with achievement, because achievement implies masculine characteristics such as aggressiveness and competitiveness. The resulting fear of success causes intrapsychic conflict for women in achievement circumstances, which inhibits their achievement strivings and leads them to perform below their ability levels.

On the basis of this theory, Horner (1973) advanced three major hypotheses. First, fear of success should be more common among women than among men, due to differential sex role socialization. Second, fear of success is most likely to be aroused in situations that heighten the potential negative consequences of success – specifically, competitive achievement situations in which the task is male-stereotype oriented (such as one reflecting competitive competence or leadership ability) and in which the competitor is a male. Third, women likely to achieve success – high ability, achievement-oriented women – should show more fear of success than low ability, nonachievement-oriented women, since high likelihood of success activates fear of success.

Horner's original empirical study to evaluate these hypotheses has been the target of a great deal of criticism (Murphy-Berman, 1975; Tresemer, 1977; Zuckerman & Wheeler, 1975) and seems to provide little sound evidence in support of the theory. Subsequent research has also failed to confirm certain hypotheses. Few studies have reported a high incidence of fear of success among women or the predicted gender difference in the prevalence of the motive (Tresemer, 1977; Zuckerman & Wheeler, 1975). However, the weight of the evidence does support Horner's notions about the conditions that inhibit the performance of females. That is, a number of studies have found that females tend to show performance decrements when moving from a noncompetitive to a mixed-sex competitive trial on a male-oriented task (Heilbrun, Kleemeier, & Piccola, 1974; Karabenick & Marshall, 1974; Morgan & Mausner, 1973). Nonetheless, most studies have found no relation (Eme & Lawrence, 1976; Feather & Simon, 1973; Morgan & Mausner, 1973; Peplau, 1976; Romer, 1975) or an inverse relation (Heilbrun et al., 1974; Sorrentino & Short, 1974) between fear of success and performance decrement.

Some researchers have argued that a central problem with Horner's theory is the assumption of an unconscious motive – fear of success – that is unnecessary and difficult to measure reliably. Canavan-Gumpert and colleagues (1978) have contended that women do, as Horner suggests, face conflicts between achievement needs and female role demands, but that such conflicts are conscious and are sometimes resolved in ways that prevent performance decrement. This less dynamic "conscious conflict" interpretation of Horner's theory rejects the notion that performance decrements in females stem from success anxiety generated by an unconscious motive, instead attributing such decrements to the relatively conscious conflict between the anticipated positive and negative consequences of success for women in our society. Thus, success and failure may be seen as taking on a range of possible incentive values, including positive value, negative value, and simultaneous positive and negative values. In addition, by affecting these incentive values, task characteristics – including whether a task is competitive or not, whether a task involves competition with a male or with another female, and whether a task measures stereotypically masculine or feminine qualities – can heighten the likelihood of performance inhibition.

Achievement behavior as a function of gender differences in value orientation

Similar to the conscious-conflict reinterpretation of Horner's theory is a theory that has emerged out of research with mixed-motive game paradigms, such as the Prisoner's Dilemma game. Across various tasks, females play less optimally than do males (e.g., Bedell & Sistrunk, 1973; Hottes & Kahn, 1974; Kahn, Hottes, & Davis, 1971; McNeel, MnClintock, & Nuttin, 1972), and they vary their behavior more than do males in response to the sex of the opponent, the sex of the experimenter, and the perceived attractiveness and personality characteristics of the opponent (Bedell & Sistrunk, 1973; Hottes & Kahn, 1974). Such evidence suggests that when females fail to perform as optimally as males in competitive achievement situations, they are engaging in strategic performance depression. That is, it is argued that they intentionally depress their performance in order to achieve particular social goals, such as impressing one's opponent (Kahn et al., 1971) or conforming to feminine sex role demands (Benton, 1973; Morgan & Mausner, 1973).

Basically, the proponents of the strategic performance depression theory hypothesize that females, faced with a choice between satisfying either achievement needs or social needs, opt for social gratification, unlike males. Females play the "achievement" game to lose when losing offers success in the social sphere. Females would be expected to depress their performance deliberately when the likelihood of succeeding is high (thereby creating the need to lower performance in an intentional fashion), and when the anticipated negative consequences of success (e.g., being disliked due to violation of sex role demands) outweigh the anticipated positive consequences (e.g., the intrinsic pleasure generated by success). By contrast, if expectancy of success were low (thereby eliminating the need to perform poorly intentionally), or the value attached to success were on balance more positive, then strategic performance depression would be less likely to occur.

That females will forego the satisfaction of achievement needs to attain social outcomes presumably reflects gender differences in value orientation. In other words, females are socialized to be primarily "socially oriented," while males are socialized to be primarily "achievement oriented" (cf., Maccoby & Jacklin, 1974). According to Horner's theory, females who perform poorly in competition strive to win, but are inhibited by unconscious conflict and the attendant anxiety about success. According to the strategic performance depression theory, however, such females knowingly elect not to try to their full capacities, and should feel reasonably satisfied upon failing, since unlike males, they simply do not *value* winning as much as social success.

Gender differences in expectancies

We have considered how individual differences in motives and values have been hypothesized to underlie gender differences in achievement behavior. Another line of reasoning has focused on the other principal variable stemming from the Atkinson-McClelland model – expectancies. Specifically, Deaux (1976) developed a theory of gender differences in achievement behavior in which the main determinant of such differences is variation in initial levels of confidence. First, females tend to approach achievement tasks with lower expectations of success than do males. These gender differences in confidence develop through a process of "self-stereotyping," whereby males and females internalize stereotypic images of males as more adequate, competent, and aggressive competitors than females. Second, these initial expectancies are hypothesized to produce outcome attributions that maintain the expectancies, even in the face of disconfirming evidence. For males, with high expectancies of success, actual success on a task will confirm their expectancies and be attributed to high ability; whereas failure will be inconsistent with high expectancies and will therefore be attributed to a temporary cause, such as bad luck or low effort (cf. Weiner et al., 1972). By contrast, females, with their lower expectations of success, should find actual success discrepant with their expectations and tend to attribute it to transient causes such as good luck; whereas failure is consistent with their lower confidence and readily attributable to the stable cause of lack of ability. Finally, Deaux argued that over an extended period of time, expectancies determine the level of performance on achievement tasks by affecting the motivation to engage or persist in certain tasks and thus by shaping the degree to which one develops skills in those areas. Hence, in the long run, low expectancies would have a debilitating effect on ability and performance, and high expectancies a facilitative effect.

Unfortunately, Deaux's theory is difficult to evaluate because in most studies that have found sex differences in achievement behavior and attributional patterns, the role of expectancies as a determinant of those outcomes has not been clearly assessed. However, there is considerable evidence that males express higher expectancies than females prior to engaging in achievement tasks; and this difference emerges quite early developmentally (Dweck & Elliott, 1983), well before the emergence of any associated differences in achievement. Indeed, while higher achievement in boys is associated with higher expectancies of success, higher achievement in girls is actually associated with *lower* expectancies (e.g., Stipek & Hoffman, 1979). The early development of expectancy differences is consistent with Deaux's suggestions that expectancies stem from gender self-stereotyping and precede other gender differences in achievement behavior.

Integration of perspectives on undermotivation

Our brief foray into the literature on gender differences in achievement behavior has served its purpose of bringing forward a range of ideas about conditions that are undermotivating. To this end, the McClelland-Atkinson theory identified three major variables that are implicated in achievement motivation – unconscious motives, values attached to outcomes, and the perceived expectancies of attaining those outcomes. Unfavorable levels on these variables may bring about undermotivation, in the sense they elicit suboptimal effort.

First, unconscious motives may contribute to undermotivating circumstances. Thus the motive to avoid failure may predominate over the motive to achieve success, or the motive to avoid success may lead to conflict that partly neutralizes the motive to achieve success. Second, when success in the situation entails both attractive and unattractive outcomes, the relative values that the individual attaches to those outcomes may inhibit optimal achievement. Thus for some individuals the social cost of success may outweigh its intrinsic benefit, leading to reduced effort. Third, low expectancy of success may likewise lead an individual not to try optimally, and in addition may have self-fulfilling qualities. Thus people with low expectancies of success may perceive real success as mere luck, but internalize failure in such a way as to make future effort relatively unattractive.

In contrast, the theories reviewed also suggest situational factors that should enhance the performer's desire for success and tendency to strive to achieve that outcome. Specifically, certain levels of incentive value and expectancy would be expected to heighten the motivation to succeed.

First let us consider incentive value. As we have seen, recent theorists on achievement motivation have questioned Atkinson's original assumptions that incentive value is exclusively dependent on expectancy and that success and failure are unmixed or univalent outcomes. The incentive value of an outcome depends on a number of factors in addition to expectancy, including the anticipated consequences of achieving it. The work on female achievement motivation indicates that these consequences are both extrinsic, such as the social and material gains and losses associated with success and failure, and intrinsic, such as the degree of pride generated by mastery or competence. Thus both anticipated intrinsic and extrinsic consequences for success appear to contribute to the incentive value of an outcome. Concerning the extrinsic consequences, it would appear that when the negative situational consequences of success or the positive consequences of failure are minimized, the motivation to strive for success is enhanced. Concerning intrinsic consequences, these appear to be the most motivating when the task provides a measure of a central and personally valued ability, in which case success and failure have an impact on self-esteem.

Turning to expectancy, our review of the various theories on achievement motivation provides two basic hypotheses about the level of expectancy (high, mixed-moderate, or low) likely to generate the maximum motivation to strive for success in an achievement situation. The first hypothesis is that the motivation to strive for success increases as the likelihood of achieving success decreases. This hypothesis reflects the assumption central to the Atkinson-McClelland theory that expectancy and value are inversely related, such that the importance of success increases as the difficulty of achieving it increases. On the basis of this reasoning, then, one might predict that the performer's desire to achieve success would be greatest on a high difficulty task (low expectancy situation), moderate on a moderately difficult task (mixed expectancy situation), and least on a low difficulty task (high expectancy situation). However, the other hypothesis is that the mixed expectancy situation, meaning the one in which success and failure are equally probable outcomes, maximizes the wish for success. Again according to the Atkinson-McClelland theory, the mixed expectancy condition is supposed to be more likely than high or low expectancy circumstances to arouse the dominant achievement motive, and more "diagnostic" of the level of the actor's effort and skill. It may be that the mixed expectancy condition heightens both the attractiveness of success and the aversiveness of failure, thus creating a highly motivating situation. Hence, there are reasonable grounds for arguing that either the mixed expectancy or the low expectancy condition is likely to maximize the motivation to strive for success on an achievement task.

Perspectives on overmotivation

Unfortunately, situations that maximize motivation do not necessarily maximize performance as well. There are some grounds to believe that beyond a moderate level, further increases in motivation may lead to decrements in performance. The theoretical underpinnings of this hypothesis come from arousal theory – specifically, the argument that internal arousal has an inverted-U relation to performance (Duffy, 1957; Malmo, 1959; Yerkes & Dodson, 1908). Since achievement motivation should be fairly closely linked to the level of internal arousal, it follows that highly motivating circumstances may drive an individual's level of arousal beyond the optimal level and thus actually lower performance.

This intriguing hypothesis has received some attention in the achievement motivation literature, especially in the research of Samuel and his colleagues. In a series of very similar experimental studies, subjects worked in either a "stressful" or "relaxed" environment on problems for which they experienced success or failure (Samuel, 1977; Samuel, Baynes, & Sabeh, 1978; Samuel, Soto, Parks, Ngissah, & Jones, 1976). The stressfulness of the environment was manipulated essentially via generalized expectancies – half the subjects believing most anyone was very likely to do well on the task (supposedly inducing stress due to evaluative pressure), the other half believing that no one would find the problems easy. The researchers hypothesized that failure in a stressful setting should be the most arousing and success in a relaxed setting the least arousing; thus the subjects in these conditions should subsequently perform less well than the other two groups of subjects. In the terminology used here, the successful, relaxed subjects would be regarded as undermotivated, and the unsuccessful, stressed subjects as overmotivated.

The performance results were generally consistent with the arousal hypothesis; and a measure of arousal based on five self-report bodily symptoms showed a fairly clear inverted-U relation to performance (collapsing across experimental conditions). Unfortunately, the researchers were unable to show that the arousal measure was affected as predicted by the experimental manipulations, thus casting some doubt on the assumption that internal arousal mediates the link between situational factors and performance. Samuel (1980) has also shown that personality scores indicative of "upset mood" – and, one might presume, arousal – exhibit a rather weak tendency toward an inverted-U relation with IQ-test scores.

The arousal variables used in these studies are not unproblematic, however. For example, they have peculiar and strongly nonnormal distributions; and they were administered after the performance tasks and thus may be regarded as a reaction to performance, rather than a mediator of it. Another problem is that it is difficult to relate the situational manipulations used in the experimental studies to the classic achievement motivation variables reviewed earlier. In fact, in some ways the conceptual thrust of the situational manipulations does not seem to bear the interpretive weight the researchers place on it. For example, the very important combination of "stressful" atmosphere and failure on the pretrial has the seemingly obvious connotation to the subjects that they are unintelligent – a violation of expectancy condition somewhat difficult to relate to the other work on achievement motivation reviewed here. In addition, this clear connotation, since it requires *both* conditions interactively, does not accord well with the researchers' claim that stressful atmosphere and failure at the preliminary task "each make an independent, additive contribution to an examinee's state of internal arousal" (Samuel et al., 1978). Nonetheless, despite some problems of this sort, the work is suggestive and provocative.

Why might excessive motivation disrupt performance?

If indeed arousal is an important mediator between situational factors and performance decrement in achievement contexts, through what mechanisms does this mediation take place? One approach to this question has been via test anxiety theory (e.g., Sarason, 1980), which is based on a Hullian Habit x Drive model. Basically, the idea is that situational cues can elicit a drive state – "test anxiety" – which in turn sometimes activates task-relevant and productive responses, but often activates task-irrelevant and interfering responses instead. Particularly when the task is difficult and the individual's response hierarchy is dominated by task-irrelevant responses, high drive levels should lead to responses incompatible with optimal performance (e.g., self-preoccupation).

A more thoroughgoing theoretical approach to the mechanisms that may underlie overmotivation has been offered by Humphreys and Revelle (1984). These researchers make two central assumptions. The first is that in an achievement task, situational manipulations, as well as individual differences, influence two core motivational states – arousal level and on-task effort. The second assumption is that these two motivational states in turn affect two basic component processes in information-processing tasks – sustained information transfer, and short-term memory. Situational manipulations are seen as differentially affecting arousal and effort. For example, the authors argue that the kinds of manipulations used in the achievement motivation literature probably chiefly affect on-task effort, and have little or no impact on arousal (a perhaps questionable assumption). Likewise, performance tasks are seen as differing importantly in the amount of sustained information transfer versus short-term memory resources required.

Based on these assumptions, Humphreys and Revelle forge an elegant theory: The curvilinear relation between motivation and performance represents two opposing monotonic processes. On the one hand, higher arousal and on-task effort both bring about increases in the resources available for the sustained-information-transfer components of a task. On the other hand, higher arousal also brings about decreases in the resources available for the short-term-memory components of the task, whereas higher effort is hypothesized not to affect short-term memory. The superimposition of these two processes produces an inverted-U relation between motivation and performance.

Basically, then, overmotivation effects are attributed to excessive levels of arousal and their debilitating effect on short-term memory. However, Humphreys and Revelle show that according to the theory, high effort (reflecting high achievement motives and cognitive situational influences) should increase the likelihood of an overmotivation effect. This is because high-effort subjects quickly reach the limit on any further improvement in sustained information transfer that increased arousal can afford, while at the same time the increased arousal erodes the subjects' short-term memory functioning.

Humphreys and Revelle also address the role of anxiety, in a fashion strongly akin to test anxiety theory. They argue that anxiety has both a worry or cognitive component, and a somatic tension or drive component. Increases in the cognitive component produce reductions in on-task effort, due to interference from self-appraisal and negative self-statements. By contrast, increases in somatic tension raise arousal. Under some conditions, the increase in arousal due to anxiety could improve performance; however, more often, and especially with a complex task with high memory requirements, increases in anxiety would lead to decrements in performance.

It is interesting to reflect back on the experimental studies of Samuel and his colleagues (e.g., Samuel et al., 1978) in the light of this model of the effects of anxiety. After subjects experienced failure in a stressful atmosphere, performance decrements may have been due more to reductions of on-task effort than to the increases in arousal that the researchers hypothesized but did not obtain. Of course, one would still need to explain why failure appears to lead to improved performance under relaxed conditions, compared to success. However, failure would verify the low expectancies generated by the relaxed condition, and therefore, by indicating clearly that the task was challenging, may have raised the incentive value of the task. Thus there are indeed grounds to suspect that the experimental manipulations did not work principally by differentially raising internal arousal, as opposed to affecting more cognitive processes.

In a similar vein, Baumeister and Showers (1986) deemphasize arousal as an explanation of overmotivation effects and instead point to disruptions of on-task attention. Their chief concern is with overmotivation effects in sports performance under pressure, colloquially termed "choking"; but they draw interesting attention to commonalities between such effects in sports and in intellectual achievement contexts. Akin to Humphreys and Revelle, they argue that a decline in performance under pressure may be explained by distraction due to worry – that is, reduced attention to on-task cues and increased attention to task-irrelevant cues. However, they distinguish this possibility from that of performance deficits due to self-focused attention or self-awareness. For example, conscious attention to the process of performance may interfere with and slow down skills best executed automatically, since the person may not consciously know how he or she does something and may deliberate fruitlessly over alternatives. Similarly, attention to the potential goals or outcomes of performance – such as imagining the victory celebration to come – might interfere with on-task behavior, since they have little to do with the ongoing task.

In summary, overmotivation effects have been hypothetically attributed to a number of mediators. These include arousal, distraction due to worry, and self-focused attention. These factors do not appear to be mutually exclusive, and as the Humphreys and Revelle model suggests, may well occur together.

Integrating under- and overmotivation: the concept of optimal pressure

Our research was intended to integrate a number of previous perspectives on achievement behavior. Our own approach makes use of the classical achievement motivation variables, but takes account of their new guises in more recent work such as the sex-differences literature. Our particular focus is on variation in situational factors that affect motivation and performance, rather than on individual differences in traits. In addition, we take an approach in which undermotivation and overmotivation effects are viewed as a function of different levels of the same set of variables; in this respect our work builds on the research of Samuel and his colleagues (e.g., Samuel et al., 1978), although we examine the effects of a quite different set of independent variables from those researchers.

Baumeister and Showers (1986) usefully define "pressure" as "the presence of situational incentives for optimal, maximal, or superior performance" (p. 362). As they suggest, pressure is not just arousal, but has an essential phenomenological component, in the sense that the individual is aware of the incentive in question. In addition, there are a number of possible forms or sources of such pressure; Baumeister and Showers tentatively suggest that when they occur together, they may be additive.

Borrowing from classical expectancy-value theory, we would argue that the expectancy and incentive value of success in a given achievement situation combine to create varying degrees of pressure on the individual; and that this pressure increases as success becomes more attractive and failure more aversive. Expectancy, meaning the subjective estimate of the likelihood of success or failure, affects the pressure to strive for success by contributing to the positive incentive value of success and the negative incentive value of failure. Despite the inverse relation that may generally exist between expectancy and value, we anticipated that a condition of mixed expectancy (50–50 chance of success), by heightening the importance of success and the threat of failure simultaneously, would be likely to create more pressure to strive for success than a condition of high expectancy, in which both the value of success and the threat of failure are low, or a condition of low expectancy, in which the value of success is high but the threat of failure is low.

Turning to incentive value, although it was defined by Atkinson simply as the attractiveness of success or the unattractiveness of failure (both determined by expectancy), recent theories concerning female achievement motivation have introduced the notion that success and failure may be bivalent. That is, success may sometimes have unattractive properties and failure attractive ones. In addition, we would argue that while some incentives are *intrinsic,* such as enacting one's high ability, others are extrinsic or *situational,* such as rewards or punishments. Hence, incentive value may be defined more broadly as the attractiveness or unattractiveness of success, compared to failure, as determined by the anticipated intrinsic and situational consequences of experiencing those outcomes.

Thus we are considering three distinct sources of pressure: expectancy of success, the intrinsic value of success, and the situational consequences of success. We hypothesize that these three components are roughly *coequal* determinants of the positive value of success and negative value of failure; and that they *combine additively* to determine the amount of pressure to strive for success created by a given achievement circumstance. Furthermore, we hypothesize that performance on an achievement task bears a *curvilinear relation* to total pressure. That is, a very low level of

Table 10.1. *Pressure sources in the expectancy by intrinsic value by social consequence conditions*

	Intrinsic value high		Intrinsic value low	
Expectancy	Situational consequences of success: positive	Situational consequences of success: negative	Situational consequences of success: positive	Situational consequences of success: negative
High	+2	+1	+1	0
Mixed	+3	+2	+2	+1
Low	+2	+1	+1	0

situational pressure should lead to undermotivation and suboptimal performance; moderate pressure should lead to optimal levels of motivation and hence performance; and finally, very high pressure should generate overmotivation and performance decrements.

These predictions are outlined in Table 10.1. Each cell has been assigned a pressure value based on the number of sources of pressure to succeed bearing on that cell. High intrinsic value, positive situational consequences, and mixed expectancy were each assumed to convey one unit of pressure; and their alternative conditions were assumed to convey none. The resulting sums are obviously somewhat oversimplified, but do represent the key predictions that decrements in performance are likely to occur in overmotivating (+3) and undermotivating (0) conditions, while optimal performance is expected when motivation is moderate (+2 or +1).

An illustrative study of the dynamics of optimal, suboptimal, and supraoptimal pressure

In an experiment, we independently manipulated these three sources of pressure – intrinsic value, situational consequences, and expectancy – and observed their effects on performance. The subjects were forty-eight male and forty-eight female high school students, half of which came from a public school and half from a private academy. Although students from the two schools tend to share relatively high socioeconomic backgrounds and positive orientations to achievement, the private academy is smaller and more academically demanding and competitive, as suggested by the higher average academic aptitude and achievement of its students.

The intrinsic value of success was manipulated by describing the ability to be assessed either as "creativity" (high value) or "puzzle-solving ability" (low value), each accompanied by a brief definition. These descriptions were selected in a preliminary study because creativity was perceived as significantly more important than puzzle-solving ability by both sexes; and neither males nor females were very certain of their ability on either dimension, a valuable characteristic given the need to manipulate subjects' expectancies of success on measures of these abilities.

The expectancy of success was manipulated by providing both fictitious norms about task difficulty and a practice task in which the subject's degree of success appeared to confirm the norms. This procedure combined the main two manipulations used in earlier research, and, again as in previous research, yielded three distinct levels of expectancy: high expectancy of success; mixed or moderate expectancy, in which success and failure seemed equally likely; and low expectancy of success. More specifically, subjects were told that "by a random draw" they had been asigned the "high," "moderate," or "low" difficulty test; and then they were given a "practice trial" on which there was "about a 95% overlap between performance on this task and on the actual test."After bogus scoring of this task, subjects were informed that their "chances of succeeding on the actual test" were "15%," "51%," or "85%."

The situational consequences of success were manipulated so as to appear either positive or negative. Consequences of a social nature were selected to allow us to test concurrently the predictions of the fear of success and strategic depression models, which identify social costs and benefits as particularly powerful determinants of achievement behavior. Subjects were told, "If you succeed on the test, you will be asked to serve as an experimental assistant" in another study by acting "as a peer-tutor for a subject in this study." Half of the subjects were then informed that subjects in the other study "are quite pleased to have the assistance of peer tutors," with the tutor being very well liked, respected, and appreciated. By contrast, the other half of the subjects were told that subjects in the other study "react quite negatively," the tutor being very disliked, resented, and distrusted.

At this point in the procedure, the actual test took place, performance on which constituted the key dependent measure in the experiment. Subjects had three minutes to "study and remember as much as they could" about a literary passage, whereupon they were asked to answer a set of questions, some of which elicited their general impressions and others their retention of information in the passage. A preliminary study showed that subjects tended to view this task as neither very high nor very low in difficulty, and were not too certain of its difficulty level, conditions presumably favorable to the continuing plausibility of the expectancy of success manipulation.

In accord with a trend in the literature to employ memory tasks as the dependent measure in studies of achievement motivation (see Canavan-Gumpert et al., 1978; Eme & Lawrence, 1976; Heilbrun et al., 1974; Karabenick, 1977), the question which elicited free recall of information was of primary interest. The recall measure was calculated by scoring each detail recalled from the passage for degree of exactness, assigning higher credit to exact recall, and then summing scores across details to get a composite score. Here it may be noted that results on an additional dependent measure – the subject's number of correct responses to a set of seven true-false questions, a measure of recognition memory – were broadly consistent with those reported here for the free recall measure.

Finally, following the test, subjects were given some questions concerning their affect and attention; these results will be mentioned briefly.

Results

The free recall measure, based on both the quality and quantity of recalled information, was the chief dependent measure in this study. Expectancy of success, intrinsic value of success, and social consequences of success were the independent variables, along with sex of subject and high school of subject. According to the optimal pressure theory, the nonlinear combined effects of the three sources of pressure should lead to higher-order interactions – most clearly, a three-way interaction. Indeed, an analysis of variance on these data yielded significant higher-order interactions; however, the influence of expectancy was more complex than anticipated, as it tended to interact with the subject variables of sex and high school. Let us first look at the results for intrinsic value and social consequences, then proceed to the more complex picture afforded by considering expectancy as well.

Means for the significant interaction of intrinsic value and social consequences are provided in Table 10.2. It is important to note that the combination of these two factors theoretically generated three levels of pressure to strive for success: a two-pressure condition (the cell of high intrinsic value and positive social consequence), a pressure-absent condition (the cell of low intrinsic value and negative social consequences), and two single-pressure conditions (the two other cells), as noted by integers under the cell means in Table 10.2. The means show that when intrinsic value of success was high, performance was significantly better in the face

Table 10.2. *Mean recall scores obtained by subjects in the intrinsic value by social consequence conditions*

	High intrinsic value	Low intrinsic value	Social consequence means
Positive	19.92[a]	27.46[b]	23.69
Negative	26.42[b]	23.29[a b]	24.86
Intrinsic value means	23.17	25.38	

Note: In this and subsequent tables, means not sharing a common superscript are significantly different at the $p < .05$ level or beyond.

of negative social consequences for success than in the face of positive social consequences. Moreover, when the intrinsic value of success was low, the anticipation of positive social consequences showed some tendency to improve performance compared to the anticipation of negative consequences, although not quite to a statistically significant degree.

These findings clash with the predictions of fear of success and performance depression theories, which hold that negative social consequences depress performance, particularly on highly valued tasks. In contrast, the results are broadly consistent with our optimal pressure model of performance; better performance occurred in conditions with one positive motivational pressure than in those with two pressures or none.

A little more complicated were the results for expectancy, as there was both a significant three-way interaction with sex and high school, and a significant four-way interaction with intrinsic value, social consequence, and high school. Means for the interaction of expectancy with sex and high school are provided in Table 10.3, whose marginals also reflect two significant main effects – females performed better than males overall, as did private academy students over public school students. The most striking feature of this pattern of means is that public school females in the high expectancy condition performed quite a bit lower than they did in the mixed and low expectancy conditions, unlike their public school male counterparts. This is consistent with theories on fear of success and performance depression, which would suggest that the high expectancy condition, the one in which success is a likely outcome, should elicit success avoidance for females and not males. However, inconsistent with these theories are both the overall tendency for females to outperform males and the pattern of performance demonstrated by private school females.

Table 10.3. *Mean performance scores obtained by subjects in the Expectancy × Gender × High School conditions*

	High School				
	Private		Public		Expectancy
Expectancy	Male	Female	Male	Female	group means
High	22.50[b c]	30.50[d e]	20.13[a b c]	19.13[a b]	23.06
Mixed	25.00[b d c]	24.63[b c e]	14.25[a]	31.88[d e]	23.81
Low	27.13[c d]	31.86[d]	14.88[a]	29.88[d e]	25.94
Gender × High School means	24.87	29.00	16.42	26.80	
High School means	26.94		21.61		

The means for the interaction of expectancy, intrinsic value, social consequence, and high school are provided in Table 10.4, again accompanied by integers denoting the respective numbers of pressure sources. The pattern of means found in the intrinsic value by social consequence interaction, discussed above, emerged clearly in the high expectancy condition for private academy students and the low expectancy condition for public school students. That is, in both instances subjects tended to perform better in anticipation of negative social consequences than positive ones when the intrinsic value of success was high; and they tended to perform better in anticipation of positive social consequences than negative ones when the intrinsic value of success was low.

Considering the other means obtained for private academy students, it was found that contrary to our assumption that high and low expectancy should be equivalent in motivational pressure, the low expectancy condition yielded a unique set of findings. Private school students in the low expectancy condition performed uniformly high in recall. In the mixed expectancy condition, it was found that private academy students performed optimally in the presence of one motivational pressure, while the augmentation of pressure depressed performance to a minimal level in the three-pressure cell. The difference between the single-pressure and the three-pressure cells was significant, and is of course consistent with the optimal pressure model.

Turning to the other means for public school students, it was found that

Table 10.4. *Mean recall scores obtained by subjects in the expectancy by intrinsic value by social consequence by high school conditions*

	Private				Public				
	High intrinsic value		Low intrinsic value		High intrinsic value		Low intrinsic value		
Expectancy	Positive	Negative	Positive	Negative	Positive	Negative	Positive	Negative	
	ae	f	bef	ae	ac	af	ae	ae	
High	21.50	36.25	28.25	20.00	15.00	23.00	20.50	20.00	23.06
	2	1	1	0	2	1	1	0	
	ad	aef	aef	ef	ae	ae	af	af	
Mixed	17.75	22.75	24.75	34.00	21.00	19.75	27.00	23.50	23.81
	3	2	2	1	3	2	2	1	
	def	def	bef	fce	ab	af	f	a	
Low	30.25	31.00	27.50	29.25	14.00	25.75	36.75	13.00	25.94
	2	1	1	0	2	1	1	0	
	23.17	30.00	26.83	27.75	16.67	22.83	28.08	18.83	

the high and low expectancy conditions again had unexpectedly different effects on recall. In the high expectancy condition, while negative social consequences tended, though not significantly, to heighten performance more than positive ones in the high intrinsic value condition as expected, no differences emerged due to social consequence in the low intrinsic value condition. In addition, in the mixed expectancy condition, although mean differences were not significant, the pattern of means suggest a tendency for positive social consequences to lead to higher recall than negative consequences, particularly in the low intrinsic value condition.

Overall test of the optimal pressure model

The expectancy by intrinsic value by social consequence by high school interaction is quite intriguing because it involves the three independent variables of primary interest. That is, the combination of the expectancy, intrinsic value, and social consequence variables theoretically yielded conditions ranging in pressure from a minimum of zero, to an intermediate level of one or two pressures, to a maximum level of three pressures to strive for success. Here we would like to present another perspective on the combined effects of these factors – an analysis in which more assumptions need to be made, but in which the overall fit of the results to the model is much clearer.

We used planned comparisons to test directly for differences in recall at different levels of pressure. In the comparisons conducted, means of conditions hypothetically "equal" in the number of pressure factors were combined, using weighted coefficients, to provide better estimates of recall at each level of pressure. Underlying this analysis were the assumptions that the pressure sources were equal in magnitude and additive in their effect on motivation. The associated means are plotted in Figure 10.1. The curves in the figure were plotted for each high school using mean recall scores at 0, 1, 2, and 3 levels of pressure. The clear implication of these curves is that the high school samples responded in roughly similar fashions to the achievement pressures, demonstrating better recall in the single-pressure condition than in any other, and showing decrements in performance with 0 and 2 pressure circumstances.

Turning to the planned comparisons, it was found that private academy students performed significantly better in the single pressure conditions than in either the three-pressure or the two-pressure conditions. Public school students performed significantly better in the single pressure conditions than in either the zero pressure or the two pressure conditions. Finally, taking the liberty of collapsing across high schools given the rather

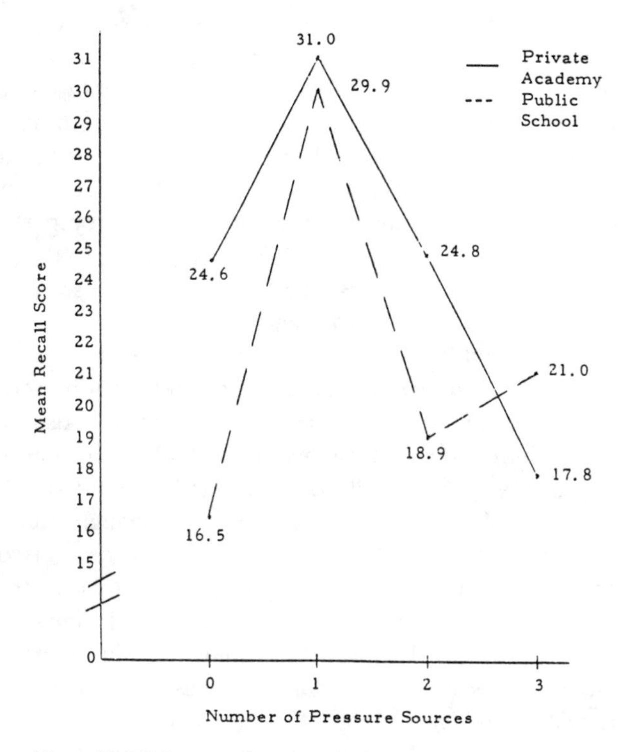

Figure 10.1. Mean recall scores obtained in the Expectancy × Intrinsic Value × Social Consequence × High School interaction.

minimal interaction of the performance curves, it was found that subjects performed significantly better in the single-pressure conditions than in those that reduced the motivation to strive for success to zero pressures or augmented it to two or three pressures.

In summary, this somewhat rough but direct test of the optimal pressure model indicates that subjects tended to perform best in the presence of one motivational pressure, whereas further augmentation or reduction of pressure resulted in lower performance. These trends were moderated to some degree by the high school attended by the subject. However, as can be seen in Figure 10.1, these school-moderated effects had minimal impact on the pressure-performance trends.

Post-test measures of affect and attention

Subjects' retrospective reports of anxiety level and ability to concentrate during the test trial tended to yield complex interactions with the subject variables – sex and high school. Concerning anxiety, the significant sex by high school interaction indicated that among private school subjects males reported less tension than females (2.42 vs. 3.25 on a seven-point scale), whereas in the public school subjects, it was the reverse, with males reporting more tension than females (3.71 vs. 2.71). The somewhat higher tension in private academy females is consistent with fear of success theory; however, contrary to its predictions, private school females outperformed all other groups of subjects. It is also notable that in contrast to the private school females, the relatively high tension reported by public school males corresponded with relatively low performance.

The other significant interaction for anxiety involved intrinsic value, social consequence, and high school. Public school students reported more anxiety with two sources of pressure (4.08 in the high value, positive consequence cell) and with no source of pressure (4.42 in the low value, negative consequence cell) than in the single-pressure conditions (2.67 in the low value, positive consequence cell, and 3.25 in the high value, negative consequence cell). The puzzling piece of this pattern is, of course, the relatively high anxiety in the no-pressure condition. The private academy students showed somewhat opposite trends, although the means (2.75, 3.17, 3.83, and 3.17, respectively) were not significantly different.

Turning to subjects' retrospective reports of focused versus wandering attention, there was a significant main effect of expectancy, with subjects feeling more focused in the low expectancy condition than in either the high or mixed expectancy conditions (2.75 vs. 3.25 and 3.56, respectively, on a seven-point scale). However, this main effect was qualified by a significant interaction of expectancy, intrinsic value, social consequence, and high school. Simple main effects for expectancy were insignificant for all but two of the various combinations of the other three variables. In the high value, positive consequence condition for private academy students, self-reported focus was better under low than under high or mixed expectancy (2.25 vs. 4.50 and 4.75); and this was true for public school students as well, but in the high value, *negative* consequence condition (1.75 vs. 4.00 and 4.75, respectively). These rather large differences once again illustrate the pervasive moderator impact of high school on subjects' subjective reports.

Conclusions and speculations

Let us summarize the basic thrust of these results and use them to revisit and reflect upon the theoretical perspectives introduced earlier. The most important finding was that the number of pressure sources present in the achievement situation bore an inverted-U relation to performance level. Specifically, it was found that in the presence of a single incentive to succeed, performance tended to be at its highest, whereas both the absence of achievement pressure and the presence of multiple sources of pressure produced performance decrement. Performance decrement under no sources of pressure we would label as undermotivation, and decrement under multiple sources of pressure as overmotivation.

This key overall finding is intriguingly comparable to the results obtained by Samuel and his colleagues (e.g., Samuel et al., 1978) and broadly consistent with the optimal pressure model that we advanced. However, the question remains how best to explain this pressure-performance relation. It may be recalled that Samuel and his colleagues favored arousal as the mediating mechanism, a moderate level of which was hypothesized to be optimal for performance. Humphreys and Revelle also assigned a primary role to arousal, but devoted an important secondary role to worry, which was hypothesized to reduce on-task attention. Finally, Baumeister and Showers largely rejected arousal as an explanation and favored disruption of attention, hypothesized to stem from worry and also from self-awareness, as the mediating mechanism.

Unfortunately, it has to be admitted that the results for the affect and attention measures in our study are not really illuminating about these possibilities, since the effects obtained were intricately intertwined with subject characteristics and did not generally parallel the performance results closely. To some extent, this may simply reflect difficulties with post-task introspective measures generally (cf., Quattrone, 1985).

Nonetheless, we can at least attempt to characterize the main possibilities clearly. The first possibility is that the *total level* of pressure is crucial, largely because of its effect on arousal. That is, as the number of achievement pressures increased from zero to three, the magnitude of motivation experienced by the performer may have increased from low to medium to high. In this sense, two sources of relatively weak pressure might be regarded as equivalent to one source of strong pressure.

The second major possibility is that the *number of sources* of pressure is crucial, largely because of its effect on attention. The single-pressure conditions may have provided the performer with a singularity of focus which facilitated concentration and performance; whereas the multiple-pressure conditions may have apportioned the focus of the performer among multiple goals, leading to distraction, worry, and self-focus. In this case, it is the multiplicity of sources of motivation that is essential, rather than their combined level.

The latter explanation of our results may be contrasted interestingly to the work of Baumeister (1984), who argues that self-focus in the *process* of performance interferes with the optimal execution of skills. That is, "choking" may be due to focusing on inward states that are extraneous to optimal performance. By comparison, our work may indicate that self-focus on the *goals* of performance is also important. That is, focus on one goal boosts performance; but too many goals may diffuse one's attention and lower performance.

This distinction between a performer's inward focus on the *goal* versus the *process* of performance may be a critical one for discerning the impact of motivation on performance. To the extent that inward self-focus augments attention to a single desired goal state, it should facilitate performance. If, on the other hand, multiple goal states are activated by inward focusing, it will likely diffuse a performer's attention and intrude on performance. With regard to inward *process-based* self-focus, one might conjecture that each step in the conjured process sequence possesses the potential for activating concern and worry with different goals (i.e., looking good, demonstrating knowledge, succeeding, remembering critical information, etc.). By increasing the probability of multiple goal foci, process self-focus will frequently intrude on actual performance. In short, self-focus is not, in and of itself, a performance-intruding process, but it can facilitate performance when inward reflection centers the performer on singular goal states.

The role of individual differences

Subject characteristics – namely, sex and high school – played a fairly prominent role in the results of our study and merit some discussion. In particular, self-perceptions of affect and attention seemed to have more to do with these subject variables than with the manipulations of the pressure variables. This may suggest that there are important individual differences in reactions to achievement situations, differences that may eventually constitute constraints on applying the optimal pressure model.

For instance, there were some indications in the results that private academy females, who are high achieving compared to their public school counterparts, are especially resilient in the face of pressure, being able to tolerate relatively high anxiety while maintaining high performance. This pattern is the opposite of the one originally posited by Horner in her fear of success theory; and it probably reflects the kinds of socialization experiences these females are afforded, in which achievement is nurtured.

Of the pressure manipulations in our study, expectancy was most clearly and pervasively moderated by subject characteristics, especially high school. Rather than the mixed expectancy condition being most favorable, as suggested by value-expectancy theory, low expectancy seemed especially focusing and performance enhancing for the private academy students. This may reflect social comparison processes in self-evaluation. Specifically, the highly talented private academy students may compare themselves to high achieving others, such that the norms provided have a different meaning to them. They may know that they are quite good on difficult tasks; therefore the low expectancy situation (an especially hard task for the average performer) is especially motivating, and the mixed expectancy situation (50–50 for the average performer) is not particularly challenging. Hence, expectancy may have somewhat different dynamics in high ability groups compared to mixed ability groups.

In general, the socialization experiences shared by members of a group may generate a propensity to experience particular incentives in particular ways. Thus it might be possible to reconcile an optimal pressure model with gender-based achievement models by gleaning from the gender-based models the hypotheses that they raise about differential responsiveness to achievement cues that may stem from being male or female. For example, the strategic performance depression theory raises the notion that for females social concerns are more salient as determinants of motivation than are intrinsic incentives, while the opposite may characterize males. While such considerations may constrain the optimal pressure model somewhat, we believe the same underlying explanation of pressure-performance relations would hold for both genders.

It may well be that the unique bivalent connotations of success for females alluded to by Horner, Deaux, and other commentators and researchers render females particularly vulnerable to overmotivation effects when compared to males. If difficult achievement circumstances naturally arouse intrinsic ability concerns, then the social concerns that accompany female achievement may operate as inducers of superfluous arousal. Indeed, the tendency for female achievement attributions for success to underplay ability self-attribution may be a reasonably adaptive strategy. This attribution tendency may signal reduced female attention to intrusive ability concerns and thus promote a more optimal focus on single but extrinsic motivators of performance.

On the other hand, the performance of the private academy females in our study might indicate that high achieving females develop the capacity to reduce attention to superfluous extrinsic incentives when pursuing goals related to intrinsic ability. One might conjecture that for a subset of highly talented females, the pervasive exposure to multiple sources of achievement pressure renders them particularly resilient to arousal arising from extrinsic sources during achievement encounters. Much like the star athlete who learns through continual exposure to either blot out the influence of the crowd or to use that influence as a motivator, the academically talented female might be prone to develop strategies to handle superfluous sources of pressure. It certainly would be interesting to explore empirically the arousal-adaptive strategies of talented females who are "pressure resilient" and those who are "pressure sensitive" in subsequent research.

Guarding against superfluous incentives – some examples

Finally, we may suggest tentatively some examples of how the insights from this research, after further research and refinement, might be employed in real-life settings for assessment and intervention of achievement problems by teachers, coaches, and therapists. First, consider an athlete entering a competition. His or her desire for success is likely to be fueled by a number of sources: the wish for the intrinsic pleasure of performing well, the wish to please the coach, the wish to impress the audience and win the glory and trappings of the winner. We would argue that the performer who cognitively alters the situation to focus on a single important goal is most likely to perform optimally. One athlete might focus on the self-evaluative, intrinsic value dimension, while minimizing attention to the other pressure sources. This is the player who thinks, for instance, "I'm going to concentrate on selecting good shots and placing the ball where I intended to hit it. I will not be concerned at the moment with whether my opponent returns the shot or misses it or whether the shot looked spectacular to the audience or whether I end up winning the match. I only want to try to play my game and do what I know how to do." Another athlete might focus on a social goal: "I will play my best to please my coach, who has helped me so much over the years. I'm less concerned at the moment about what I might gain from winning or what this one match might reflect about my ability. I want to win it for him." With focus on one such goal, attention can shift to the task demands, and anxiety stemming from having many good reasons to win is reduced. Conversely, we would argue that the athlete who pursues several goals at once is likely to succeed at none.

Similarly, in the classroom, an anxious child who is performing below ability level may be laboring under a multiplicity of incentives for success: the wish to be able and competent, to please his or her teacher, to win a promised award from his or her parents, to gain respect from onlooking peers, and so on. His or her motivation may be high, but the multiple goals may feel overwhelming and unattainable to the child, who is consequently distracted from the demands of the task.

Indeed, children who encounter achievement problems in school frequently warrant the concerned scrutiny of teachers and parents alike. In addition, they are also likely to meet with implicit and explicit evaluations from their peers. In short, such children frequently are invested with too many reasons to perform adequately (to please parents or teachers, to feel better about their own abilities, to elicit more positive evaluations from peers, etc.). As a consequence, it is likely that overmotivation initially ensues and compromises performance. After repeated bouts of superfluous arousal resulting in less than optimal performance, such children might indeed become achievement-avoidant in order to minimize their pervasive multiply determined arousal in achievement circumstances. It could be conjectured that "underachieving" children progress from initial states of overmotivation to subsequent states of undermotivation in the wake of the many external pressures and incentives that are brought to bear on their achievement. Focusing such a child on a single goal is a strategy that might better facilitate improved performance. Determining the most effective goal may require sensitivity to individual differences; and such differences in responsiveness to various sources of achievement pressure may prove to vary systematically with subject characteristics such as gender, attitudes about achievement, and norms for social comparison.

Of course, with other individuals performing below their ability levels the problem may be the more traditional one of being undermotivated; and they may need help in adopting and valuing a clear, highly motivating goal – moving from no pressure to one pressure. Nonetheless, in conclusion, we would like to emphasize what seem to be the drawbacks of too many incentives. A framework of superfluous rewards may not only undermine interest, as in the well-known research of Lepper and Greene (1978), but also result in superfluous sources of motivation and thus decreased performance. Accordingly, to end on an optimistic note, we might amend an old aphorism. If at first you don't succeed, try, try again – but with each try you might want to do it with fewer and fewer good reasons to succeed.

References

Atkinson, J. W., & Feather, N. J. (Eds.). (1966). *A theory of achievement motivation*. New York: Wiley.

Atkinson, J. W., & Litwin, G. H. (1960). Achievement motive and test anxiety as motives to approach success and to avoid failure. *Journal of Abnormal and Social Psychology, 60*, 52–63.

Baumeister, R. F. (1984). Choking under pressure: Self-consciousness and paradoxical effects of incentives on skillful performance. *Journal of Personality and Social Psychology, 46,* 610–620.

Baumeister, R. F., & Showers, C. J. (1986). A review of paradoxical performance effects: Choking under pressure in sports and mental tests. *European Journal of Social Psychology, 16,* 361–383.

Bedell, J., & Sistrunk, F. (1973). Power, opportunity costs, and sex in a mixed motive game. *Journal of Personality and Social Psychology, 25,* 219–226.

Benton, A. (1973). Reactions to demands to win from an opposite sex opponent. *Journal of Personality, 41,* 430–442.

Canavan-Gumpert, D., Garner, K., & Gumpert, P. (1978). *The success-fearing personality: Theory and research with implications for the social psychology of achievement.* Lexington, MA: Lexington Books.

Deaux, K. (1976). Sex and the attribution processes. In J. Harvey, W. Ickes, & R. Kidd (Eds.), *New directions in attributional research* (Vol. 1). New York: Wiley.

Duffy, E. (1957). The psychological significance of the concept of "arousal" or "activation." *Psychological Review, 64,* 265–275.

Dweck, C. S., & Elliott, E. S. (1983). Achievement motivation. In E. M. Hetherington (Ed.), *Handbook of child psychology: Vol. 4. Socialization, personality, and social development* (4th ed.). New York: Wiley.

Eme, R., & Lawrence, L. (1976). Fear of success and academic underachievement. *Sex Roles, 2,* 269–271.

Feather, N. J., & Simon, J. G. (1973). Fear of success and causal attribution for outcome. *Journal of Personality, 41,* 525–542.

Frieze, I. H., Parsons, J. E., Johnson, P. B., Ruble, D. N., & Zellman, J. L. (1978). *Women and sex roles: A social psychological perspective.* New York: Norton.

Heilbrun, A. B., Kleemeier, C., & Piccola, G. (1974). Developmental and situational correlates of achievement behavior in college females. *Journal of Personality, 42,* 420–436.

Horner, M. (1973). A psychological barrier to achievement in females: The motive to avoid success. In D. McClelland & R. Steele (Eds.), *Human motivation: A book of readings.* Morristown, NJ: General Learning.

Hottes, J., & Kahn, A. (1974). Sex differences in a mixed motive conflict situation. *Journal of Personality, 42,* 260–275.

Humphreys, M. S., & Revelle, W. (1984). Personality, motivation, and performance: A theory of the relationship between individual differences and information processing. *Psychological Review, 91,* 153–184.

Kahn, A., Hottes, J., & Davis, H. L. (1971). Cooperation and optimal responding in the prisoner's dilemma game: Effects of sex and physical attractiveness. *Journal of Personality and Social Psychology, 17,* 267–279.

Karabenick, S. (1977). Fear of success, achievement and affiliation dispositions and the performance of men and women under individual and competitive conditions. *Journal of Personality, 42,* 220–237.

Karabenick, S., & Marshall, J. M. (1974). Performance of females as a function of fear of success, fear of failure, type of opponent and performance-contingent feedback. *Journal of Personality, 42,* 220–237.

Lepper, M. R., & Greene, D. (Eds.). (1978). *The hidden costs of reward.* Hillsdale, NJ: Erlbaum.

Maccoby, E., & Jacklin, C. (1974). *The psychology of sex differences.* Palo Alto, CA: Stanford University Press.

Malmo, R. B. (1959). Activation: A neuropsychological dimension. *Psychological Review, 66,* 367–386.

McNeel, S. P., McClintock, C. G., & Nuttin, J. M. (1972). Effects of sex role in a two person mixed motive game. *Journal of Personality and Social Psychology, 24,* 372–380.

Morgan, S. W., & Mausner, B. (1973). Behavioral and fantasied indications of avoidance of success in men and women. *Journal of Personality, 41,* 457–470.

Murphy-Berman, V. (1975). Motive to avoid success: A test of basic assumptions. *Representative Research in Social Psychology, 6,* 37–44.

Peplau, L. (1976). Fear of success in dating couples. *Journal of Personality and Social Psychology, 2,* 249–258.

Quattrone, G. A. (1985). On the congruity between internal states and action. *Psychological Bulletin, 98,* 3–40.

Romer, N. (1975). The motive to avoid success and its effect on performance in school age males and females. *Developmental Psychology,* 689–699.

Samuel, W. (1977). Observed IQ as a function of test atmosphere, tester expectation, and race of tester: A replication for female subjects. *Journal of Educational Psychology, 69,* 593–604.

Samuel, W. (1980). Mood and personality correlates of IQ by race and sex of subject. *Journal of Personality and Social Psychology, 38,* 993–1004.

Samuel, W., Baynes, K., & Sabeh, C. (1978). Effects of initial success or failure in a stressful or relaxed environment on subsequent task performance. *Journal of Experimental and Social Psychology, 14,* 205–216.

Samuel, W., Soto, D., Parks, M., Ngissah, P., & Jones, B. (1976). Motivation, race, social class, and IQ. *Journal of Educational Psychology, 68,* 273–285.

Sarason, I. G. (1980). Introduction to the study of test anxiety. In I. G. Sarason (Ed.), *Test anxiety: Theory, research, and applications.* Hillsdale, NJ: Erlbaum.

Sorrentino, R. M., & Short, J. A. (1974). Effects of fear of success on women's performance at masculine versus feminine tasks. *Journal of Research in Personality, 8,* 277–290.

Stipek, D. J., & Hoffman, J. M. (1979). *Children's perceptions of the causes of failure.* Unpublished manuscript, University of California, Los Angeles.

Tresemer, D. W. (1977). *Fear of success.* New York: Plenum Press.

Weiner, B., Frieze, I., Kukla, A., Reed, L., Rest, S., & Rosenbaum, R. M. (1972). Perceiving the causes of success and failure. In E. E. Jones et al. (Eds.), *Attribution: Perceiving the causes of behavior.* Morristown, NJ: General Learning Press.

Yerkes, R. M., & Dodson, J. D. (1908). The relation of strength of stimulus to rapidity of habit formation. *Journal of Comparative Neurological Psychology, 18,* 459–482.

Zuckerman, M., & Wheeler, L. (1975). To dispel fantasies about the fantasy-based measure of fear of success. *Psychological Bulletin, 82,* 932–946.

11 Self-handicapping and achievement

Janet Morgan Riggs

Educators and parents long have been plagued by the problem of underachievement in children. Many have had the frustrating experience of watching a child undermine his or her chances for a good performance simply by not trying. An apparently bright student who performs poorly as a consequence of not studying or not completing assignments may perplex his or her teachers. A coach may despair as an able athlete wastes his or her talent by not practicing enough. Clearly the question of why an individual would sabotage his or her performance this way has no simple answer. In the present chapter, the issue of underachievement is addressed from an attributional perspective in an attempt to shed light not only on the question of why some individuals come to adopt underachieving "strategies," but also on how the negative effects of such strategies might be alleviated.

Underachievement and the need for achievement

Achievement has long been a focus of interest among researchers in the field of psychology. Early research concentrated on the development of testing instruments, such as the Thematic Apperception Test, that measure an individual's need for achievement (e.g., McClelland, Clark, Roby, & Atkinson, 1949; McClelland, Atkinson, Clark, & Lowell, 1953). In subsequent years, Atkinson and his colleagues (e.g., Atkinson, 1958; Atkinson & Feather, 1966; Atkinson & Raynor, 1978) developed a sophisticated theory of achievement motivation. They suggested that resultant achievement motivation is an additive function of three components: the tendency to achieve success (T_s), the tendency to avoid failure ($T -_f$), and extrinsically motivating factors. If no extrinsically motivating factors are present, an individual is described as being high in resultant achievement motivation when his or her tendency to achieve success is stronger than the tendency to avoid failure ($T_s > T -_f$).

Much research has been devoted to defining the differences between individuals who display high and low levels of need for achievement (n Ach). Weiner and his colleagues (Weiner & Kukla, 1970; Weiner & Potepan, 1970) found that high n Ach individuals perceive their ability as being greater than do low n Ach individuals. High n Ach individuals attribute their successes to ability more frequently than do those low in n Ach; however, low n Ach individuals attribute their failures to lack of ability more often than do high n Ach individuals (Kukla, 1972). High n Ach individuals prefer tasks of intermediate difficulty (that are more diagnostic of ability than either very difficult or very easy tasks); low n Ach individuals avoid tasks that are diagnostic of ability (Atkinson & Litwin, 1960; McClelland, 1958).

Although great strides have been made in the understanding of individuals who are low or high in the need for achievement, the underachiever remains something of a mystery. At first glance, one might be tempted to equate underachievement with a low need for achievement. However, a closer look suggests that this assumption would be not only unwarranted, but misleading. First, the term "need for achievement" has been used traditionally as a personality construct, denoting an individual's relatively stable disposition to approach (or avoid) achievement-related activities. "Underachievement," however, is a term that denotes discrepancies between an individual's performance and his or her ability. An underachiever is someone whose performance does not measure up to estimations of his or her potential. Furthermore, the low n Ach individual is one whose motive to avoid failure is greater than his or her motive to achieve success. Yet by not trying, the underachiever seems to be inviting, rather than avoiding, failure.

It is clear, then, that research on need for achievement cannot be translated directly to the study of underachievement. The reasons why an individual adopts underachieving strategies still are unknown, and viable methods for decreasing the likelihood of underachievement have not been suggested. However, social psychologists, and particularly attribution theorists, have adopted a theoretical approach that may well provide insight into the understanding of underachievement.

An attributional perspective

In his seminal description of naive psychology, Heider (1958) proposed that a behavioral effect is perceived to be dependent upon two causal factors: *can* and *trying*. He described *trying* as a motivational factor, consisting of intention and exertion; *can* was described as being a combination of power and effective environmental force. Weiner and his colleagues (e.g., Weiner, Frieze, Kukla, Reed, Rest, & Rosenbaum, 1971; Weiner, Heckhausen, Meyer, & Cook, 1972) elaborated Heider's attributional schema by suggesting a two-dimensional taxonomy of the perceived causes of success and failure. Based upon the dimensions of stability versus instability and internal versus external locus of control, this taxonomy consists of four perceived determinants of performance: ability (a stable internal cause), effort (an unstable internal cause), task difficulty (a stable external cause), and luck (an unstable external cause). Weiner's conceptions of ability, effort, and task difficulty and luck are comparable to Heider's original concepts of power, trying, and effective environmental force, respectively.

Weiner's classification scheme has generated a great deal of research and has added much to the understanding of performance attributions (see Weiner, 1974). However, as Weiner has noted, this taxonomy is not altogether complete. For example, although effort is classified as an unstable cause of performance, it obviously has some stable properties as well. Most likely individuals differ on this trait, in that some people are inclined to work harder than others. Similarly, although ability is classified as a stable component, it probably is somewhat variable, depending upon a person's physical and mental state.

More recently, Darley and Goethals (1980) offered a more sophisticated analysis of people's perceptions of the causes of ability-linked performances. Their model describes how people perceive the relationships among performance, ability, motivation, task difficulty, and luck:

$$P = (A - A') \times (M \pm M') + (D \pm D') \pm L.$$

In this equation P denotes performance; A, M, D, and L denote long-term ability, motivation, task difficulty, and luck; and A', M', and D' denote the short-term components of ability, motivation, and task difficulty. Thus, their conception allows for greater flexibility in the perceived causes of performance. According to their equation, a student's performance on a test would be attributable not only to the student's intellectual ability and effort, test difficulty, and luck; it also could be attributable to factors such as illness or fatigue (that might temporarily impair ability), the student's general level of motivation, and the legibility of the test.

The Darley and Goethals model suggests that an individual conceivably could manipulate the attributions made for his or her performance. For example, the individual faced with a poor performance might wish to avoid an attribution of low ability. According to the equation, there would be several ways of doing this. One would be to excuse one's performance as being due to a transient impairment of one's ability: "I was ill when I took that test." Or the individual might cultivate an attribution of low effort: "I could have done well if I had tried." Because an abundance of factors are thought to affect performance, there is a vast array of potential causes, other than ability, to which a failing performance can be attributed. The enterprising individual need only select or convey the appropriate one.

But are people aware that they can manipulate attributions? Are they capable of capitalizing upon the complexities of the performance equation? Quattrone and Jones (1978) have collected evidence suggesting that people indeed are adept at manipulating the attributions made by others for their performances. They have shown that people are capable of trading on the attributional principles of discounting and augmentation (Kelley, 1971; 1973) so that successful performances will be attributed to ability. Relevant to this is work done by Snyder and his colleagues (e.g., Snyder, Stephan, & Rosenfield, 1976; 1978) on the topic of attributional egotism, which they describe as "the tendency to make attributions that put oneself in the best possible light" (1976, p. 435). Their research suggests that people display a general tendency to take credit for their successes and deny blame for their failures. For example, Snyder and his colleagues found that players who won a game attributed their performance more to skill and less to luck than did their losing opponents. Similarly, the players who lost the game attributed their performance more to bad luck and less to lack of skill than did the winners. Apparently individuals have little difficulty manipulating attributions for their performance in a self-serving manner.

Self-handicapping

It is perhaps not surprising that people make and project egotistical attributions for their past performances. However, Jones and Berglas (1978) suggested that individuals also may take a more active role in shaping these attributions by setting the stage so that such egotistical attribution is facilitated. This is accomplished by the adoption of self-handicapping strategies: "By finding or creating impediments that make good performance less likely, the strategist nicely protects his or her sense of self-competence. If the person does poorly, the source of the failure is externalized in the impediment. . . . If the person does well, then he or she has done well in spite of less than optimum conditions" (p. 201).

Strategies

In their insightful paper, Jones and Berglas (1978) proposed that several behaviors might serve as potential self-handicapping strategies, including drug and alcohol use, lack of sleep before an important performance, avoidance of lessons and practice, acquisition and/or use of the "sick" role, and a general reduction in effort. An increasing body of research has supported their notion that these behaviors may be adopted for the purpose of self-handicapping.

Drugs and alcohol. The first study designed to test directly the notion of self-handicapping was performed by Berglas and Jones (1978). They provided success feedback to subjects who had just completed an intelligence test. Test difficulty was manipulated so that half of the subjects were given relatively easy problems, and so experienced genuine success; the other subjects were given unsolvable problems, and thus experienced an inauthentic success, one that was not contingent upon their performance. Berglas and Jones found that males who had experienced noncontingent success were more likely to choose ingestion of a performance-inhibiting drug when faced with a future testing situation than were those males who had experienced contingent success. The researchers' rationale for this effect was that those who had experienced noncontingent success were uncertain that they would be able to duplicate their success. To preserve this previous success and the competence it implied, subjects searched for a means of externalizing the cause of a potential failure. In this case, the obvious strategy was ingestion of the performance-inhibiting drug. The cause of their anticipated poor performance could then be externalized to the drug. However, if the individual performed well on the second test, he would have overcome the effects of the drug, implying that he must be very high in ability. Similarly, Tucker, Vuchinich, and Sobell (1981) demonstrated the use of alcohol as a self-handicapping strategy in a paradigm parallel to the one used by Berglas and Jones.

Lack of practice. In a different setting designed to investigate lack of practice as a self-handicapping strategy, Rhodewalt, Saltzman, and Wittmer (1984) first identified swimmers as being either high self-handicappers or low self-handicappers by administering a questionnaire developed by Jones and Rhodewalt (1982). Rhodewalt and his colleagues found that high self-handicappers practiced less before an important swimming competition than did low self-handicappers. In this case, high self-handicappers were thought to set the stage so that a poor performance could be attributed to a lack of practice rather than to a lack of athletic ability.

Symptom reporting. The experience and reporting of internal symptoms, such as illness and anxiety, have received attention as another means of self-handicapping (Snyder & Smith, 1982). Although the idea is not new (e.g., Adler, 1913), more recent research has provided clear evidence that people use symptoms in self-serving ways. Smith, Snyder, and their colleagues have examined the self-handicapping strategies of test-anxious people, hypochondriacs, and shy people (Smith, Snyder, & Handelsman, 1982; Smith, Snyder, & Perkins, 1983; Snyder, Smith, Augelli, & Ingram, 1985). They found each of these groups to report heightened symptoms when the individuals thought that these symptoms would excuse poor performance. Similarly, Baumgardner, Lake, and Arkin (1985) found evidence for the strategic reporting of mood as a self-handicapping strategy. Although not all such symptoms can be explained from this perspective, these findings suggest yet another subtle way in which people may use self-handicapping to insulate themselves from the effects of potential failure.

The use of symptoms differs significantly from the self-handicapping strategies mentioned earlier (e.g., use of alcohol and drugs, lack of practice) in that the use of alcohol or drugs, for example, could be viewed as a more active technique of self-handicapping. The individual actually engages in a behavior that most likely will impede performance. This active form of self-handicapping seems consistent with Jones and Berglas's (1978) original notion: "By finding or creating impediments that make good performance less likely, the strategist nicely protects his sense of self-competence" (p. 201). The reporting of symptoms, however, does not necessarily require an active search for and embracing of handicaps. Rather, it consists of reporting a handicap, which may or may not be genuine. Arkin and Baumgardner (1985) have elucidated this distinction in their organizational scheme of self-handicapping: handicaps may be either acquired (e.g., drug use) or claimed (e.g., symptom reporting).

Lack of effort. Yet another form of self-handicapping that has been the focus of investigation is effort withdrawal. Jones and Berglas (1978) suggested that this might be the primary tactic used by the underachiever, who may be trading on a phenomenon described by Heider (1958):

> If "*p* tried" and "*p* does not cause" are given, we infer "*p* cannot." But, if both *not a* and *not c* are given, we cannot make any inference with respect to the absence or presence of *b*. Thus, if a person does not succeed (*not c*) and we know that he did not try (*not a*) we cannot conclude anything about his ability (*b*). (p. 116)

Research by Frankel and Snyder (1978) supports the notion that effort withdrawal may be self-serving. Their subjects, who first were exposed to a series of unsolvable problems, solved more problems more quickly on a subsequent test when that test was described as being highly difficult, as opposed to moderately difficult. Frankel and Snyder reasoned that failure at a moderately difficult task is perceived to be more damaging to one's self-image than failure at a highly difficult task. Wishing to avoid further damage to their self-esteem, subjects faced with a moderately difficult task withdrew effort. In a related study, Pyszczynski and Greenberg (1983) found subjects' intentions to exert effort on a task to follow a similar pattern of self-handicapping.

An attempt to look more directly at effort expenditure in evaluative performance contexts was made by Riggs (1982). Subjects were high school students, some of whom had been classified as underachievers because their achievement test scores indicated that their grade point averages should have been higher. Subjects were told that they could exert some control over the presentation time of test problems by squeezing a hand dynamometer. The experimenter said that the amount of force they applied to the dynamometer would provide a direct measure of the amount of effort they exerted during the test. It was found that underachieving students who thought that effort affected performance exerted less effort (as determined by pressure on the dynamometer) and performed less well (as determined by number of problems answered correctly) than did other subjects. This finding is consistent with the notion that underachievers strategically may withdraw effort when they believe that it will provide a ready explanation for poor performance.

The use of each of the aforementioned strategies of self-handicapping, particularly those that are acquired, ensures that the individual will not achieve to his or her fullest capacity. Observers may shake their heads in despair as the individual repeatedly sabotages his or her chances for success. However, the self-handicapper may feel secure in the knowledge that an illusion of competence has been maintained, despite a poor performance.

Etiology of general strategy

The obvious question is, why would an individual be driven to the adoption of such strategies? Why would a person deliberately undermine his or her chances for success? Jones and Berglas (1978) suggested two scenarios that might initiate a cycle of self-handicapping. The first focuses on the notion that rewards can have two different meanings: exchange and signification. In the first case, a reward may be acknowledgment of and compensation for the costs of a behavior. If a child cleans his or her room, a parental reward of thanks or a treat may be interpreted as a simple exchange. However, rewards also may be interpreted as signifying love and esteem. Children (as well as adults) may have trouble determining whether a reward is offered as a simple exchange or as a symbol of love and acceptance.

According to Jones and Berglas, this confusion, coupled with the fear that one is not unconditionally loved, may lead an individual to adopt one of two opposing strategies. One strategy is to avoid poor performance at any cost, thereby assuring that rewards will not be withdrawn and that evidence of the conditionality of love cannot emerge. The individual using this tactic might be called an overachiever. He or she exerts great effort to avoid failure. Of course, failure under this condition deals a tremendous blow to the competence-image. Heider (1958) stated that "the most convincing raw material for the perception that '*o* cannot do it' is to see someone trying very hard and not succeeding" (p. 118). Thus trying, in this case, may lead to a greater fear of failure and increased effort.

The alternative strategy is underachievement, which may be adopted by the individual who believes that love is conditional on ability, rather than on performance. This individual may go to great lengths to avoid a situation in which performance would imply a lack of ability. By handicapping his or her performances, the individual may fail, but will be able to avoid a low ability attribution and possible withdrawal of love. This analysis, then, explains the behavior of both overachievers and underachievers. Both are motivated by the fear that love is conditional on performance and/or competence. The overachiever deals with this fear by exerting high levels of effort in order to avoid failing performances, while the underachiever withdraws effort so that the blame for a potential failure can be diverted away from low ability.

A second scenario offered by Jones and Berglas is that a strategy of self-handicapping may be adopted by the individual who has experienced success, but who is uncertain how he or she attained that success and thus uncertain whether it can be repeated. The child may think that parental love is contingent upon the competence this success implies. Afraid of shattering this positive image and thereby losing that love, he or she may stage future performances so that blame for a potential failure will be externalized to something other than his or her inherent ability. Evidence supporting this scenario comes from a variety of studies in which subjects' tendency to self-handicap has been measured after they have been exposed to performance-contingent versus noncontingent success (e.g., Berglas & Jones, 1978; Kolditz & Arkin, 1982; Tucker et al., 1981). Consistently, self-handicapping has been found to occur most frequently among those who have experienced noncontingent success. Wanting to protect the positive image won from their previous success, and afraid that they will not be able to repeat that success, these individuals may self-handicap so that a future failure can be attributed to the handicap rather than to a lack of competence.

In both scenarios, Jones and Berglas suggest that preoccupation with one's image of competence is crucial to the development of a disposition toward self-handicapping. If belief in one's ability is precarious, the fear of clearly exposing this lack of competence may be great enough to lead the individual to adopt such a self-protective strategy.

Individual differences in self-handicapping

It is clear that some individuals are more prone to adopting self-handicapping strategies than are others. Jones and Rhodewalt (1982) developed a scale to assess such individual differences. The diagnostic effectiveness of this scale was validated by the finding of Rhodewalt and his colleagues (1984) that individuals who scored high on this scale were more likely to self-handicap than those who scored low.

Other research has pointed to several individual-difference variables that seem to be associated with self-handicapping. For example, Weidner (1980) found that individuals with Type A personality characteristics were more likely to self-handicap than Type Bs. Why might the coronary-prone Type A behavior pattern be related to the tendency to self-handicap? The Type A individual typically is more aggressive, hard-working, achievement-oriented and fearful of failure than the Type B individual (Burnam, Pennebaker, & Glass, 1975; Friedman, 1977; Gastorf & Teevan, 1980). It is not surprising, then, that potential failure would be particularly disquieting to Type As, who might deal with this threat by self-handicapping.

As Snyder and Smith (1982) have noted, certain clinical populations seem particularly prone to self-handicap, or at least to adopt certain self-handicapping tactics. The probable links between self-handicapping and drug and alcohol use, hypochondria, test anxiety, and social anxiety have been demonstrated in a variety of studies (e.g., Berglas & Jones, 1978; Smith et al., 1982; Smith et al., 1983; Snyder et al., 1985; Tucker et al., 1981).

One might expect that uncertainty with regard to self-evaluation also would be related to the tendency to self-handicap. Recently, Harris and Snyder (1986) found that males who were uncertain about their self-esteem prepared less well for an upcoming test than did males who were certain of their self-esteem. However, level of self-esteem had no significant effect upon self-handicapping. Based on their findings they suggest that "it may not be how much sense of personal worth one has, but rather how firmly one senses that personal worth that is the key [to predicting self-handicapping]" (p. 457).

Finally, gender differences in self-handicapping have received some attention. Berglas and Jones (1978) and Snyder and his colleagues (1985) found self-handicapping effects among males but not among females. However, others have observed self-handicapping among females as well (e.g., Baumgardner et al., 1985; Pyszcynski & Greenberg, 1983; Smith et al., 1982; Smith et al., 1983). It is likely that differences in performance context and type of strategy available may influence which gender is most likely to self-handicap. Perhaps females are less likely to use acquired handicaps than are males. Or, as Snyder and Smith (1982) suggested, perhaps females are more likely to self-handicap in person-oriented contexts, while males are more likely to self-handicap in task-oriented contexts.

Facilitating conditions

Perceived probability of success. Although differences between individuals may affect self-handicapping, a variety of situational variables also seem to play a role in determining whether an individual will adopt a self-handicapping strategy. As Jones and Berglas suggested, some experience with success probably is necessary to produce a tendency to self-handicap; without such experience, the individual would have no positive competence image to protect. However, it also appears that a recent experience with failure may promote self-handicapping, as the individual strives to avoid additional failures that might damage his or her competence image (Frankel & Snyder, 1978; Baumgardner et al., 1985).

Most likely the key lies in the expectations that an individual's past experience has established for future performance. Following either a noncontingent success or a failure experience, individuals may think that their chances for future success are low. Their response is to arrange future situations so that failure may be attributed to something other than a lack of ability (Pyszczynski & Greenberg, 1983).

Uncertainty of self-evaluation. Related to this perceived probability of success is the degree to which the individual feels confident about and in control of the performance context. While certainty about self-evaluation may be examined as an individual-difference variable (Harris & Snyder, 1986), it also may vary as a function of the situation. For example, experience with noncontingent success probably leads to self-handicapping because it produces uncertainty about one's ability to repeat that success. Other factors that generate uncertainty about one's performance and about self-evaluation may also promote self-handicapping. Soder and Riggs (1986) have demonstrated that receiving bogus physiological feedback that is inconsistent with one's actual experience increases the tendency to self-handicap. In this experiment, subjects were attached to an apparatus that supposedly measured galvanic skin response and gave them bogus feedback about their tension level while taking a test. Subjects were given either solvable or insolvable problems, but all received success feedback. Before taking another test, they could choose how long they wanted to work on a mentally fatiguing task that most likely would interfere with their subsequent performance. The self-handicapping effects among subjects who had been given insolvable problems were greater when they received feedback suggesting that they were feeling relaxed rather than tense. However, the reverse was true for subjects who had been given solvable problems; these subjects were more likely to self-handicap if told they were feeling tense rather than relaxed. The inconsistency between what subjects were told and what they actually experienced magnified the tendency to self-handicap. It is possible that any factor that introduces uncertainty concerning self-evaluation will increase the probability of self-handicapping.

Ego-relevance. A third factor that seems to be crucial in producing self-handicapping is the performance context. If this context is important to the individual and if failure poses a threat to the individual's self-esteem, he or she is more likely to self-handicap. Evidence for this comes from a variety of studies. For example, Rhodewalt and his colleagues (1984) found self-handicapping among swimmers only if an upcoming swimming meet was important to them. In the work by Smith, Snyder and their colleagues on the use of symptoms by test anxious, hypochondriacal, and shy people (Smith et al., 1982; Smith et al., 1983; Snyder et al., 1985), self-handicapping was found only in evaluative contexts, that is, in situations in which subjects thought some underlying ability (e.g., general or social intelligence) was being measured. Pyszczysnki and Greenberg (1983) found self-handicapping in the form of an intention to exert less effort only when subjects perceived an impending test to be ego-relevant. These findings are not surprising, since performing poorly on a test that measures something insignificant does not pose a threat to one's self-esteem. Only when the individual faces the possibility of failure in an important performance context will he or she be likely to adopt a self-handicapping strategy.

Perceived viability of strategy. In predicting self-handicapping, another critical factor seems to be the potential effectiveness of a particular strategy. That is, a particular self-handicapping strategy is likely to be adopted only if the individual believes that that particular handicap will provide a viable excuse for poor performance (Smith et al., 1982; Smith et al., 1983; Snyder et al., 1985; Baumgardner et al., 1985). Riggs (1982) revealed further support for this notion in an investigation of the effort expenditure and performance of academic underachievers. Underachievers who thought that effort influenced performance exerted less effort and performed less well in a testing situation, compared to underachievers who thought that effort had little influence on performance.

It is worth noting that Smith and his colleagues (1982) found that test-anxious subjects adopted an alternative self-handicapping strategy when the credibility of test anxiety as an excuse for poor performance was discounted; in this case, highly test-anxious subjects reported that they exerted less effort on the test. Taken together, these findings suggest that the likelihood of adopting a particular self-handicapping strategy will decrease as the credibility of the handicap is undermined. However, discrediting a particular excuse may not reduce an individual's general tendency to self-handicap; rather, this may prompt a search for an alternative strategy which will allow for the desired attributions.

Incentive for successful performance. A fifth factor that recently has been found to influence the probability of self-handicapping is the incentive for good performance. What happens when the importance of a successful performance is raised in the eyes of the potential self-handicapper? In an experiment modeled after that done by Smith and his colleagues (1982), Greenberg, Pyszczynski, and Paisley (1985) told their low and high test-anxious subjects either that the individual who scored highest on a test would receive five dollars (low incentive) or twenty-five dollars (high incentive). Although they replicated the earlier findings in the low incentive condition, the effect disappeared in the high incentive condition. This suggests that when successful performance itself becomes highly important, self-handicapping may no longer be desirable. Rather, the individual may focus his or her attention on achieving maximally instead of on manipulating attributions for performance.

Availability of a performance-enhancing option. Two other factors that may influence self-handicapping are worth considering, although the evidence for both is mixed. The first is whether a performance-enhancing option is available to the potential self-handicapper. Tucker and colleagues (1981) suggested that self-handicapping is likely to occur only if such a performance-enhancing option is unavailable. In their investigation, subjects who had been exposed to contingent or noncontingent success were allowed to consume as much alcohol and/or study as much as they wanted before taking a second test. While noncontingent-success subjects tended to consume more alcohol than contingent-success subjects, this effect was not statistically significant. However, when the performance-enhancing option of studying was not offered, noncontingent-success subjects consumed significantly more alcohol than did contingent-success subjects. The researchers interpreted these findings as an indication that noncontingent success will produce self-handicapping "only when subjects are denied access to a viable performance enhancing strategy for avoiding anticipated failure" (p. 228). This conclusion is a bit surprising given the finding (e.g., Berglas & Jones, 1978; Kolditz & Arkin, 1982) that noncontingent success produces a greater likelihood of choosing a performance-inhibiting drug over a performance-facilitating drug when subjects anticipate a retest. Tucker and colleagues explained this difference by suggesting that taking a performance-facilitating drug is not a viable and familiar alternative to self-handicapping. In any case, there clearly is a need for further investigation of the impact of performance-enhancing options on the disposition to self-handicap.

Perceived publicity. A final factor which may influence the occurrence of self-handicapping is the public versus private nature of the performance context. Again, this is an area in which the evidence has been mixed. Originally, Jones and Berglas (1978) suggested that the primary impetus for self-handicapping was in the motivation to protect one's self-image:

> Handicapping is a self-defending maneuver whose significance is probably augmented by the presence of an audience, but we emphasize that the public value of the strategy is not its original impetus. This lies in the exaggerated importance of one's own private conception of self-competence and the need to protect that conception from unequivocal negative feedback even in the absence of others. (p. 202)

In support of their contention, Berglas and Jones found self-handicapping to occur in their drug-choice paradigm whether or not subjects thought that the experimenter administering the second test would know their test scores. Kolditz and Arkin (1982), however, have presented evidence that self-handicapping might be primarily a self-presentational strategy.

Baumgardner and her colleagues (1985) focused on a different aspect of the private versus public dimension of self-handicapping: the publicity of a past failure. They found that self-handicapping did not occur when subjects thought that the experimenter was aware of their prior failure. This lack of self-handicapping the authors attributed to the individual's spoiled public identity; he or she had no positive public image to protect. However, these findings contradict those of Frankel and Snyder (1978), who found that self-handicapping occurred following a poor performance of which the experimenter was aware. The results of these two studies are difficult to reconcile; the subject clearly merits further investigation.

In summary, a variety of situational factors seem to influence the likelihood that an individual will adopt a self-handicapping strategy. The perceived probability of success, the certainty of self-evaluation, the ego-relevance of the task, the viability of a given self-handicapping strategy, and the incentive for good performance all seem to be important determinants. Two additional factors that invite further research are the presence of performance-facilitating alternatives and the publicity of performances and handicaps.

The onset of self-handicapping – adolescence?

Recent research has focused on the circumstances under which a variety of self-handicapping techniques might be employed. There is little evidence, however, to suggest at what point during one's lifetime one might be prone to develop self-handicapping strategies. Do these techniques arise during childhood? Or are the required attributional maneuvers too sophisticated for children? Furthermore, when does the motivation to self-handicap emerge?

Research on the development of children's attributions has suggested that young children probably do not have the cognitive sophistication necessary for complex strategic self-handicapping (see Ruble & Rholes, 1981, for a review of this literature). For example, it has been found that five- and six-year-olds perceive effort and ability as necessarily varying together (e.g., Kun, 1977). This type of schema seems to preclude the use of the self-handicapping strategy of effort withdrawal. In addition, experience with failure, as compared to success, does not produce the effect on the self-attributions of young children that it does on older children (Ruble, Parsons, & Ross, 1976). However, even very young children probably engage in rudimentary forms of self-handicapping. For example, children who flatly refuse to engage in an activity may do so because they fear failure. By rejecting the activity altogether, they may be adopting an ego-protective strategy that allows them to avoid failure. Of course, the consequences may be severe for the child who carries this behavior to the extreme. By avoiding certain activities, the child may never give him- or herself the opportunity to develop particular skills and talents.

The motivation to engage in self-handicapping probably increases dramatically during adolescence, when many behaviors that fall under the rubric of self-handicapping (e.g., substance abuse, underachievement) are manifested. Adolescence marks a transition from childhood to adulthood, during which children face a variety of challenges. Havighurst (1972) has listed a series of eight developmental tasks that the adolescent must master. These include a wide range of achievements, from the development of socially responsible behavior to the adoption of a masculine or feminine role, from attaining emotional independence from adults to preparing for a career. These challenges are accompanied by heightened peer pressure and a desire to be accepted by others. During this time, therefore, the motivation to self-handicap may become particularly strong. Confronted with this series of challenges and concerned with establishing and maintaining a positive self-image, the adolescent who fears failure may resort to self-handicapping.

Academic achievement in adolescence

Weiner's (1980) discussion of academic underachievement is germane to the notion that adolescence is a time when individuals may be particularly prone to handicap their performances. Although such factors as cultural influences and learning disabilities may explain why some adolescents do not perform as well as they could, it is likely that self-handicapping contributes to this behavior as well. Weiner noted that the parents of underachievers often set high academic goals for their children. It is quite possible that these children fear that they will never be able to achieve these lofty goals, which will result in a loss of parental esteem. Such children may fall into a pattern of self-handicapping, which precludes the achievement of these goals but provides a viable excuse for unsatisfactory performance. Weiner suggested that "these young people carefully hedge their bets. They rarely risk making a mistake, they consistently deny having exerted themselves even when they have, and they pride themselves on what they have been able to accomplish with minimal effort ('I got a C without even cracking a book')" (p. 462). He called this style of behavior passive-aggressive, because of its "purposeful inactivity." We might expect that the tendency to adopt such a strategy would be strongest at those points at which the child is most fearful of failure. Such points might include stepping from junior high to high school or from high school to college, or moving into a higher "track" class. To cope with these situations, individuals might resort to Weiner's purposeful inactivity, drug and alcohol abuse, or complaints of test anxiety.

However, not all adolescents deal with challenging situations in self-defeating ways. What, then, differentiates an adolescent who self-handicaps from one who copes differently? Probably a configuration of the factors discussed in the previous sections produces the disposition in certain

Table 11.1. *Mean reported and actual effort expenditure*[a]

	Actual Effort[b]	Reported Effort[c]
Underachievers	490.8	74.4
Overachievers	405.6	88.7

[a]Means are adjusted for the effects of subjects' hand strength and achievement level.
[b]Kilograms of force applied to dynamometer.
[c]Percentage of total effort expended.

individuals to self-handicap: an expectation of failure, the ego-relevance of the task, a fear that the love of significant others is conditional, and so on.

Riggs (1982) and Preston (1983) attempted to investigate directly tenth and eleventh graders' tendency to handicap their academic performances. As previously mentioned, Riggs designed a paradigm in which students thought they were taking a test that measured conceptual ability. Subjects were instructed that they could exert some control over the presentation time of digit-symbol substitution problems on a computer screen by squeezing a hand dynamometer. They were told that for some problems the harder they gripped the handle, the longer they would have to study the problem before having to answer; for other problems, the presentation time would be determined randomly. (In reality, subjects had no control over problem presentation times; all times were randomly determined.) Subjects' actual effort expended and perceived effort expended during the test were then measured. Based on discrepancies between their achievement-test scores and grade-point averages, subjects were classified as overachievers and underachievers. The most striking results were found in the control condition, in which subjects were given no further instructions about the test. Quite unexpectedly, underachievers tended to exert relatively *more* effort than did overachievers. However, underachievers tended to report exerting *less* effort than did overachievers (see Table 11.1). Preston (1983) replicated this finding in a similar paradigm; in fact, the effects in her study were even stronger than those reported by Riggs.

In this experimental context, discrepancies between actual effort and reported effort probably reflected more than a self-presentational tactic. Because subjects were led to believe that their true effort was being measured, they knew that they would not be able to deceive the experimenter about true effort expended (Jones & Sigall, 1971). It is likely, then, that the discrepancy between actual and self-reported effort reflected a true misperception or self-deception on the part of the subjects.

One possible explanation for underachievers' underestimation of effort expenditure is that underachievers are polished attributional egotists (Snyder et al., 1978). Underachievers may exert great effort in order to enhance the likelihood of success, yet convince themselves that they have not tried very hard. This allows them to attribute success to ability rather than to effort. Of course, failure still could be attributed to a lack of effort.

However, there is an alternative explanation for this disparity between actual and reported effort that is not self-serving in nature. Rather, it rests upon the assumption that underachievers' parents repeatedly have told them that they could do well if only they would try. It is possible that these children have received this kind of feedback even when they *have* been trying hard. After all, parents probably like to think of their children as being bright and capable. If their children do not perform well, parents might prefer to attribute their children's performance to a lack of effort rather than admit that their son or daughter has anything less than superior (or at least average) ability. These children then may become confused when assessing the effort they put into performance contexts and may be swayed by their parents' perceptions. That is, these children actually may come to regard themselves as giving less than 100 percent of their effort. Thus, underachievers' underestimation of their effort expenditure may be traceable to a learned misperception.

Some of Preston's data are consistent with this explanation. She found that the absolute difference between actual and estimated effort expenditure was greater for underachievers than for overachievers. This suggests that underachievers were less accurate in their estimates than were overachievers. Furthermore, in a questionnaire administered to parents of her subjects, Preston found that mothers of underachievers were more likely than mothers of other students to attribute their son's or daughter's poor grade on a test to not studying enough.

Either explanation – attributional egotism or learned misperceptions – could account for the disparity between effort expended by underachievers and their self-reports. Both explanations suggest that under some circumstances, those labelled as underachievers actually are not withdrawing effort but only *appear* as if they are. They or their parents may explain a performance that does not meet expectations by attributing it to low effort. However, the real source of the problem could be, for example, an ability to score well on standardized tests that does not carry over into typical school grading situations. High achievement-test scores thus lead to an erroneous expectation of successful academic performance. A handy rea-

Table 11.2. *Mean performance, reported effort expenditure, actual effort expenditure, and reported trying*[a]

	Overachievers		Underachievers	
	Ability Attribution ($P = A \times e$)	Effort Attribution ($P = a \times E$)	Ability Attribution ($P = A \times e$)	Effort Attribution ($P = a \times E$)
Performance	32.9	44.3	42.3	29.8
Reported % of Effort Expended	87.8	87.6	90.5	84.3
Actual Effort Expended (kg)	426.5	452.3	441.2	417.4
Reported Trying	8.0	9.2	9.2	8.0

[a]Means are adjusted for the effects of subjects' hand strength and achievement level.

son for a performance that does not meet those expectations is low effort expenditure.

In an attempt to relate these results to the theoretical framework on which the experiment was based, Riggs performed a series of internal analyses on her data. Subjects were classified according to their response to the question: "To what extent do you think test scores are affected by how hard a person grips the handle?" Those whose responses were above the median were classified as effort attributors. That is, these subjects' responses suggested that they perceived that effort exerted on the dynamometer had an effect upon test scores ($P = a \times E$). Those subjects whose responses were below the median were classified as ability attributors, since presumably they perceived their efforts as having little effect upon test scores ($P = A \times e$).

Perhaps the most striking finding was uncovered in the analysis of subjects' correct responses to the test problems. The significant achievement by attribution interaction is shown in Table 11.2. Overachievers classified as effort attributors answered more test problems correctly than did overachievers classified as ability attributors. However, underachievers classified as effort attributors tended to answer *fewer* test problems correctly than did those underachievers in the ability attribution group. Consistent with this interaction were the correlations between number of correct responses and rating of the extent to which gripping the dynamometer influenced test scores. A significant positive correlation between these variables was found among overachievers, $r = +.39$. That is, the more effective overachievers perceived gripping the dynamometer to be, the more problems they answered correctly. However, this relationship was not found among underachievers. In fact, there was a tendency for underachievers to answer *fewer* questions correctly, the greater the perceived effect of gripping the dynamometer, $r = -.37$.

Internal analyses also were performed on the major dependent variables: self-perceptions of effort expended and actual effort expended. Overachievers classified as effort attributors tended to exert more effort (as measured by the dynamometer) than did overachieving ability attributors. However, underachievers classified as effort attributors tended to exert *less* effort (and reported exerting less effort) than did underachieving ability attributors (see Table 11.2).

A significant interaction also was obtained when the same internal analysis was performed on responses to the question: "How hard did you try while taking this test?" Overachievers in the effort-attribution condition reported trying harder than did overachievers in the ability-attribution condition. However, the reverse was true for underachievers (Table 11.2). The general patterns exhibited in Table 11.2 are fairly consistent. Underachieving effort attributors generally tried less hard and performed more poorly than did underachieving ability attributors. However, overachieving effort attributors generally tried harder and performed better than did overachieving ability attributors.[1]

Given this collection of findings, some conjectures might be made about the basic differences between these adolescent overachieving and underachieving groups. Turning first to the underachieving group, the effect is consistent with a self-handicapping analysis. Underachievers exhibited a self-handicapping strategy only when that behavior could protect self-esteem. If performance was perceived to be affected by effort expenditure, then the individual could adopt a strategy of effort withdrawal, thereby ensuring that a poor performance could be attributed to something less threatening than low ability. However, underachievers who perceived performance to be a pure indicator of ability did not have this option. Rather, they had nothing to lose and everything to gain by trying their hardest to avoid failure, because failure under any circumstances would indicate a lack of ability. This finding is quite consistent with those of Smith, Snyder,

[1] It is worth noting that in this experiment there was a positive relationship between effort expenditure and actual performance, despite the fact that effort exerted on the dynamometer had no effect upon problem presentation time. Subjects were divided by a median split into high and low performance groups. Subjects who performed relatively well were found to have exerted significantly more effort on the dynamometer than subjects who performed relatively poorly. This effect suggests that there was indeed a relationship between physical effort exerted on the dynamometer and mental effort (e.g., attention and concentration) exerted on the test problems themselves.

and their colleagues, who found symptom-reporting to decrease when it was not perceived to be a viable excuse for poor performance.

But why do these patterns of effort and performance not parallel those of overachievers? One explanation is that the performance decrements of overachieving ability attributors were caused by feelings of lack of control or helplessness. It is not surprising that the perception that the dynamometer had little effect on test scores would cause them to grip it less tightly. After all, why waste the effort if it has little to do with test scores anyway? Supporting this notion was the general tendency for overachievers to perceive their effort as controlling duration time on fewer of the problems than did underachievers.

Why overachievers would be more susceptible to feelings of helplessness than underachievers can only be conjectured. One possibility is that overachievers have perceived their efforts to be fruitful in the past. They may believe that trying hard has kept them from failing, thus allowing them to exert some degree of control over their performance outcomes. They might be, therefore, particularly sensitive to situations in which this control is absent, leading to feelings of helplessness. The finding of actual performance decrements under these circumstances seems analogous to those found in studies of learned helplessness (e.g., Thornton & Jacobs, 1971; Hiroto & Seligman, 1975) and lack of control (e.g., Glass & Singer, 1972).

Of course, the nature of such internal analyses does not allow one to make clear cause-effect inferences. However, it does appear that there is some relationship between one's perceptions of the causal role of effort in performance and one's effort expenditure and performance. The relationship seems to be a positive one for overachievers. Perceiving effort to be an effective influence upon performance is accompanied by increases in effort expenditure and performance among overachievers. However, this relationship appears to be a negative one for underachievers. Perceiving effort to have an effect upon performance seems to be accompanied by the adoption of the self-handicapping strategy of effort withdrawal and subsequent decrements in performance among underachievers.

Conclusions

The roots of underachievement clearly are numerous and varied. Underachievement can occur in a wide variety of settings, from the academic to the social to the athletic to the vocational. It can manifest itself in any type of behavior that precludes maximal performance, from not studying to overindulging in alcohol to not practicing to experiencing symptomatology to simply not trying. Certainly it cannot be assumed that an individual who is not performing up to his or her potential is attempting to manipulate the attributions for his or her performance; a host of other factors may come into play. However, a self-handicapping analysis might provide one perspective on why some individuals fall into an underachieving pattern.

The impetus for adopting a self-handicapping strategy cannot be pinned to any single cause. However, an underlying factor that seems critical is an overriding concern with one's competence-image. The individual who is uncertain about his or her abilities and fears exposure of a lack of competence may become motivated to adopt a self-protective strategy. Adoption of a self-handicapping strategy allows the individual to set the stage so that poor performance can be attributed to the handicap, rather than to a lack of ability. The extent to which this is a conscious process is unknown and probably varies from individual to individual. However, the person who is provided with excuses for poor performance by others, or who finds through experience that such excuses are viable, may begin to fall into a self-handicapping cycle. Self-defeating behaviors may not be consciously chosen over and over again; rather, with time they may become habitual.

What can be done to preclude the adoption of self-handicapping strategies? Clearly, more research needs to be done before this question can be answered adequately. However, current research does suggest some possibilities. Divesting the individual entirely of such self-protective strategies probably is impractical and impossible. In fact, it may do more harm than good to rob the individual of those strategies that protect his or her self-esteem. Instead of attacking the symptom, a more fruitful approach might be to address the underlying problem – the individual's doubt about his or her basic worth or competence. Although feedback from significant others needs to be contingent on performance, love should not be withdrawn in the absence of good performance (Jones & Berglas, 1978). A child or adolescent (or adult) needs to know that he or she is accepted and respected for what he or she is, rather than for what he or she could be. This type of environment should lead to the development of a positive self-image, rather than to the establishment of a precarious one that may foster self-defeating behavior.

References

Adler, A. (1913). Individual psychologische behandlung der neurosen. In D. Sarason (Ed.), *Jahreskurse fur arztliche fortbildung*. Munich: Lehmann.

Arkin, R.A., & Baumgardner, A.H. (1985). Self-handicapping. In J.H. Harvey & G. Weary (Eds.), *Attribution: Basic issues and applications* (pp. 167–198). New York: Academic Press.

Atkinson, J.W. (Ed.) (1958). *Motives in fantasy, action, and society*. Princeton: Van Nostrand.

Atkinson, J.W., & Feather, N.T. (Eds.) (1966). *A theory of achievement motivation*. New York: Wiley.

Atkinson, J.W., & Litwin, G.H. (1960). Achievement motive and test anxiety conceived as motive to approach success and motive to avoid failure. *Journal of Abnormal and Social Psychology, 60,* 52–63.

Atkinson, J.W., & Raynor, J.O. (1978). *Personality, motivation, and achievement*. New York: Wiley.

Baumgardner, A. H., Lake, E. A., & Arkin, R.A. (1985). Claiming mood as a self-handicap: The influence of spoiled and unspoiled public identities. *Personality and Social Psychology Bulletin, 11,* 349–357.

Berglas, S., & Jones, E.E. (1978). Drug choice as a self-handicapping strategy in response to noncontingent success. *Journal of Personality and Social Psychology, 36,* 405–417.

Burnam, M.A., Pennebaker, J.W., & Glass, D.C. (1975). Time consciousness, achievement striving, and the Type A coronary-prone behavior pattern. *Journal of Abnormal Psychology, 84,* 76–79.

Darley, J.M., & Goethals, G.R. (1980). People's analyses of the causes of ability-linked performances. In L. Berkowitz (Ed.), *Advances in experimental social psychology, Vol. 13* (pp. 1–37). New York: Academic Press.

Frankel, A., & Snyder, M.L. (1978). Poor performance following unsolvable problems: Learned helplessness or egotism? *Journal of Personality and Social Psychology, 36,* 1415–1423.

Friedman, M. (1977). Type A behavior pattern: Some of its pathophysiological components. *Bulletin of the New York Academy of Medicine, 53,* 593–604.

Gastorf, J.W., & Teevan, R.C. (1980). Type A coronary-prone behavior pattern and fear of failure. *Motivation and Emotion, 4,* 71–76.

Glass, D.C., & Singer, J.E. (1972). *Urban stress*. New York: Academic Press.

Greenberg, J., Pyszczynski, T., & Paisley, C. (1985). Effect of extrinsic incentives on use of test anxiety as an anticipatory attributional defense: Playing it cool when the stakes are high. *Journal of Personality and Social Psychology, 47,* 1136–1145.

Harris, R.N., & Snyder, C.R. (1986). The role of uncertain self-esteem in self-handicapping. *Journal of Personality and Social Psychology, 51,* 451–458.

Havighurst, R. J. (1972). *Developmental tasks and education* (3rd ed.). New York: McKay.

Heider, F. (1958). *The psychology of interpersonal relations*. New York: Wiley.

Hiroto, D. S., & Seligman, M. E. P. (1975). Generality of learned helplessness in man. *Journal of Personality and Social Psychology, 31,* 311–327.

Jones, E. E., & Berglas, S. (1978). Control of attributions about the self through self-handicapping strategies: The appeal of alcohol and the role of underachievement. *Personality and Social Psychology Bulletin, 4,* 200–206.

Jones, E. E., & Rhodewalt, F. (1982). *Self-handicapping scale*. Unpublished manuscript, Psychology Departments, Princeton University and University of Utah.

Jones, E. E., & Sigall, H. (1971). The bogus pipeline: A new paradigm for measuring affect and attitude. *Psychological Bulletin, 76,* 349–364.

Kelley, H. H. (1971). *Attribution in social interaction*. Morristown, NJ: General Learning Press.

Kelley, H. H. (1973). The processes of causal attribution. *American Psychologist, 28,* 107–128.

Kolditz, T. A., & Arkin, R. A. (1982). An impression management interpretation of the self-handicapping strategy. *Journal of Personality and Social Psychology, 43,* 492–502.

Kukla, A. (1972). Attributional determinants of achievement-related behavior. *Journal of Personality and Social Psychology, 21,* 166–174.

Kun, A. (1977). Development of the magnitude-covariation and compensation schemata in ability and effort attributions of performance. *Child Development, 48,* 862–873.

McClelland, D. C. (1958). Risk-taking in children with high and low need for achievement. In J. W. Atkinson (Ed.), *Motives in fantasy, action, and society* (pp. 306–321). Princeton: Van Nostrand.

McClelland, D. C., Atkinson, J. W., Clark, R. A., & Lowell, E. L. (1953). *The achievement motive.* New York: Appleton-Century-Crofts.

McClelland, D. C., Clark, R. A., Roby, T. B., & Atkinson, J. W. (1949). The projective expression of needs. IV: The effect of need for achievement and thematic apperception. *Journal of Experimental Psychology, 39,* 242–255.

Preston, E. A. (1983). *The role of effort expenditure in academic achievement.* Unpublished doctoral dissertation, Princeton University.

Pyszczynski, T., & Greenberg, J. (1983). Determinants of reduction in intended efforts as a strategy for coping with anticipated failure. *Journal of Research in Personality, 17,* 412–422.

Quattrone, G. A., & Jones, E. E. (1978). Selective self-disclosure with and without correspondent performance. *Journal of Experimental Social Psychology, 14,* 511–526.

Rhodewalt, F., Saltzman, A. T., & Wittmer, J. (1984). Self-handicapping among competitive athletes: The role of practice in self-esteem protection. *Basic and Applied Social Psychology, 5,* 197–209.

Riggs, J. M. (1982). *The effect of performance attributions on choice of achievement strategy.* Unpublished doctoral dissertation, Princeton University.

Ruble, D. N., Parsons, J. E., & Ross, J. (1976). Self-evaluative responses of children in an achievement setting. *Child Development, 47,* 990–997.

Ruble, D. N., & Rholes, W. S. (1981). The development of children's perceptions and attributions about their social world. In J. H. Harvey, W. J. Ickes, & R. F. Kidd (Eds.), *New directions in attribution research*(Vol. 3). Hillsdale, NJ: Erlbaum.

Smith, T. W., Snyder, C. R., & Handelsman, M. M. (1982). On the self-serving function of an academic wooden leg: Test anxiety as a self-handicapping strategy. *Journal of Personality and Social Psychology, 42,* 314–321.

Smith, T. W., Snyder, C. R., & Perkins, S. C. (1983). The self-serving function of hypochondriacal complaints: Physical symptoms as self-handicapping strategies. *Journal of Personality and Social Psychology, 44,* 787–797.

Snyder, C. R., & Smith, T. W. (1982). Symptoms as self-handicapping strategies: The virtues of old wine in a new bottle. In G. Weary & H. L. Mirels (Eds.), *Integrations of clinical and social psychology* (pp. 104–127). New York: Oxford University Press.

Snyder, C. R., Smith, T. W., Augelli, R. W., & Ingram, R. E. (1985). On the self-serving function of social anxiety: Shyness as a self-handicapping strategy. *Journal of Personality and Social Psychology, 48,* 970–980.

Snyder, M. L., Stephan, W., & Rosenfield, D. (1976). Egotism and attribution. *Journal of Personality and Social Psychology, 33,* 435–441.

Snyder, M. L., Stephan, W. G., & Rosenfield, D. (1978). Attributional egotism. In J. H. Harvey, W. Ickes, & R. F. Kidd (Eds.), *New directions in attribution research* (Vol. 2, pp. 91–117). Hillsdale, NJ: Erlbaum.

Soder, L. A., & Riggs, J. M. (1986). *Self-handicapping and affect.* Unpublished manuscript, Gettysburg College, Gettysburg, PA.

Thornton, J. W., & Jacobs, P. D. (1971). Learned helplessness in human subjects. *Journal of Experimental Psychology, 87,* 367–372.

Tucker, J. A., Vuchinich, R. E., & Sobell, M. B. (1981). Alcohol consumption as a self-handicapping strategy. *Journal of Abnormal Psychology, 90,* 220–230.

Weidner, G. (1980). Self-handicapping following learned helplessness treatment and the Type A coronary-prone behavior pattern. *Journal of Psychosomatic Research, 24,* 319–325.

Weiner, B. (1974). *Achievement and attribution theory.* Morristown, NJ: General Learning Press.

Weiner, B., Frieze, I., Kukla, A., Reed, L., Rest, S., & Rosenbaum, R. M. (1971). *Perceiving the causes of success and failure.* Morristown: General Learning Press.

Weiner, B., Heckhausen, H., Meyer, W. U., & Cook, R. E. (1972). A conceptual analysis of effort and reanalysis of locus of control. *Journal of Personality and Social Psychology, 21,* 239–248.

Weiner, B., & Kukla, A. (1970). An attributional analysis of achievement motivation. *Journal of Personality and Social Psychology, 15,* 1–20.

Weiner, B., & Potepan, P. A. (1970). Personality characteristics and affective reactions towards exams of superior and failing college students. *Journal of Educational Psychology, 61,* 144–151.

Weiner, I. B. (1980). Psychopathology in adolescence. In J. Adelson (Ed.), *Handbook of adolescent psychology* (pp. 447–471). New York: Wiley.

12 Divergent approaches to the study of motivation and achievement: The central role of extrinsic/intrinsic orientations

Ann K. Boggiano and Thane S. Pittman

The chapters in this volume are clearly diverse and encompass a wide array of consequences for children with different motivational orientations. Taken together, they point to a theoretical stance that can no longer be ignored by social developmental psychologists concerned with issues relevant to motivation and achievement. For instance, the findings discussed in these chapters point to the need to reconsider the critical importance of affect. As posited by Zajonc (1980), the strong emphasis on understanding cognitive processes during the past twenty years has diminished psychologists' attempts to explore the critical role of affect as a mediator of behavior, and in particular of motivation and achievement. Perhaps invoking Bem's (1972) self-perception theory or the discounting principle to interpret "overjustification" effects has diminished researchers' concern with affect as it relates to intrinsic motivation and other achievement variables. Nevertheless, affect has been seen more recently as a central factor influencing performance (see Chapters 5 and 11, this volume) and feelings about peers (Chapter 3, this volume). Moreover, affect is inexorably intertwined with perceptions of self-determination, competence, and self-esteem (Chapter 2), which in turn affect motivation and achievement (Chapter 7). The chapters in this volume also make clear the critical need for research on motivation from a developmental perspective (Chapters 3, 5, and 8).

Although contributors to this volume have concentrated primarily on effects of different motivational orientations, there are several other interesting approaches to understanding achievement and motivation. Like research in the motivation orientation arena, these other approaches emphasize affect and motivation as well as cognition as important factors influencing the learning process. Researchers have begun to seek the processes and outcomes of motivation and achievement by considering children's *reasons* for undertaking activities generally, and for undertaking school-related activities in particular (see also Chapter 10).

One intriguing theoretical analysis developed by Dweck and colleagues (e.g., Dweck & Elliott, 1983; Dweck & Leggett, 1988) points to two divergent goals adopted by children as mediators of the helpless versus mastery-oriented achievement patterns. According to Dweck, children's differential reactions to uncontrollable situations – for example, failure – may result from different reasons for undertaking achievement tasks. Mastery-oriented children pursue *learning* goals: they initiate activities to refine their skills and develop competence. Conversely, helpless children may adopt *performance* goals: achievement situations are viewed primarily as evaluations of their ability, thereby leading them to need either to "prove" evidence of competence or to avoid indications of inadequacy. Moreover, contexts that engender learning goals should facilitate mastery-oriented behaviors, regardless of differential perceptions of ability, whereas those that make performance goals salient should lead to the helpless pattern, if the child has a low perception of his or her ability or competence (see Dweck & Leggett, 1988, p. 259). Support for this proposition is provided in one recent study (Elliott & Dweck, 1988). Further, given that the child feels incompetent, the belief that intelligence is fixed or unchangeable would, according to the theory, tend to exacerbate negative responses to situations in which performance goals were most salient.

Another interesting and innovative approach to understanding motivation and achievement in children has been developed by Nicholls (1984). According to this theoretical vantage point, to the extent that a child adopts an ego-orientation, the primary goal is to demonstrate to self and others that one's ability is superior. Conversely, undertaking a task-orientation toward learning involves interest and commitment to learning for its own sake and a desire to understand and integrate material, rather than simply to memorize facts. The data show clearly that students with a task-orientation perform significantly better on academic tasks than do students with an ego-orientation (Nolen, 1988).

It is the position of the present authors that there are considerable similarities among these three approaches. All underscore the reasons for *initiation* of academic activities (e.g., evaluation, self-enhancement, tangible rewards, ego-involvement, performance goals), and undertaking activities for these extrinsic reasons has been shown to have dramatic effects both on the process of learning and the quality of the outcome. Moreover, there is evidence that all these maladaptive approaches generate negative affect (e.g., feelings of pressure, anxiety, defensive attributions).

Despite these similarities, the position taken here is that ego-involvement and an emphasis on performance goals are a subset of manipulations that produce states that can be subsumed within an extrinsic motivational orientation framework. For example, Ryan (1982) has demonstrated that ego-involvement undermines motivation to a greater extent than does task-involvement. And the effects of performance goals and feedback depend on whether the feedback is perceived as informational or controlling (see Boggiano & Barrett, 1991; Chapter 6, this volume; Plant & Ryan, 1985; Koestner, Zuckerman, & Koestner, 1987). Insofar as ego or self-involvement is viewed as controlling, motivation and achievement will be impaired (see Pittman, Davey, Alafat, Wetherill, & Kramer, 1980). Thus, ego-involvement is one example of a manipulation engendering an extrinsic motivational orientation.

Most importantly, it is not only evaluation or factors that enhance ego-involvement or performance goals that have negative consequences for the learning process. Even trivial incentives that lead children to shift their focus from the task per se to an extrinsic reason for task performance produce clear detrimental effects on subsequent motivation and performance level. That is, the offering of marshmallows, stickers, candy, a good player award, deadlines, and even saying "You should do well" impairs subsequent motivation and/or performance quality (Boggiano et al., 1988; Ryan, 1982). Thus, an extrinsic motivational orientation is comprised of ego-involvement and performance goals, among many other manipulations engendering an extrinsic set.

Although researchers in these chapters have pointed to the negative effects of students' adopting an extrinsic motivational orientation, there may be more dramatic consequences to overall adjustment than previously considered. Not only do extrinsic students display a number of cognitive, motivational, and behavioral deficits associated with helplessness (see Chapter 9, this volume), but extrinsics also evidence emotional deficits such as depression and a maladaptive attributional style. Moreover, when presented with an induction in which thoughts about a failure experience were made salient, extrinsics report stronger feelings of self-blame and hopelessness – consistent with the emotional deficit hypothesis (Boggiano, Barrett, & Silvern, 1991). Indeed, our recent research with fourth graders indicates that there is a significant correlation between motivational orientation and depressed affect: more negative mood, lower self-worth, greater feelings of hopelessness, and lower energy were associated with more extrinsic orientations, whereas intrinsic orientations were associated with the opposite feelings. We currently are examining the causal relation between children's feelings of depression and the development of an extrinsic motivational orientation – a question important both from a theoretical and a practical standpoint.

To summarize, an extrinsic motivational orientation appears more global than ego-involvement and performance goals, and may be relatively easy to engender in students. There is evidence, for example, that an extrinsic motivational orientation develops only six weeks after exposure to a controlling teacher (Chapter 2, this volume). Moreover, this orientation often has dramatic effects on a wide array of achievement related behaviors and strongly influences performance and affective states. The proposition, of course, is not to argue that socializing agents should never entice a child to perform activities for extrinsic reasons. The evidence at hand indicates that an extrinsic motivational orientation affects performance, motivation, and affective states when activities are interesting and offer the promise of mastery over challenge. Performance of mundane and rote tasks may well profit from the availability of extrinsic incentives.

Where does this lead our educators and social developmental theorists who are concerned with ways of optimizing motivation and achievement? What research directions have been or should be undertaken to attenuate the negative effects of an extrinsic motivational orientation in students – which in fact, accelerates as students progress through school (Harter, 1978; 1981)? Several innovative approaches are under way.

One intriguing approach, developed by Lepper and his colleagues, is the observation of expert human tutors who have devised ways of having students perceive themselves with a strong personal sense of control. Interestingly, these tutors themselves exert significant amounts of control over their students' work – with enormous success. Students feel personally responsible for learning in a context that is relevant to the content of material taught and level of challenge afforded (Lepper, 1988).

A second interesting approach researched for a number of years is peer tutoring. Overall, the findings indicate highly beneficial results for the tutor – both affectively and motivationally – that resemble the ability to integrate and conceptualize material in a more effective manner when actively teaching rather than being a passive recipient (Benware & Deci, 1984).

An additional important question related to the issue of altering motivational orientation is whether motivational orientation is malleable. To address this issue, we are conducting a three-year longitudinal study examining whether motivational strategies used by parents moderate the impact of those used by teachers on children's development of a particular motivational orientation. A second major question addressed in this longitudinal study centers on the malleability of children's motivational orientation, depending on exposure over the school years to teachers using primarily controlling versus autonomous strategies to motivate their students. For instance, if children are taught by teachers using controlling techniques over several years, will they continue to maintain an extrinsic set even when subsequently exposed to teachers using autonomy-promoting strategies?

We also are conducting an intervention study with elementary school children to explore ways to increase children's resistance to the detrimental effects of extrinsic constraints (see Chapter 4, this volume). Clearly, however, further research is called for in the areas of both the antecedents of a particular motivational set and the malleability of an extrinsic approach to learning. Taken together, these intervention approaches may contribute to students' enhanced deeper processing of material, reduce a sense of functional fixedness, and extend students' control over ways of mastering the learning process. At the very least, we need to shift drastically our educational philosophy, as exemplified by J. Sulzer (Miller, 1984): "Obedience is so important that all education is actually nothing other than learning how to obey." Use of controlling strategies as a "cure" may indeed be worse than the "disease" in terms of the consequences for the development of critical thinking in children.

References

Bem, D.J. (1972). Self-perception theory. In L. Berkowitz (Ed.), *Advances in experimental social psychology* (Vol. 16). New York: Academic Press.

Benware, C.A., & Deci, E.L. (1984). Quality of learning with an active versus passive motivational set. *American Educational Research Journal, 21,* 755–765.

Boggiano, A.K., & Barrett, M. (1991). Maladaptive achievement patterns: The role of motivational orientation. Unpublished manuscript. University of Colorado, Boulder.

Boggiano, A.K., Barrett, M., & Silvern, L. (1991). Predicting emotional concomitants of learned helplessness: The role of motivational orientation. Unpublished manuscript, University of Colorado, Boulder.

Boggiano, A.K., Main, D.S., & Katz, P.A. (1988). Children's preference for challenge: The role of perceived competence and control. *Journal of Personality and Social Psychology,* 54, 134–141.

Dweck, C.S., & Elliott, E.S. (1983). Achievement motivation. In P.H. Mussen (Ed.), *Handbook of child psychology* (Vol. 4). New York: Wiley.

Dweck, C.S., & Leggett, E.L. (1988). A social-cognitive approach to motivation and personality. *Psychological Review, 95,* 256–273.

Elliott, E.S., & Dweck, C.S. (1988). Goals: An approach to motivation and achievement. *Journal of Personality and Social Psychology, 54,* 5–12.

Harter, S. (1978). Effectance motivation reconsidered: Toward a developmental model. *Human Development, 21,* 34–64.

Harter, S. (1981). A model of mastery motivation in children: Individual differences and developmental changes. In W. A. Collins (Ed.), *Aspects of the development of competence: The Minnesota Symposium on Child Psychology* (Vol. 14, pp. 215–225). Hillsdale, NJ: Erlbaum.

Koestner, R., Zuckerman, M., & Koestner, J. (1987). Praise, involvement, and intrinsic motivation. *Journal of Personality and Social Psychology, 53,* 383–390.

Lepper, M.R. (1988). Motivational considerations in the study of instruction. *Cognition and Instruction, 5,* 289–309.

Miller, A. (1984). *For your own good.* New York: Farrar, Straus, & Giroux.

Nicholls, J.G. (1984). Conceptions of ability and achievement motivation. In R. Ames & C. Ames (Eds.), *Research on motivation in education* (Vol. 1). New York: Academic Press.

Nolen, S.B. (1988). Reasons for studying: Motivational orientation and study strategies. *Cognition and Instruction, 5,* 269–287.

Pittman, T.S., Davey, M.E., Alafat, K.A., Wetherill, K.V., & Kramer, N.A. (1980). Informational versus controlling verbal rewards. *Personality and Social Psychology Bulletin, 6,* 228–233.

Plant, R. & Ryan, R.M. (1985). Intrinsic motivation and the effects of self-consciousness, self-awareness, and ego-involvement: An investigation of internally controlling styles. *Journal of Personality, 53,* 435–449.

Ryan, R.M. (1982). Control in the intrapersonal sphere: An evaluation theory. *Journal of Personality and Social Psychology, 43,* 450–461.

Zajonc, R.B. (1980). Feeling and thinking: Preferences need no inferences. *American Psychologist, 35,* 151–175.

Name index

Subject index